D0915724

Slavery and Jeffersonian Virginia

ROBERT McCOLLEY

SLAVERY
AND
JEFFERSONIAN
VIRGINIA

Second Edition

UNIVERSITY OF ILLINOIS PRESS

Urbana   Chicago   London

Publication of the first edition of this work was supported by a grant from the Oliver M. Dickerson Fund. The Fund was established by Mr. Dickerson (Ph.D., Illinois, 1906) to enable the University of Illinois Press to publish selected works in American history, designated by the executive committee of the Department of History.

Second edition, 1973

Cloth: ISBN 0–252–00346–2
Paper: ISBN 0–252–00347–0

IN MEMORY OF GRANT MCCOLLEY

CONTENTS

PREFACE TO
THE SECOND EDITION

In recent years there has been a remarkable outpouring of works on slavery and such related subjects as abolitionists, racism, and West African history. If one theme may be outstanding among the many that run through these works, it has been a concern for finding, with sympathy as well as precise information, the range of experience that made up the lives of blacks in the New World. One of the methods that has proved especially helpful has been the systematic comparison of slavery and freedom in the many colonies and nations of the Americas. Of course the comparative method is no more guaranteed than any other to produce accurate results, and some of the early essays in the field are remarkable chiefly for the degree to which they have been qualified or even overturned. Ultimately, if present trends continue, scholars will assemble all of the pieces in the grand history of the Afro-American. This process is already far enough advanced that it is possible to write about the origins of the black population of Virginia in a way that would have been quite impossible eight years ago. Because my book of 1964 had no such discussion, it seems especially desirable to add one now, as a preface to the new edition.

The textbooks tell us that the first Negroes to arrive in

Virginia—or in any English colony of North America—came on a Dutch ship, numbered twenty, and were not slaves at all but only servants for a fixed period of time. This information is partly accurate, partly conjectural, and wholly misleading. It leaves the impression that an unexpected foreign ship quite accidentally traded black laborers to Virginians who had not expected them, and through their innocence and inexperience of slavery, were disposed to treat them just like their indentured white servants.

In fact, certain gentlemen in Virginia and Bermuda had invested in a privateering venture against the Spanish West Indies, which involved the nameless "Dutch man of war" and an English ship long familiar in the colonies, the *Treasurer*. Plundering the Spanish Main had been an important source of wealth for Englishmen in the recent past, but the official policy of both James I and the Virginia Company opposed this practice. But early colonists even more than later ones had a way of ignoring their government's policies when it appeared profitable to do so. Far from being innocent of the existence of slavery, these early colonizers knew perfectly well that slave labor greatly helped many of the Portuguese and Spanish colonies show a profit. The blacks they brought back to Virginia (the *Treasurer*, by the way, carried fourteen additional slaves to the Bermuda investors) were almost certainly slaves kidnapped from the Spanish. That the Englishmen who engaged in this business did so to improve the status of these blacks (by specifying that they should be free after a few years' labor) hardly squares with their general disposition to pursue wealth at all costs. As Edmund S. Morgan has recently argued, the early planters of Virginia had a distinct bent toward modifying the English institution of indentured servitude into something much more like slavery. They also knew how to seize offending Indians and sell them into slavery.[1]

---

[1] The best and wisest discussion of the first blacks in Virginia is in Wesley Frank Craven's *White, Red, and Black: The Seventeenth Century Virginian*

The word "slave" itself was a term of violent abuse in the first half of the seventeenth century; in one letter preserved in the records of the Virginia Company a survivor of an Indian massacre refers to the murderers of his friends and relatives as "slaves"; they were nothing of the sort, it was simply the strongest epithet he could find to hurl at them. But then the offensive word was unnecessary, because the term "Negro" in the American colonies carried with it the connotation of slavery. When, as was sometimes the case, a black was free, or an indentured servant, qualifying adjectives were added, as in the case of John Philip, a "free Christian Negro," probably a sailor just passing through Virginia in 1624.

An old argument, most persuasively set forth by James C. Ballagh, held that slavery could not really exist until a body of positive laws existed to support the institution. That may have been true for Kansas in the 1850's, but in the early history of American colonization quite the opposite was the case—planters introduced slavery and then eventually made up codes of law to govern the institution. It was also typical of early slavery that, even though it rested on a racial basis, it was never entirely closed. Free blacks, or blacks contracted to labor for a period of years, generally appeared at the same time slaves did.

The status of the very first blacks in Virginia is an intriguing question, and all the more so because of the many contradictory theories that have been woven around the not always understood facts. Even so, those early beginnings of slavery were of minor historical importance, except as they illustrated the growing importance of Negro slavery in the tropics. In 1648 there were approximately 15,000 whites and 300 blacks in Virginia; the latter were a mere 2 percent of the total, and

(Charlottesville, 1971). On the rapacious nature of early Virginia planters, see Edmund S. Morgan, "The First American Boom: Virginia 1618 to 1630," *William and Mary Quarterly* third series, XXVIII (April, 1971). No further annotation follows for this preface, but the points raised here can be traced in the scholarly works listed in the Supplementary Bibliography.

therefore of minimal significance to the colony. By this time, however, the sugar boom in the Carribbean had been under way for several years, and Englishmen from London, Bristol, and the Americas now began to show a great interest in both the slave trade and the use of slave labor. To ask when and how slavery started in Virginia is therefore somewhat to ask the wrong question, for the tobacco business was not, by itself, enough to drive the British into slaving as a major enterprise. The sugar business was.

It was only after the British had established a regular flow of slaves to the New World that Virginia was able to make regular importations. This was during the last third of the seventeenth century, and even then the supply naturally went mainly to the Caribbean. After the rise of Liverpool in the eighteenth century slavers with several hundred blacks visited the Chesapeake on a regular basis. That the Virginia planters wished to increase their stock of slaves was proved by a law of 1660 which offered special trading privileges to Dutch ships bringing slaves to Virginia. This act was swept away by the Navigation Acts of Charles II, but his chartering of the Royal Africa Company helped provide the labor the Virginians craved. From 1661 onward the Virginians had passed a number of laws concerning slavery; one of the most significant of these was an act toward the end of the century which prohibited slave-owners from emancipating their slaves. Only in 1705, as part of a general revision and rationalization of the laws of the commonwealth, did Virginia get a coherent body of law governing slavery. This stood, with minor revisions, until the next overhauling of the laws, which followed the Declaration of Independence.

Blacks were a minor part of the Virginia labor force in the seventeenth century. From 1640 to 1700 importations probably averaged only forty to fifty a year. From 1700 to the American Revolution, on the other hand, the average was between perhaps eight and nine hundred each year. It was, obviously, during the eighteenth century, the "Golden Age," that Afro-American slavery became the basis of the Virginia economy, and Afro-Americans became almost half the population of the commonwealth. On its own terms, the introduction of blacks into Virginia was quite rapid. Yet compared to the sugar islands, Brazil, or even South Carolina, the introduction of blacks into Virginia was very gradual, and blacks never outnumbered whites.

The native African usually acculturated rapidly in Virginia, because he was most likely to be surrounded by white Virginians, blacks who were natives of Virginia, or blacks who, though born in Africa, had lived in Virginia for several years, and had become fluent in English and familiar with Virginia customs. The systematic research of Robert E. and B. Katherine Brown has proved that the holding of slaves was very widely dispersed in colonial Virginia. More than half of the blacks lived on family farms in groups of from one to ten, and the larger groups invariably included several young children. The farmers who owned these smaller groups of slaves had to work along with them. Only on the large plantations were blacks likely to suffer from the rather stifling life of the field hand kept at monotonous routines and deprived of variety in work and social experience. But the large plantations also had complex and challenging tasks which often supplied a generous measure of personal liberty for skilled blacks. A recent student of black Virginians, Gerald Mullin, has found work allotment to be the most significant factor in the acculturation of slaves, and, not surprisingly, Mullin has also found that the workers who were most well off—the artisans and the boatmen—were the most rebellious of Virginia's slaves. They knew enough of freedom to hunger for it.

The rapid increase of blacks in North America has been so much taken for granted that only recently, with the development of comparative studies of slavery, has it been noted as something remarkable. At the high level of policy, formed by the leaders of church and state, the Spanish and Portuguese were much more concerned than the British about protecting marriage and fostering orderly family life among their slaves, just as they were more positive in their policy of encouraging emancipation. But official policy had little to do with mere survival; all of the tropical sugar colonies, whether Spanish, Portuguese, French, or British, had to import slaves to maintain their labor force, for they killed workers faster than the work force increased by natural means. In Virginia, Maryland, and North Carolina, on the other hand, the Afro-Americans nearly doubled each generation.

The leading reason for this may have been that the colonies in the temperate zone were simply healthier; they were certainly less crowded than the islands, and less frequently visited by ships bringing new diseases. Perhaps the food supply was most important: except for occasional spells of drought, the Chesapeake region produced a surplus of food and exported it regularly; the sugar islands had the opposite situation, they depended on importations to complete their food supply. Many sugar planters calculated that it was simply cheaper to buy full-grown slaves than to raise them from infancy, with the result that they positively discouraged breeding—often by purchasing only male slaves. Again, Virginia planters found that it was cheaper to raise slaves than to purchase them, or at least that it was more profitable to have a female slave spend part of her time bearing children than all of it working in the fields.

Another reason for the rapid increase of the slave population in Virginia was its ability to absorb as slaves an unknown but certainly important proportion of white and Indian blood. In the tropics the institution of concubinage was widespread: though black women were scarce, white women were even scarcer, and white overseers, mechanics, and even businessmen lived openly and more or less permanently with black mistresses. Domestic intimacy often encouraged them to free the children of these unions, and, as Marvin Harris has pointed out, mulattoes were badly needed in these societies to assume intermediate managerial roles. For economic as well as domestic reasons, then, mulattoes assumed an intermediate position in the tropics, free but, compared to the pure whites, restricted in their privileges. So far as interracial mating occurred it had the tendency to increase the free population.

In Virginia, by contrast, interracial mating was always surreptitious; concubinage no doubt existed, but it was never permitted the open and widespread status it held in the tropics. The reason for this is surely not that North Americans were, as certain French naturalists charged, less ardent for their females. Rather it was that (again, by comparison with the tropics) white Virginia men lived in a reasonably and increasingly well-balanced middle-class society in which there were enough girls for them to marry. Virginia was not, like Jamaica, a place to make a quick fortune before settling in England; it was a permanent home where men cleared their farms, raised their families, and made provision for their children's estates. Concubinage was pushed to the fringe in colonial Virginia by the triumph of regular marriage. It was this regular family life among most of the white planters that caused, in turn, the regular family life of their slaves. The statutes of colonial Virginia, to be sure, gave no protection to slave families, but social custom did. Both religion and economic self-interest encouraged the planter to promote domesticity among his slaves. Married slaves with children were more productive in the fields, the children were intrinsically valuable, and parents were much less likely to run away or rebel than single slaves.

Throughout the colonial era, however, there were always thousands of white servants in Virginia who were unable to marry until their indentures expired. They were usually of the age where the mating instinct is strongest. They were liable to harsh punishments for the crime of fornication, and punishment fell especially hard on white girls guilty of fornication with black men. Even so many white girls committed this particular indiscretion, and became pregnant; by law their mulatto offspring were then bound out as servants to the age of thirty-one. From time to time such a mulatto went to court to sue for his freedom; no doubt many others were raised and treated as slaves, never knowing that they had a white mother whose status could legally save them from life-long slavery.

A more common type of fornication was between the white male servant and the slave girl. The children of such unions always became slaves, following the condition of their mothers. Therefore interracial mating had exactly the opposite effect of the institution in the tropics; it reduced the descendants of Europeans to slavery, instead of elevating the descendants of Africans to freedom. In Virginia there was, overall, a far greater need for labor than for managerial talent; there was no economic or social need to be served by creating a mulatto class with partial and restricted freedom. The Virginia slave code made no distinction between Negroes and mulattoes. Within the world of Virginia plantation slavery, however, mulattoes, as natives with familiar manners and rather more familiar looks, rose to the top of whatever work hierarchies existed.

By the time of the American Revolution Virginia had a population of slaves that was predominantly Virginia-born and widely dispersed throughout the commonwealth. Although a few white Virginians believed in emancipation on religious and humanitarian grounds, the consensus was emphatically to preserve domestic slavery while cutting off forever the importation of new African slaves. The blacks of Virginia therefore belonged to an expanding population of whites, who hoped, as they moved westward across the continent, to divide their growing stocks of slaves among their equally growing broods of children. This was a sort of slave-holding white democracy, with the potential of developing into something quite different when (as then seemed remote) all the good land had been taken up.

This is the point in history where this book begins. Except for correcting two or three minor factual or printing errors, the main text is that of 1964; were I to rewrite the book today I could only guarantee that it would be longer. The University of Illinois Press has graciously consented to the addition, at the end, of certain documents and statistics which should help fill out the particular message of this work. The new preface owes much to the distinguished books which are listed in the Supplementary Bibliography, and is also derived from a study I have been working on at the invitation of Colonial Williamsburg, Inc., concerning the colonial Virginia Negro. Thanks are now due to Arthur Zilversmit and William Freehling, fellow students of Kenneth Stampp. Thanks are also due to the University of Kentucky Library and especially Jacqueline Bull; to the Huntington Library for permission to copy and use a letter from the Pleasants Family Papers; and to Martha Friedman, history librarian, and Norman F. Nash, rare book librarian, at the University of Illinois. Finally, my thanks go to Richard Wentworth, present editor of the University of Illinois Press, and Carole S. Appel, assistant editor.

Urbana, Illinois
February, 1972

ACKNOWLEDGMENTS

For assistance in research, it is a pleasure to thank the staffs of the following repositories: the University of California Library, Berkeley, the Harvard University Library, the Illinois Historical Survey, the University of Illinois Library, the Manuscripts Division of the Library of Congress, the Virginia State Library, the Virginia Historical Society, the Library of the University of Virginia, and the Valentine Museum, Richmond.

This book is an expanded and modified version of a dissertation, "Slavery in Jefferson's Virginia," which was read by Carl Bridenbaugh, J. Rogers Hollingsworth, Seymour M. Lipset, and Kenneth M. Stampp, all of whom deserve the warmest thanks for their critical interest. The present version has been saved from errors and infelicities by Dominic Candeloro, William B. Goodman, Robert W. Johannsen, Diane Kelsey McColley, and Sherman Paul. The faculty seminar of the History Department, University of Illinois, listened to an earlier version of the first chapter, and offered valuable advice. The Research Board of the Graduate College, University of Illinois, provided a fellowship for research in the summer of 1961, and funds for typing. My thanks to all of these, and to the staff of the University of Illinois Press, especially Donald Jackson, the editor, and Mrs. Bruce McDaniel, editorial assistant.

Champaign, Illinois   *Robert McColley*
February, 1964

LC	Manuscripts Division, Library of Congress
UVL	Library of the University of Virginia
VHS	Virginia Historical Society, Richmond
VSL	Virginia State Library, Richmond
DAB	*The Dictionary of American Biography*
JNH	*The Journal of Negro History*
Burnett	E. C. Burnett, ed., *Letters of Members of the Continental Congress*, 7 vols. (Washington, D.C., 1921–34).
Catterall	Helen T. Catterall, ed., *Judicial Cases Concerning American Slavery and the Negro*, volume I: Cases from the Courts of England, Virginia, West Virginia, and Kentucky (Washington, D.C., 1926).
Hening	William Waller Hening, *The Statutes at Large in Virginia*, vols. IX-XIII (Richmond, 1821–23, and Philadelphia, 1823).
Shepherd	Samuel Shepherd, *The Statutes at Large in Virginia, 1792–1806*, being a continuation of Hening, 3 vols. (Richmond, 1835).

INTRODUCTION

General histories of the United States customarily discuss slavery as it existed in the thirty years preceding the Civil War. Monographs on slavery have also concentrated on this most controversial period. Historical accounts of the first two hundred years of slavery are rare; those that exist are dated or are highly specialized and polemical.

This book originated in a desire to understand the grass-roots origins of Jeffersonian politics in Virginia. An extensive search through the sources of Jeffersonian Virginia led to these conclusions: that the social history of the ruling class has been fully and intelligently set down in such works as Carl Bridenbaugh's *Myths and Realities*, Charles Sydnor's *Gentlemen Freeholders*, and John R. Alden's *The South in the American Revolution*, and also in a number of modern biographies of the great Virginians of the Revolutionary and early national period. What one misses in these excellent books is a full portrayal of the powerful and varied influences of slavery on the life, the thought, and the politics of Jeffersonian Virginians.

In the absence of any careful consideration of slavery in the early national period, a number of plausible myths have survived. One of these holds that slavery was declining from economic causes and might have collapsed entirely had it not been for the cotton boom which developed early in the nineteenth century. A related myth holds that before cotton created overwhelming economic incentives for the perpetuation of slavery, there existed among the ruling class of the South, and especially that of Virginia, a broad humanitarian desire for emancipation. Consequently, Eli Whitney's cotton gin and the short-staple cotton plant stand forth in our general histories as the perverse but impersonal agencies which continued slavery unnaturally into the liberal nineteenth century.

It is certainly true that leading Virginians denounced slavery as a curse upon their land during the Jeffersonian period, just as it is obvious that those parts of the United States where free labor prevailed were growing far more rapidly in wealth and population than were the slaveholding regions. But it is surely false to infer that these circumstances were alone sufficient to guarantee an early end to slavery. After all, cotton cultivation did not become generally profitable until after the War of 1812. The severe economic difficulties of Virginia had recurred from the time of Bacon's Rebellion and had reached a crisis before the American Revolution. The liberal impulses let free by the Great Awakening and the Revolution itself provided as strong a humanitarian sentiment for emancipation as ever existed in the South. Finally, cotton cultivation was never to be a source of profit for Virginia itself. From 1776 until 1815 all the forces that should have destroyed slavery in Virginia could operate without restriction from a decisive cotton influence. And yet this forty-year period saw slavery fixed more securely on the Virginians at its close than at its beginning. So much was this the case that Thomas Jefferson, who had carefully composed a plan for gradual emancipation in the years immediately following the Declaration of Independence, wrote at the end of his life: "On the subject of emancipation I have ceased to think because [it is] not to be a work of my day."[1]

Frequently cited as evidence of the decrepitude of slavery in the early national period is the enormous migration out of Virginia, especially that part of it which involved the removal of the poorer elements to states and territories where slavery was outlawed. But at the very same time that Virginians were settling the Old Northwest, other Virginians were settling territories which became the slave states of Tennessee, Kentucky, Mississippi, Alabama, Louisiana, and Missouri. The years of slavery's supposed decline were in fact the years of its greatest expansion. And if economic shortcomings compelled the westward movement, it was still the case that slavery was more warmly embraced and less frequently attacked in new territories than in the old Atlantic states. An indication of the expansive strength of slavery may be seen in the powerful, though ultimately unsuccessful, attempts to overthrow the Ordinance of 1787 and to introduce slavery into Indiana and Illinois. Finally, while the free states of 1820 contained a larger population than the slave states, a glance at a map will demonstrate that slavery controlled many more square miles of the United States than free labor. The gentlemen who precipitated the crisis of 1819 had adequate reason for wishing to check the further advance of slavery. Indeed, slavery might easily roll back the area of free labor, for it was then still possible that Illinois would amend its constitution, as sovereign states certainly might, to allow the introduction of slavery there.

A study of slavery in the Jeffersonian period should therefore concern itself with explaining the capacity of slavery to endure and to expand in an age whose ideology strongly op-

---

[1] Thomas Jefferson, *The Works of . . .* , edited by Paul Leicester Ford (New York, 1905), X, 362.

posed it, and whose general economic trends pointed to its obsolescence. Such a study reveals that slavery was a social and economic institution of such power that it sustained and extended an economic system whose demands went far to determine the domestic and foreign policy of the "agrarian" party in our early history. For the agrarian politics of Jefferson, while possibly benefiting the small freeholder, very clearly served the interests of the plantation system, at least as the planters conceived their interests. It is difficult, for instance, to comprehend on ideological grounds the attachment of the Jeffersonian Republicans of Virginia to France after 1794. On the other hand, the planter's ancient desire for the widest possible markets fully explains the enduring desire for friendly relations with France, even at the cost of affronting imperial Britain. On the domestic scene, the planter's desire for the maximum control of his economic destiny explains his virulent hostility to the Hamiltonian program of funding and banking, a hostility most vigorously argued in the polemics of John Taylor of Caroline. Taylor, it should be remembered, was not an advocate of the independent democratic freeholder. He was a forthright apologist for the plantation system based on slave labor, and in explaining the blessings of slavery for white master and Negro servant alike he fully anticipated the later "sociology" of George Fitzhugh. Charles Beard and Vernon Parrington have celebrated to two generations of receptive scholars Taylor's indictment of monied interests, but in doing so they have obscured his promotion of the theory of slavery as a positive good.

Jeffersonian studies, indeed, are still largely under the influence of the giants of progressive historiography: Beard, Turner, and Parrington. For these men and their followers the party of Jefferson preserved and developed agrarian democracy in opposition to the Hamiltonian system of favoring and promoting modern capitalism. If they noted that the southern Jeffersonians were slaveowners, their slavery seemed incidental and separable from their agrarianism. The aggression of capitalism against farmers and workers, still embryonic in the early national period, seemed to the progressive historians more significant, and certainly more odious, than the palpable exploitation of slaves which flourished and grew through the Jeffersonian era. The explanation for this distortion can of course be found in the progressive era itself. When the tendency of the middle class was to worship American capitalists — a tendency which culminated in the innocent blasphemy of Bruce Barton, delineating the Christlike qualities of various corporation presidents — outraged intellectuals could hardly resist the temptation to advance a more democratic system of values. Yet the anthropological wisdom of their age urged that the Negro was, as southerners had always said, an inferior order of humanity. Weary of bloody-shirt interpretations of the American Civil War, the progressive historians were soft on slavery and slaveholders and at the same time very hard on capitalists and capitalism.

But the ideological climate of the nation has changed. The dream of the average man is no longer to earn a fortune of at least a million dollars; the autocratic captains of industry of the earlier age are rapidly being replaced by college-educated business administrators who are aware of public as well as corporate responsibilities, and who are often more "liberal" than farmers and laborers on such urgent contemporary issues as foreign affairs and civil rights. Inevitably, the historian who today rethinks the problems of early America must shed the preoccupations of the progressive era and replace them with those of his own. Jefferson and his contemporaries may have set down great maxims of liberty, they may have struck courageously against special and undeserved privileges, but they also accepted, as the *Notes on Virginia* demonstrate, doctrines of racism. Coupled to simple economic interest, these have kept the American Negro in a subordinate position throughout our national history.

The position underlying this study is the contemporary one that the Negro is a human being, with the innate capacities to think and work, to love and hate, to do good or do evil, that are shared by all humanity. It follows from this that Negro slavery, at any stage of American history, was a tragic and vicious system which warped to some extent everyone having occasion to become involved with it. Such a position does not and should not imply that white southerners were peculiarly depraved. Trapped by slavery, many southerners mitigated or even battled its evils by deeds more admirable than the mere advocacy of Negro rights by outsiders. Furthermore, while avoiding the romantic image of the "happy nigger" advanced in the Magnolia Blossom school of southern fiction and history, one must also avoid the equally romantic notion of Negro slaves perennially seething with a sense of injustice and incipient rebellion — a notion most persuasively advanced, perhaps, in Herbert Aptheker's *American Negro Slave Revolts*. One of the cruelest consequences of American Negro slavery was its efficacy in convincing the slave that he was as ignorant, helpless, and dependent as his masters said he was.

Finally, there is no point in replacing the vague references toward slavery in Jefferson's Virginia with a latter-day abolitionist tract. Though chattel slavery was brutal we must accept the testimony of honest men from all over the greater community of Western civilization that nowhere was it milder than in Virginia. Indeed, then as now, life was brutal for most people in most places, and the slave of Virginia enjoyed a measure of its blessings. The tragedy of the Virginia slave was not that he was starved and beaten, but that, surrounded by the opportunities of rich and empty lands, and of free institutions, he and his children were bound forever to their master's will. And there was the complementary tragedy of the master, himself a believer in human freedom, who had become so trapped by racist fears and profit-motives that he must deny his own noblest ideals by asserting the justice, or at least the necessity, of holding property in man.

CHAPTER

ONE

A Plantation Economy

Whenever one seriously looks for the motives of human behavior, it appears that matters economic, social, political, or personal are so intertwined and interdependent as to make the discussion of any one category seem shallow and artificial. Still, without accepting Marx's laws of history, investigators of the American past are always well advised to study the economic basis of the time and place that interests them. The American nation originated in the commercial expansion of Europe; some of our early establishments were entirely dedicated to amassing wealth, and in none of them was this motive greatly subordinated. When Calvin Coolidge described the business of America as business, he spoke with remarkable historical accuracy.

The American tradition of seeking and compiling wealth has gained our people a reputation for materialism. But this must be seriously qualified. If Americans are preeminent in the accumulation of material goods, they are still notably inefficient in the preservation and care of their property. So much is this the case that the act of acquisition itself often seems the most meaningful part of our economic life. Though there is here an undeniable element of materialism, it may well be that the primary motive is the quest for personal power and dignity, expressed in earlier societies by the development of military and political skills which permitted an elite to enjoy comfort and ease at the expense of impoverished masses. The ruling middle class of America, if it has often seemed deficient in the cultural refinements of the ruling classes of older civilizations, has at least had two virtues: it has been a productive as well as a ruling class, and it has not been notably exclusive.

Guardians of romantic southern traditions have often argued that southern civilization was less preoccupied with accumulating wealth than Yankee civilization. Certainly it is true that wealthy southerners usually surpassed their northern cousins in the cultivation of courtly manners and aristocratic leisure, at least before the Civil War. But the economic surplus which permitted so much gracious living in the Old South was itself the product of an agrarian capitalism intensely exploitive of land and labor. This agrarian capitalism was based on the raising of staple crops for export, and used Negro slaves for labor. It flourished and grew, with a minimum of minor and local setbacks, from the Declaration of Independence to the firing on Fort Sumter.

So much has been written about the decrepitude of slavery in the Jeffersonian period that some general points should be made at the outset. It was in the nature of American plantation development that the land would always be more sparsely settled, other factors being equal, than would be the case in free-labor areas. Southern states early revealed that they were falling behind northern states in both population and in the total production of wealth. While this might alarm southerners of broad views, and cause them to identify slavery as the malign influence, it did not for that reason change the overall pattern of individual decisions which created the growth and expansion of the Virginia economy. For if the per capita income of Virginians, including slaves, was less than that of northern denizens, it was still the case that the slaveholding planter was in a comfortable economic position, and his was the class of men that ruled Virginia.[1]

Geography and climate had their telling influences on the economy of Virginia. A generous rainfall and the watershed of the Blue Ridge created a large number of streams, navigable by small craft above the fall line and by larger craft below. The Tidewater region of Virginia may best be described as a series of peninsulas reaching out into Chesapeake Bay, affording innumerable harboring facilities and access to the Piedmont along the James, York, Rappahannock, and Potomac river systems. Before the industrial era Virginia depended almost entirely on these generous water facilities for her transportation. Virginia settlers were planters from the time of the establishment of tobacco as a salable crop, and from that time forward the settlement of Virginia was scattered and diffuse. But it was not without pattern and reason. The two important qualities of a plantation site were fertility and easy access to transportation. Even within the seventeenth century the small population of Virginia was

---

[1] For a discussion of sources on the economy of Virginia during the early national period and the uses here made of them, see the essay on sources preceding the bibliography.

stretched thinly across hundreds of miles of river frontage.[2]

No part of Virginia was better suited to commercial agriculture than the Tidewater. Its accessibility to oceangoing vessels and its long growing season gave its planters a permanent advantage over their compatriots above the fall line. For given the same skill in management and comparable soil fertility, the Tidewater planter could retain as profit the extra charges upcountry planters paid for transportation. Nevertheless, in the early national period the Tidewater barely maintained its population, while the Piedmont grew rapidly. The ascendancy was symbolized at the beginning of the period by the transfer of the seat of government from Williamsburg to Richmond. A generation later it was further stressed by the creation of the University of Virginia at Charlottesville, in Jefferson's own Albemarle County, an act which also represented the triumph of republicanism over monarchy and of secularism over Anglican Christianity. The third and fourth major zones of Virginia, the Shenandoah Valley and the mountains, were increasingly remote from the major highways of Atlantic commerce, and therefore poorly suited for the plantation system. These areas were characterized by small farms, worked either without the aid of slave labor, or with small numbers of slaves. Many settlers came into these regions from Pennsylvania, and had little sympathy for Old Virginia east of the Blue Ridge. The western counties were to provide an interesting political challenge to the plantation area of Virginia in the early national period, but they were never able to weaken the firm control by the planters of the state government.[3]

---

[2] For the early growth of Virginia, see Wesley Frank Craven, *The Southern Colonies in the Seventeenth Century, 1607–1689* (Baton Rouge, 1949), especially Chapter 5. Craven suggests that resistance by the Indians along the James contributed to the coastal dispersion; see especially pp. 172–173.

[3] The standard account is Charles Henry Ambler, *Sectionalism in Virginia from 1776 to 1861* (Chicago, 1910).

The Tidewater was bound to be overtaken by the Piedmont, because the latter was much the larger area, a vast triangle with a broad base along the southern border of Virginia, and its sides following the Blue Ridge on the west and the fall line on the east until these lines met and merged at the falls of the Potomac. Furthermore, the southern boundary of Virginia was a political rather than a natural dividing line, and much of the North Carolina Piedmont was bound economically and culturally to Virginia. A significant cause of the eclipse of Tidewater Virginia was soil exhaustion; yet, as will be discussed below, this need not have been decisive. The inescapable defect of the Tidewater was its pestilential effect on its inhabitants. Those who were acclimatized were still less healthy than their compatriots west of the fall line, and newcomers had chances of survival little better than those of the original settlers of Jamestown. When Wilson Cary Nicholas, a friend and neighbor of Jefferson's in Albemarle County, sought and obtained the position of collector at Norfolk, his brother John urged him to resign. "What can induce you," he wrote, "to the risk to which you expose your own and your family's health — a West India climate with a homebred yellow fever. I am not personally acquainted with the place, but I know so many instances of its proving fatal to people who were not bred there . . . that I consider it as morally impossible that so numerous a family as yours should escape."[4]

The state of medical science was still such that one's best course was to stay healthy. William Janson, an Englishman who settled for a while in Norfolk, was fortunate enough to

---

[4] John Nicholas to Wilson Cary Nicholas, 17 June 1804, W. C. Nicholas Papers, LC. Also, on sickness in Tidewater Virginia, Dr. Robert Miller of Yorktown to Dr. James Minor of Louisa County, 14 November 1807, James Minor Papers, UVL; Johann David Schoepf, *Travels in the Confederation*, translated and edited by Alfred J. Morrison (Philadelphia, 1911), II, 51; Benjamin Latrobe, *The Journal of Latrobe* (New York, 1905), 11.

survive the yellow fever that seized him during one of the town's periodic epidemics. Janson credited the "judicious" treatment of his doctor: "I was copiously bled in the first instance, and blisters were applied to my legs, my feet, and the back of my neck." Further benefits were "strong doses of calomel, and . . . of bark." [5] While agues and fevers plagued the people of Tidewater Virginia, travelers remarked that the farther they proceeded above the fall line, the healthier and more robust they found the citizens. [6] Surely the obvious advantage of upland Virginia for comfort and longevity must have contributed to the slow decline of the Tidewater.

In New York state the expanding hinterland caused the rapid growth of New York City; the growth of Pennsylvania was comparably beneficial to Philadelphia and to Baltimore, which dominated the trade of the Susquehanna River. Virginia, with her diffuse population and numerous river systems, had no such prosperous and cultured cities. For most of the colonial period the only center of Virginia trade was the British Isles, whence came the ships which visited the scattered county tobacco warehouses and private wharves of the Tidewater. With the extensive and increasing settlement of upland Virginia there finally developed a number of towns worthy of the name, characteristically situated on or near the falls of the major rivers: Alexandria, Fredericksburg, Richmond, and Petersburg. The twin towns of Norfolk and Portsmouth were the only consequential settlements with a different situation. Their commanding position at the mouth of Chesapeake Bay made them a natural entrepôt for smaller vessels in the Tidewater trade, and the extensive pine forests of their vicinity supported a significant shipbuilding industry. Although the immediate hinterland of these towns pro-

---

[5] Charles William Janson, *The Stranger in America*, edited by Charles S. Driver (New York, 1935), 394–395.

[6] Isaac Weld, Jr., *Travels Through the States of North America* (London, 1800), I, 210.

duced little surplus for export, the difficulties of navigating Albemarle Sound brought much of the trade of North Carolina through Norfolk, especially after the completion of the Great Dismal Swamp Canal.[7]

At the beginning of our national period mercantile operations were still so scattered that the German physician, Dr. Johann Schoepf, remarked, "The entire commerce of Virginia has for long been almost altogether in the hands of European houses who have maintained their ware-houses and factors here. Among the Virginians few have concerned themselves in trade beyond the keeping of little shops here and there, and throughout the whole province there are still hardly any houses who would be disposed, or in a position, to undertake large affairs."[8] The Jeffersonian era saw some modification of this situation. Local merchants of imposing stature appeared in the fall-line towns as the expansion of Virginia required within the state itself an increase in the handling of commodities. This was most true of Richmond, for the Piedmont areas drained by the James secured the new capital the largest producing hinterland of all. By the end of the Jeffersonian period Richmond had become the first true city in Virginia.

The trade of Virginia was characteristic of an era devoted almost exclusively to commercial agriculture. Every description of manufactured article was imported and exchanged for staple commodities. The classic staple of Virginia was tobacco, but in the early national period Virginia planters turned increasingly to the cultivation for export of wheat, corn, and other foodstuffs. Lumber, livestock, and naval stores were also significant products of parts of the state.

---

[7] Médéric-Louis-Elie Moreau de Saint-Méry, *Moreau de St. Méry's American Journey*, translated and edited by Kenneth Roberts and Anna M. Roberts (New York, 1947), p. 51. François-Alexandre-Frédéric, Duc de la Rochefoucauld-Liancourt et d'Estissac, *Voyage dans les États-Unis d'Amerique*, vol. IV (Paris, 1799), pp. 255–256, 260–262, 270, 301–303.

[8] Schoepf, *Travels*, II, 59.

Every settled portion of Virginia was connected by road, creek, river, or bay to the commercial network, even including the transmontane Shenandoah Valley, whose commerce, however, was circuitously routed through Baltimore and Philadelphia.[9] Practically every merchant in the Virginia trade was obliged to handle the same sprawling stock of imported goods, and also to deal in all of the major export commodities. Traders differed in size and reliability, but were not significantly specialized as to inventories.

The merchants were divided roughly into three spheres of operation, however. The typical Tidewater merchant was a planter who carried on a retail trade in his immediate neighborhood, or else he was simply the hired agent of a British company operating a retail store and warehouse. The goods of either would come and go by water, usually directly to or from the British Isles. The merchants of the fall-line towns were sometimes willing to sell on a retail basis, but their major activity was wholesale trade. Robert Gamble of Richmond aptly described the function of this class in a letter of 1804 to Thomas Massie, a planter:

I have been in the habit for a number of years of acting as an agent between James Maury, Esq. of Liverpool, and his friends in this country, and any tobacco you forward to be shipped to him or other matters you are interested in shall be carefully attended to. I have since last fall, in order to enable me more distinctly and promptly to wind up a considerable and extensive scene of transactions under various firms, etc., taken my son Robert Gamble, Jr., into partnership, under the firm of Robert Gamble and Son, who will endeavor to execute any orders you may favor us with, as much to your satisfaction as any house here can do. In addition to a large double warehouse I built some years ago for the purpose of receiving, storing, and selling my friends' produce, I am finishing three other Brick Houses, to be covered with slate . . . which will

---

[9] La Rochefoucauld-Liancourt, *Voyage*, V, 51. The count claims that Richmond merchants lost the trade because they lacked sufficient capital to extend the long loans favored by Shenandoah merchants.

enable us to receive very extensively our friends' flour, tobacco, etc. . . . We have been able from extensive correspondence to obtain the very best rates as commission merchants for what has been confided to my care. We import largely and sell, except in particular articles, by wholesale only. Any article by *piece* or *dozen* can of course be had as low as merchants are furnished with who purchase to sell again. Our business extends to sugars, coffee, and other groceries, by the barrel, loaf, bag, etc.[10]

The third sphere of mercantile activity was above the fall line, and was, like that of the Tidewater, largely retail. Here one would not find the factors of British houses, but only planters who were also merchants. Their business was chiefly with the small planters of their neighborhoods, for great planters like Massie or Thomas Jefferson would order their supplies directly from the wholesalers of the fall line. Lacking the custom of the rich these inland merchants would not trade in finé wines, elegant furniture, or other items consumed only by the aristocracy. But otherwise they would stock the full array of imported goods, in addition to trading in local commodities such as flour, salt pork, corn meal, whiskey, and coarse clothing. Here are some of the items stocked by a retail merchant located in the southwestern part of the Virginia Piedmont: cotton, welch plains, corduroy, striped Holland, Irish linen, thread, men's and women's shoes, pewter dishes, basins, and plates, shoe hammers, awl blades, steel spurs, stock locks, men's and boys' hats, stockings, "ladies blue and white hats with trimmings," shoe buckles, ivory combs, a fiddle (price: seven shillings and sixpence), teaspoons, forks, knives, table knives, shoe knives, milling pins, scissors, ink powders, broad hose, sewing needles, darning needles, thimbles, boxes of wafers, handkerchiefs, paper, spelling books, Bibles, colored ribbons, salt, rum, pins, combs, buttons, nails, sugar, tea, German steel, "fashionable hat bands," alum salts, and green rugs. Through tree-clogged creeks and mud-rutted

---

[10] Letter of 27 August 1804, Massie Papers, VHS.

roads the irrepressible spirit of commerce brought the blessings of civilization to the frontiers of Virginia.[11]

The entire network of trade depended ultimately on the
fields of Virginia on the one hand, and on the enterprise of
British traders and manufacturers on the other. Virginia's
leaders were more than ungrateful to their British benefac-
tors, but their faith in their fields was boundless. Virginians
chose to define themselves not as businessmen or traders, but
as agrarians. Yet they have labored under a historical reputation of having been poor husbandmen.[12]

The most striking evidence that the Virginians used their
land badly was the rapidity with which they abandoned it.
In America the exploitation of land to its total exhaustion was
not, of course, peculiar to Virginians or even to slaveholding
planters. The extensive planting made possible by gangs of
slaves, however, enabled slaveholders to consume land more
quickly than the northern yeomen, restricted to the labor of
their own families and occasional hired men. Related to the
abuse of land was the Virginians' careless treatment of farm
animals. Travelers objected that the animals were normally
allowed to roam at large and were rarely provided adequate
fodder in cold weather. Thus they were likely to roam
farthest from home when the weather was at its worst. Rarely
was any effort made to preserve manure. Foreigners, accustomed to the intensive and careful cultivation practiced in
Europe, were shocked by the sloppiness of Virginia's agriculture. Dr. Schoepf remarked with disgust: "The whole com-
pass of the Virginian husbandry consists in first, raising a good
supply of maize for the planter's family, his Negroes, and his

---

[11] Various accounts, Pocket Plantation Papers, UVL.

[12] Avery O. Craven, *Soil Exhaustion as a Factor in the Agricultural
History of Virginia and Maryland, 1606–1860* (Urbana, 1925), stresses
the wastefulness of Chesapeake agriculture and the ineffectuality of
reform prior to 1820. Craven's evidence was selected to present the
bleakest picture possible, but so long as the reader is on guard, this
is the best work on the agricultural practices of the time.

cattle; then, tobacco and a little wheat for keeping up appearances; and, for the rest of the year, doing nothing at all."[13]

But outraged as he was with the Virginians' neglect of their animals, of fodder crops, of fences and barns and gardens, Dr. Schoepf found himself admiring the virtuosity of the better tobacco planters in their cultivation of that difficult plant.[14] The growing, curing, packing, and shipping of choice tobacco were complex and delicate processes, and the skill of Virginians in handling their huge annual tobacco crop was admired by practically every French and British traveler who has left us an opinion. Almost as frequently remarked was the skill of the Virginia gentry in breeding horses for racing and hunting. Furthermore, if manuring and crop rotations were not the rule in Virginia, they were practiced by some of the planters at least, and their use was spreading.[15] The agricultural revolution of eighteenth-century England was no secret to the Virginia gentry. The fairest conclusion about the quality of Virginia agriculture might run as follows: intensive use of the land was rare in a country where there was always more land than labor to tend it. At any given time, a large portion of the plantations would be newly or recently established enterprises, requiring the largest possible immediate return to cover the cost of acquisition. Virginia agriculture was essentially commercial, and therefore centered on the production of staple crops as large as possible in the shortest practical time. And the expansive, speculative nature of Virginia agriculture led the typical planter to employ his hands more in the clearing of new lands than in the careful maintenance of old ones. Such a system might well seem careless and wasteful to Europeans, as, in the long run, it surely was from any point of view. But few Virginians thought about the

[13] Schoepf, *Travels*, II, 89.

[14] *Ibid.*, pp. 73–74.

[15] Weld, *Travels*, p. 152; La Rochefoucauld-Liancourt, *Voyage*, IV, 292; William McKean Letterbook, VHS, letter of 17 July 1810.

long run as seriously as they thought about the rapid accumulation of a fortune and the payment of their debts.

The production of tobacco was the oldest and most competitive activity in Virginia. It had long since become clear that profits were relatively certain only if the tobacco were of the highest grade, and the grading was usually scrupulous and accurate, entrusted as it was to state-appointed inspectors. In the later eighteenth century the Virginians became increasingly involved in the production and export of foodstuffs, especially wheat, and their skill with grains increased proportionally as their cultivation of them expanded.[16] The quantities of wheat sent to market by Virginia planters belied the quaint notion that slave labor could not compete with free labor in this kind of agriculture. However, Virginia did ultimately fall behind Pennsylvania and New York as a grain exporter, and the reason was related clearly enough to the presence of slaves, though not to their efficiency as agricultural laborers. In the North the development of large cities was accompanied by the building of modern and efficient mills, and wheat was increasingly exported in the form of flour. But Virginia's trade was too diffuse to support milling establishments on a grand scale, and even where excellent locations were available, as at Richmand, the money of Virginia, as everywhere in the South, always tended to go into land and slaves rather than into manufacturing or processing industries. This was clearly a liability of the plantation system. Yet so long as men preferred to invest in land and slaves rather than in other forms of business capital, it is hardly reasonable to conclude that the slave-based plantation system was moribund.

The slave was fundamental in the large economic affairs

---

[16] Merrill Jensen, *The New Nation* (New York, 1950), pp. 236–237; John Tayloe Minute Book 1811, 1812, VHS, accounting for the sale of his crop of 7,003 bushels of wheat; La Rochefoucauld-Liancourt, *Voyage*, IV, 260, 261.

of Virginia. One hardly can find an instance of productive activity in which Negro slaves were not engaged. Their wide use points much more to their adaptability than to the occasional view that the Negro slave was a lazy and indifferent worker, suited only to the simplest and most monotonous tasks. As was mentioned above, tobacco culture itself was hardly simple. The plants had to be started from seedlings, then carefully transferred to their separate "hills." In an age without modern pesticides, they were protected from their natural enemies by a conscientious cultivation, and each plant was carefully pruned back so that its growth would all go into the broad lower leaves. In harvesting, curing, and packing the leaves great care was required to avoid tearing or bruising the sensitive weed.

While slave labor engaged in the growing of staples, other slaves attended to the auxiliary work of getting them to market. Negro coopers built the sturdy barrels known as hogsheads, each of which held one thousand or more pounds of tightly packed tobacco leaves. Negro blacksmiths forged the metal hoops that held these hogsheads together in their long and unavoidably rough voyage to Europe. Negro teamsters delivered the crops to the nearest available water, where Negro boatmen would pole or sail them along to the warehouses where they would await consignment to foreign buyers. At the various docks and marketplaces of Virginia, slaves attended to the hauling, loading, and unloading of the incoming and outgoing merchandise. Slave sailors even manned the ships engaged in the coastal and West India trades, though a wary legislature forbade that slaves constitute more than one-third of a crew, or serve as captains of vessels.[17]

---

[17] William Waller Hening, *The Statutes at Large in Virginia,* XI (Richmond, 1822), 404; *Virginia Argus,* 18 February 1804, advertising "for cash, a very VALUABLE NEGRO FELLOW, who has been accustomed to go by water." See Schoepf, *Travels,* II, 97.

During the American Revolution the state of Virginia used publicly owned slaves, probably acquired by confiscating them from Tories, to work the lead mines.[18] After the war some of them were freed for meritorious service. In times of peace slaves were equally conspicuous in public works. They built the roads, bridges, and ditches of the Old Dominion, such as they were. Slave labor also produced the first great public improvement of the state, the Great Dismal Swamp Canal. Slaves worked in the early coal and iron mines of Virginia, cut and milled timber, manufactured bricks, and milled grain. An enterprising Irishman named Bloom successfully employed his slaves in a cord and leather business at Norfolk. His hides came from the Virginia hinterland, he processed them entirely with Negro labor, and he shipped them to the British Isles.[19] Even Thomas Jefferson, sometime foe of manufacturing, set twelve of his young slaves, aged ten to sixteen years, to fabricating nails. By underselling the local merchants he foiled the "effort of the general system of Scotch policy to suppress every attempt at domestic manufacture."[20]

The model plantation itself exacted far more than simple cultivation from its hands. It hardly requires demonstration here that slaves in the household provided a full range of domestic services. Negro slaves also attended to the elegance and comfort of plantation life as grooms, teamsters, blacksmiths, and coachmen. They churned butter in the dairy, cured bacon and hams in the smokehouse, spun yarn, wove cloth, and made shoes. In Virginia east of the Blue Ridge slaves filled practically all the jobs available to skilled as well as to unskilled labor. The only general exceptions to this rule were the self-employed farmers with few or no slaves and the

[18] Benjamin Harrison to Thomas Madison, 12 December 1782, in H. R. McIlwain, ed., *Official Letters of the Governors of the State of Virginia* (Richmond, 1929), III, 399.

[19] La Rochefoucauld-Liancourt, *Voyage*, IV, 272.

[20] Quoted in Joseph I. Shulim, *The Old Dominion and Napoleon Bonaparte* (New York, 1952), pp. 20–21.

expert ships' carpenters of Norfolk.[21] Some travelers regarded the slaves as lazy and indifferent workers, while others thought them overworked, but all agreed that they accounted for most of the work that was accomplished.

It is probably true that the slave labor of Virginia was, on the average, less productive than the free labor of the North. But it is surely false to infer from this that slave labor must, on that account, be driven out of existence. For in individual cases, the productivity of slave labor depended not on a statistical abstraction, but on the managerial skill of the planter. Thus a Tidewater planter could boast to his French visitor that each of his eight slaves had netted over $300 one year in the production of wheat.[22] On the other hand, poor management could result in losses. Dr. Schoepf told of planters who were so improvident that when their corn crop failed they were left without food for their slaves, and were forced to court bankruptcy by buying provisions in a high market.[23] At the same time more prudent planters would diversify their crops, plant in excess of their customary need, and keep adequate reserves of provisions.

Free labor in the North naturally had a motive for efficiency missing in the slave: hard work and the saving of wages promised an early escape from the working class. But the imaginative planter could devise plenty of incentives of his own, such as the rewards of extra food, drink, clothing, and leisure, and the punishments of withholding some of these things, of demoting the slave to more menial work, and of whipping. The successful planters who profitably used their slaves were always numerous enough to preserve the system, and if an occasional Virginian abandoned the slave system, far more adopted it: the total number of slaveowners was always increasing.

---

[21] La Rochefoucauld-Liancourt, *Voyage*, IV, 270.

[22] *Ibid.*, p. 343.

[23] Schoepf, *Travels*, II, 37.

If slaves were to be expert and productive workers, how-ever, they required expert training and continual supervision. A planter could generally afford to turn over the direct super-vision of his slaves to an overseer if he owned more than ten of them.[24] This freed his time for leisure, politics, or a profes-sion, but it also threatened him with a lowered standard of performance, for overseers were a difficult lot. If a planter owned many more slaves he was practically forced to hire one or more overseers, for both the differentiation of work and the sheer extent of the larger plantations would be beyond the power of one man to supervise. Indeed, the great planter often owned plantations miles apart from one another, or even in different counties, each of which would require a resident, full-time overseer.

Unlike slaves, overseers as a class had the trait noted in the wage laborers of the North: their typical goal was the accumulation of enough capital to go into business for them-selves. Therefore if a planter should hire a truly superior overseer, he would not be likely to keep him; on the other hand, the most incompetent overseer might linger on in his job forever. The ablest planters made the best of this situation and resigned themselves to a continual recruitment of young talent. But this scarcely relieved them of managerial duties, for to a great extent they were overseers of overseers, con-tinually training and checking their young protegés.

The Virginia dynasty of Jefferson, Madison, and Monroe has often been cited as evidence that slaveholders of the early national period could not prosper. Actually the failure of these three to operate their plantations at a profit was mainly a failure of management: their continuing attention to public duties, for which they were inadequately paid, forced them to rely on overseers whom they were in no posi-tion to supervise. Jefferson, the richest and ablest agriculturist

---

[24] James Madison, *Letters and Other Writings of James Madison*, pub-lished by order of Congress (Philadelphia, 1865), III, 313.

of the three, might still have operated at a profit, but his affection for good books and fine wines, and his generosity to friends and relatives, usually caused him to live beyond his sizable income. George Washington, on the other hand, had such an enormous capacity for detail that he was usually able to manage his huge estate even when removed from it for years at a time. John Taylor, obliged to choose between a career of public service and maintaining his prosperous plantation, stayed with the plantation.

Another kind of poor management resulted from the lack of technical skill in Virginia, for slaves could only do what they were taught. For example, the merchants Graham and Havans of Richmond worked coal mines with a crew of fifty Negroes, who also tended their tobacco crop. La Rochefoucauld-Liancourt thought very little of Graham and Havans, "who were neither chemists nor mechanics, but worked blindly, and could not be enlightened by any good advice, because, perhaps, no one in all America understood the working of mines."[25] An iron manufacturer in Pittsylvania County found that even when he had produced good iron he had no market for it: the diffusion of economic activity in Virginia and the overwhelming emphasis on agriculture perennially discouraged the growth of manufacturing skills among workers and owners alike.[26]

Probably the most inefficient factor in slavery was that managerial talent normally could not be recruited from the abler slaves themselves. Independent thinking, initiative, the capacity to organize, and a wide experience of the world were dangerous traits to foster in slaves. Most Virginians properly felt that their safety required that their slaves be dependent and ignorant. Within these limitations slaves could

---

[25] La Rochefoucauld-Liancourt, *Voyage*, V, 1.
[26] Several letters from James Callaway, the iron manufacturer, to his relatives John and Ralph Smith, from 1786 through 1792, Pocket Plantation Papers, UVL.

still become expert workmen, but only under supervision. There were widespread exceptions, of course, but it was the public policy of Virginia to discourage them. A slave accustomed to directing the activity of dozens of men and their equipment was potentially the organizer of a runaway or a rebellion.

With all of the difficulties attending their use, slaves remained the basic working force in Virginia, and their value to the state may be judged by the ascendancy of slave prices over all others. Slave prices were so high in the decade before the Civil War that the prices of the Jeffersonian period have seemed low by comparison. But the difference turns out to prove that the prices of the 1850's were inflated, not that those of the earlier period were depressed. Four hundred dollars was the highest price generally paid for tractable male slaves in their late teens and in apparent good health. Only slaves endowed with exceptional skills commanded more money than this. Older or younger slaves, female slaves, and slaves known to be lazy or unruly were all priced lower. The average price paid for slaves was therefore well below $400. One major reason for the lower average was that female slaves almost always had children, and Virginians customarily sold mothers and their children together. As the child was not likely to earn his keep until the age of ten, investment in him was speculative.[27]

It is difficult to compare the prices of the early national period with those of the present, for commodities themselves have changed so much. However, a sketch of the price levels of the 1790's and early 1800's will easily demonstrate the relatively high level of slave prices. There were fluctuations and regional variations, of course, and perhaps a general upward trend of prices that continued from the late 1780's to the War of 1812. Still, the following prices are representative

---

[27] Madison, *Letters and Other Writings*, III, 315.

enough. A pound of sugar, rather a luxury in those days, cost nineteen cents, a peck of salt forty-one cents, a quart of whiskey twenty-five cents before 1800 and thirty-four cents after, a pound of beef ten cents, a pound of salt pork seven cents, and a bushel of wheat sixty cents to a dollar. A crude house could be built for $200 and a relatively commodious one for $600. A respectable house in Norfolk, where the cost of living was said to be twice that of the rest of Virginia, rented for $230 per annum. Town lots in Norfolk, sixty-six feet deep, sold for nine or ten dollars per foot of frontage. "Coarse shoes for Negroes" cost as little as three pairs for a dollar, good shoes cost from one to two dollars, and fancy shoes cost still more. A dollar a day was considered a living wage in Norfolk. In brief, the price level of the Jeffersonian period was so low that even with a price ceiling around $400 slaves were the costliest commodities in general commerce. A good field hand would cost as much as a thirty foot by sixty-six foot lot in Norfolk, or three thousand pounds of beef, or three hundred gallons of whiskey. The sale of a good slave would easily pay twice the highest annual tax assessments of the wealthiest Virginians, even when wars current or just past had raised the rates.[28]

In 1786 the tax bill of Colonel Edmund Berkeley of Middlesex County was £31.12.10.[29] Throughout the Jeffersonian period the dollar was worth six shillings, or very close to it, so this would be the equivalent of about $105. This covered assessments on an unspecified number of acres, forty slaves, twelve horses, twenty-one cattle, and four wheels. Ralph

---

[28] La Rochefoucauld-Liancourt supplies a good account of prices, especially IV, 272. Also valuable is Harry Toulmin, *The Western Country in 1793*, edited by Marion Tinling and Godfrey Davies (San Marino, 1948), especially p. 43. I have also compared prices found in the Virginia State Library's collection of county will books, and those in the personal papers listed in the bibliography.

[29] Tax receipts acknowledging payment to the Sheriff of Middlesex County, Berkeley Family Papers — Berkeley-Noland MSS, UVL.

Smith, a prosperous merchant-planter of Pittsylvania County, paid only £3.6.0 in taxes for 1788.[30] In 1815 one finds Archibald Eppes, cited by Professor Jackson T. Main as one of the one hundred wealthiest men in Virginia, paying $110 in taxes, which included an assessment of $2.80 for a pianoforte valued at $200.[31] At the other end of the economic scale George Huston of Orange County paid fifty-one cents each year from 1800 through 1809, after some prodding from the sheriff.[32] The planters of Virginia were in no danger of bankruptcy because of high taxation.

The obvious reason for the enduring high value of the slave was the enduring presence of great planters who flourished with the aid of their labor. However, the richest men in Virginia were not simply those who owned the most land and the most slaves and therefore could produce the largest crops. Ultimately the prosperity of everyone in Virginia depended on its staple exports, yet these were produced in such quantity, both in Virginia and in her sister states, that prices rarely rose high enough to yield large profits. The accumulation of wealth from agriculture alone was a slow and painstaking business, wherein the planter must practice a kind of personal mercantilism. Everything he could possibly produce on his plantation would be something less to buy from outside; if his plantation supported itself, any crop sales, no matter how low the prices, would increase his capital. Most Virginians were too advanced in their consumers' tastes to take such a grim approach to accumulation, and most of them firmly believed that in the long run — the perennial faith of American agriculturists — commodity prices would rise to profitable levels and stay there permanently.

---

[30] Pocket Plantation Papers, UVL.

[31] Item no. 465, in the Eppes Deposit, UVL. Professor Main's article, "The One Hundred," is in *William and Mary Quarterly*, 3rd series, XI (1954), 354–384.

[32] Orange County Auditor's receipt, Barbour Papers, UVL.

This very hope was a major source of profit to wealthy and able Virginians, for it was the basis of the continual expansion of the American frontier, and the profitable if risky enterprise of land speculation. Another major source of profit was trade. One of the enduring curiosities of American historiography is the identification of the commercial spirit with the North, as if the entrepreneurial spirit never existed south of Mason and Dixon's line. Although repositories of personal papers from the Jeffersonian period overflow with the records of enterprising merchant-planters, this class of citizens receives practically no attention from Jeffersonian scholarship. Most of the writing about Virginia in the early nation has been in the form of biographies, tracing the careers of eminent Virginians in military and political affairs, against a background of stable and idyllic agrarianism. During the past seventy years or so historians, with some exceptions, have been increasingly cold-blooded in their appraisal of the ruling classes of the North, while uncritically accepting the happy self-image of southern aristocrats as a relaxed and cultivated rural gentry, relatively immune to the mean motives of the marketplace. But in fact Virginians were bound to trade and speculation with an intensity unsurpassed in the North. The very profits of these activities, however, tempted many bold Virginians to plunge into them on borrowed capital, creating the inevitable cycles of boom and bust typical of entrepreneurial economies.

Because of the great scattering of commerce, only a few situations in Virginia allowed the accumulation of a great fortune in trade alone. Similarly, land speculations were long-range and uncertain investments, which often took a generation to yield their profits if they were profitable at all. The wealthy Virginian was typically a man who appreciated the customary and unavoidable small scale of any given activity in his state, and built his fortune by combining a variety of interests, no one of which could yield great wealth, but which taken altogether could do so handsomely. Thomas Elliott of Northampton County on the eastern shore was an exemplar of the pattern. He owned brick kilns and a lumber mill, a two-thirds interest in a mercantile firm, and several distilleries. He also owned several plantations. All of this property, apparently unencumbered by significant debt, he devised to his heirs, along with fourteen slaves.[33] Leneaus Bolling of Buckingham County specialized in trade, agriculture, and rentals. According to his journal he spent most of his own time tending store, entrusting the supervision of livestock, fields, and orchards to an overseer. In Buckingham and Amherst counties he rented several plantations, some of which must have been huge, considering both the value of money and the wide availability of rental lands in those days. James Smith paid Bolling but fifty dollars a year in rent for the use of his land, William Bailey paid $275, and Thomas Miller paid $500. On January 1, 1814, Bolling expected to collect around $1,600 in rent, though his tenants seemed in some cases unwilling to pay.[34]

The great political figures of Virginia were not so successful in making money, except for the most celebrated of them all, George Washington. The father of his country would willingly have been the father of all its industries. Even under the limited opportunities of the Northern Neck, Washington managed to engage in land speculation, grain and lumber milling, distilling, transportation, brickmaking, and investing in banks and canal companies. He raised crops for market also, of course, though he abandoned tobacco after the Revolution, sensing the greater profits to be made in grains.

Virginians might also amass wealth by combining planting with the learned professions of law or medicine. The danger

---

[33] Northampton County Will Book no. 32, 1802–07, VSL, pp. 255–261.

[34] Journal of Leneaus Bolling, microfilm copy, UVL. The Huntington Library holds an earlier journal by Bolling.

here was that the greater their success in their profession, the more of their business affairs had to be delegated to overseers or relatives. Patrick Henry and Thomas Jefferson provide interesting contrasts as lawyer-planters. Both rose rapidly in the legal profession as young men, and improved their plantations apace. But Jefferson gave his prime years to public service, while Henry refused to leave Virginia on any public business, and, before the Revolution was won, determined not to neglect his business affairs by holding major public office even within the state. During his lifetime Henry built a fortune, while Jefferson left his lands more encumbered with debt than they had been when he inherited them. The law could be profitably mixed with planting so long as one did not use it as a springboard into public life only, and abandon its practice in favor of underpaid political offices. A major advantage of legal expertise was the inevitable involvement of lawyers in the perpetual land speculations of the Virginia aristocracy. A lawyer-speculator could defend his own titles, in addition to profiting from the defense of those of his clients. The notorious land system of Virginia allowed buyers of public lands to secure title to a given number of acres and then locate them with their own surveys. This was a generous system, allowing the purchaser to make sure that each of his acres was as valuable as the region would yield, but it naturally led to infinite litigation.

The available methods by which Virginians grew rich reinforced the tendency of the plantation economy to diffusion. In his own neighborhood a great planter would be a small-scale monopolist, for the comparatively sparse population would support but one general store, one grain mill, a few distilleries, and perhaps only one lawyer. The extraordinary westward expansion of the plantation reflected the upward aspirations of Virginians who wanted to become, in Kentucky or Tennessee, or finally in Alabama and Mississippi, the moguls of the rich river bottoms, in possession of the best millsites, the wharf, the warehouse, and the local store. The commercial and industrial economy of the North could grow vertically as well as horizontally, as more and more kinds of enterprises developed in the older centers, but the plantation economy grew almost entirely by spreading from one river valley to another. This inevitably led to the relative decline within the Union of the state of Virginia itself, for from the beginning of the early national period the best lands for plantations were already taken up east of the Alleghenies, and both speculators and prospective grandees were looking toward the banks of the major tributaries of the Mississippi for their opportunities.

Whatever our early statesmen or later historians may have said about the economic inefficiency of slavery, the historical record demonstrates that the plantation system not only survived but dramatically extended itself in the early national period, and that the plantation system in the United States absolutely depended on slavery. Comparisons between slave labor and free labor are rather meaningless for this period, because the planter did not in fact have the alternative of hiring free white labor in any quantity, and he was unwilling to free his slaves and contract with them for wages. Immigration was light in the early national period until after the War of 1812, and most of those who came were small proprietors or skilled laborers. They sought the farms and cities of the North as being more like their homelands in climate and opportunities, and were scarcely willing to be agricultural laborers, at least for any length of time. So long as the United States was expanding, labor was relatively dear compared to Europe, and if the plantation could not achieve its maximum potential efficiency with slave labor it was likely not even to exist without it. Slave labor replaced hired and indentured servants in Virginia originally because of this economic fact.

Of course Virginia experienced some hard times during the Jeffersonian period, and slavery as a primary economic institution was related to all of them. As a plantation area, Virginia depended on foreign markets for her prosperity and always suffered when foreign trade was disturbed. Thus President Jefferson's embargo and President Madison's war resulted in bulging warehouses and unpaid bills. On the other hand, the distresses of Europe in the wars of the French Revolution otherwise benefited Virginia by increasing foreign demands for her products.

Probably the greatest economic distresses in Virginia came about because of the defective credit system. There was no federal coinage worthy of the name during the early national period, and Virginia found it extremely difficult to keep a supply of foreign coin within the state. As elsewhere in America, this led to the clipping and dividing of coins and continual bickering over their relative value.[35] Most of the transactions at the retail level and all larger transactions were accounted for on paper, and had nothing to do with specie. Retail merchants kept accounts with each of their customers which were periodically balanced by tobacco, wheat, salt pork, hides, and other staples. These commodities in larger shipments met the merchants' obligations to their own wholesalers. When a planter wanted to buy an item not available from his usual supplier and creditor, he would write out a bill of exchange, that is, a draft on the merchant with whom he had credit, and use it as payment. Bills of exchange drawn on reputable and well-established merchants could circulate indefinitely as money. Also available were the tobacco notes, secured by the government-certified tobacco deposited in warehouses for future sale and shipment. Upon deposit of his tobacco a planter would receive a certificate which he might forward immediately to his own favorite corresponding merchant, but might just as easily use as cash.

More risky was the optimistic Virginian's habit of buying land and slaves with personal promissory notes which depended on anticipated earnings for their payment. Fluctua-

---

[35] J. P. Brissot de Warville, *New Travels in the United States,* translated from the French anonymously (Dublin, 1792), pp. 437–439.

tions in trading, prices, and weather made these notes inherently unreliable, yet planters persisted in passing them on, with their own endorsements, until practically every man of consequence in the state became enmeshed in the resulting web of indebtedness and imperiled by the failure of his least reliable brethren. An eloquent example of the embarrassments produced by this system is the following letter of Bowler Cocke of Turkey Island to the prosperous Thomas Massie:

I saw Mr. John Marshall and inquired of him if he had got a judgment against me for your two bonds. He told me he believed not, but would in a few days look into the business, and if he had would give you notice of it. I requested of him to beg a further indulgence of you, for to have an execution levied on me, or my property at this time, for that sum of money, would ruin me. Depend upon it, every exertion in my power has been made, and is yet making to pay you out of the funds that ought to have [been] paid you long ago, and I have great reason to believe I shall be able to accomplish it by the spring. Mr. George Webb died in debt as an executor to my father's estate £978.23.2 [sic] with twenty years interest, and I have great reason to believe John Beckley has sold land of his to a much greater amount; besides that, I shall get judgment against a Mr. Nathan of New York in the spring for a large sum. The last time I saw my brother William he promised to do something clever in this business this winter. I expect he will because he has made a good crop and therefore has the means. Pray my dear Sir, do not order execution against me. If you do it will ruin me entirely. . . .[36]

It appears that Bowler Cocke was Massie's brother-in-law, and did secure relief, and in this he was also typical of the Virginia aristocracy. That fluid group, justly described as a cousindom, looked out for its weaker members both by the direct aid of loans and by the expert use of a legal system which favored debtors. This was not so much a question of laws, although for a while after the Revolution lands could not be seized for debts, but rather the consequence of a mar-

---

[36] Letter of 10 November 1794, Massie Family Papers, Section I, VHS.

velous sluggishness in court proceedings. It often took years to win a suit for the collection of a debt, and it happened sometimes during these delays that, while the debtor was successfully working out his difficulties, the creditor himself would go bankrupt.

If the frequent vicissitudes of the Virginia economy resulted from its being a plantation economy, dependent on foreign trade and perennially short of specie, the remedy clearly was that program of economic nationalism advocated in the new nation by Tench Coxe of Philadelphia and later by Alexander Hamilton. The development of internal manufactures and a national banking system would free the Americans from exploitation by European empires, and might also be expected to work against the institution of slavery by creating new outlets for capital. Yet it is a commonplace that Virginia politics, except for an occasional lapse, always stood against what Henry Clay later called the "American System" and urged that America remain dedicated to agriculture only. This amounted to a policy of maintaining and extending the plantation system, with its inseparable companion, Negro slavery.

CHAPTER

TWO

The Pursuit of Happiness in Jeffersonian Virginia

The social system of Virginia was as compatible with Negro slavery as the plantation economy. Social as well as economic life endured many drawbacks as a result of slavery, and at least some Virginians were well aware of them. Still, we find the Virginians of the early national period a proud and vigorous group, largely innocent of misgivings about their way of life, and practically devoid of ideas for significantly changing it.

In the fashion of aristocracies elsewhere in America, the ruling class of Virginia affected social exclusiveness, but it had no firm barriers against entry from below, and it supported the removal of legal mainstays of exclusiveness like primogeniture and entail. The majority of white Virginians, owning few or no slaves, and modest estates of less than five hundred acres, had little class consciousness under these circumstances. Their relations with the wealthy planters were usually cordial, they respected and supported the political leadership of the aristocrats, and if they were not entirely contented with their station in life, their normal ambition was to become plantation aristocrats themselves. Many of them succeeded in doing so, either in Virginia, or in the newer commonwealths of the South.

On the other hand, many of the poorer citizens of Virginia found that where the plantation prevailed they could not secure for themselves the decent lands they craved as a springboard to prosperity, so they crossed the Ohio River into the Old Northwest where slavery was prohibited. These migrants, however, were probably not conscious of having been "driven out" of the South, for it is unlikely that they regarded Kentucky and Tennessee as any more their own provinces than Ohio, Indiana, and Illinois. Anyway, those areas of the Old Northwest most heavily settled from the South eventually opposed the Republican Party in its nascent years, and they demonstrated considerable sympathy for the Confederacy during the Civil War. The ex-southerners, in short, were not notably antisoutherners. If they were sometimes opposed to slavery in principle, they were still more likely, as a class, to oppose rather than to support abolitionists and others who might undermine the southern planter.

Still less was the planters' aristocracy likely to fall victim to an outraged and alienated intelligentsia. Such intellectuals as there were within the state were loyal members of the aristocracy, and they were both proud of its traditions and jealous of its prerogatives. If they were embarrassed by slavery and eager for its early end, they were neither willing to inconvenience the slaveholder for the sake of the slave, nor to see the plantation system itself disappear. Only George Wythe, among all the eminent thinkers of Jeffersonian Virginia, was willing to reason from the fundamental principle of the Negro's rights as a human being, and to allow the claims of planters to suffer if they must. The assaults on slavery by all the other renowned intellects of Virginia were, by contrast to the positions of the mildest abolitionists, practical endorsements of the status quo.

Virginia was as free from external as from internal pressure to change. The foreign nation with which Virginia, however reluctantly, had the most contact was Britain, in whose commercial interest it remained to preserve the plantation economy. When the Federalists threatened, in the early 1790's, to fix upon the nation a program for economic transformation, the Virginia agrarians, astute as ever in politics, successfully organized a national party, swept the Federalists from office, and restored rusticity as the national ideal.

Finally it should be noted that Virginia was free of the host of modern agonies that have, since the nineteenth century, seemingly become permanent attributes of Western civilization. The goal of women was still simply to be wives and mothers, the family was still the central institution of society, and most of the relationships of life were with people rather than with routinized and necessarily impersonal bureaucracies. If petty vices were tolerated more than in some of the cooler provinces to the north, there was still full agreement about the absolutes of morality. The only disturbance of the traditional harmonies of society came in the religious life of Virginia, where the Great Awakening resumed its proselytizing of the lower classes after the Revolution and certain of the educated planters adopted the Deistic heresy. Caught between the upper millstone of reason and the nether one of evangelical piety, the Anglican Church lost the legal primacy which its indifferent organization was inadequate to defend. Conservatives might lament the loss of all power for gently persuading the support of revealed religion, but as the mass support for disestablishment came from those Virginians of the deepest religious commitment, the movement hardly seemed to threaten Christianity itself. And despite evidence to the contrary in the 1780's and 1790's, neither Deists, nor Methodists, nor any other group of dissenters seriously challenged the basic institutions of Virginia.

In describing the life of Virginians, then, we are describing a stable and relatively serene life by any standards, and certainly by those of the late eighteenth century. This very serenity explains the resistance of Virginia's leaders to any changes which might alter their comfortable world. And just as they were vigorous in the defense of Virginian values, they were active and imaginative in finding new ways to enhance those values through the reform of laws, the improvement of transportation, the securing of new markets, and the winning of the West.

A basic fact of life in Virginia was its isolation. While contemplating the relative maturity of its economy in the early national period, students are likely to think of its having become rather crowded. Yet it was easy enough in the years following the Revolution for a person to ride all day without seeing another human being. The roads were mostly paths cut through the dense woods which still covered most of Virginia. The rivers which bore the commerce of the state flowed roughly from west to east, thereby becoming an obstacle rather than a convenience to the majority of travelers, who proceeded north and south, or parallel to the Blue Ridge. A good portion of the travel accounts are taken up with the tribulations of finding one's way in Virginia. Captain Anburey has left us an example of the kind of difficulty a traveler might encounter:

. . . if perchance you meet an inhabitant and enquire your way, his directions are, if possible, more perplexing than the roads themselves, for he tells you to keep the right hand path, then you'll come to an old field, you are to cross that, and then you'll come to the fence of such a one's plantation, then keep that fence, and you'll come to a tobacco house; after you have passed that, you'll come to a road that has three forks . . . keep the right hand fork for about half a mile, and then you'll come to a creek. . . .[1]

Another traveler, Robert Hunter, Jr., learned of the hazards of travel in Virginia when his horse began to fall through the rotten planks of a bridge between Richmond and New Castle. Fortunately horse and rider were able to scramble out of the wreckage unharmed.[2] Isaac Weld, Jr., reported that of the ferries in Virginia "not one in six . . . are good and well manned. . . . As I passed along I heard of number-less recent instances of horses being drowned, killed, and having their legs broken, by getting in and out of the boats."[3]

William Wirt, in his *Letters of the British Spy,* cited the wretched condition of the roads, bridges, and ferries of Virginia as a sure indication of weakness in the state's reputed public spirit. But this was not altogether fair. Considering the size of plantations, their distance from one another, and their requirements for some sort of access to one another as well as to markets, the Virginians do not seem to have been so negligent. Each plantation must itself have been served by many miles of roads and paths, some of which had to be adequate for carriages and wagons. The state scarcely had the resources to maintain such a scattered network in first-class condition.

The wealthy planter had frequent business beyond his own plantation, especially if he were also a merchant, law-

---

[1] Thomas Anburey, *Travels Through the Interior Parts of America* (Boston, 1923), pp. 196–197. Anburey's narrative is not altogether original, urges Whitfield J. Bell in "Thomas Anburey's 'Travels Through America': A Note on Eighteenth-Century Plagiarism," *Papers of the Bibliographical Society of America,* XXXVII, no. 1 (1943) 23–26.

[2] Robert Hunter, Jr., *Quebec to Carolina,* edited by Louis B. Wright and Marion Tinling (San Marino, 1943), p. 238.

[3] Weld, *Travels,* I, 170.

yer, doctor, or officer of the government. Travel being slow, there was a demand for many taverns, for one could not always rely on open and free hospitality along every route. Harry Toulmin found a Colonel Kemp whose tavern had "altogether the appearance of a private house," which indeed, it had been, until the generous Colonel found that he must either charge his frequent guests or go bankrupt.[4] The tavern, along with the courthouse, the race track, and the market, was a focal point of the democratic element in Virginian social life, for the wealthiest planters might here talk and drink with men of lower social standing, and often solicit their votes as well. So important were the taverns that their rates and practices were strictly controlled by local government; the gentry who sat on the county courts thereby assured themselves against exploitation when the court was in session. Thus the Albemarle Court prescribed the following prices in 1792: rum and brandy were to cost four and one-half pence per gill, madeira wine should be four shillings and sixpence, dinner one shilling and sixpence, breakfast one shilling and thruppence, and lodging in a feather bed sixpence per night.[5]

Court days were always a signal for revelry. On such an occasion Robert Hunter, Jr., observed that Tappahannock was "very full, though what they come for, God knows, except it's to get drunk. No other business seems to be going on."[6] The next morning, however, there was plenty of business: a sale of Negro slaves. "Stout men of about forty years of age sold for betwixt eighty and ninety pounds. An ostler sold for £160 currency."[7] Besides supporting the progress of trade and justice, the taverns served as centers for the

---

[4] Toulmin, *Western Country*, p. 29.

[5] Albermarle County Order Book, 1791–93, VSL, entry of 10 March 1792.

[6] Hunter, *Quebec to Carolina*, p. 219.

[7] *Ibid.*, p. 228.

dissemination of information, both by gossip and by their amply papered walls and doors. From the many notices posted in taverns Dr. Schoepf observed that "the traveler gets a many-sided entertainment, and gains instruction as to where taxes are heavy, where wives have eloped or horses been stolen, and where the new doctor has settled."[8]

While the wealthy planters mixed democratically with their poorer compatriots, they preserved their aristocratic character by entertaining only their peers at home, and of course their womenfolk were largely restricted to genteel company and surroundings. The considerable distances between plantations were a justification for frequent and long visits by one or a few friends or relatives, most often female. Less frequently the planter would have an immense party lasting two or three days, when as many guests as might be packed into the house would be invited. The fabled grace and charm of Old Virginia glow through various accounts of gowns swirling through ballrooms till dawn, of feasts of ham and chicken and roast beef, of fox hunting in the afternoon or, perhaps, racing, followed by a "julap" on the veranda. More routine days might find ladies playing harpsichords or the new pianofortes, reading novels, writing letters, or sewing, while their gentlemen attended to business or to sport.

Not all planters who had the means for a cultivated and gracious life had the talent and breeding to pursue it. As in so many places before the discovery of the germ theory of disease, Virginia was a province in which the available water was wisely regarded as being unsafe, and thirsty Virginians therefore had to choose between tea, coffee, and distilled spirits, which, when mixed with water, made a safe as well as palatable drink. The ladies of Virginia seem to have universally contented themselves with tea and, if they

---

[8] Quoted in A. J. Morrison, *Travels in Virginia in Revolutionary Times* (Lynchburg, 1922), p. 50.

could afford it, wine. But many of their menfolk became so devoted to potations of rum, brandy, or whiskey and water, which they would drink from early morning till bedtime, that they staggered through life in a perpetual stupor.[9]

While the more sober and industrious planters were busy at planting, trading, litigation, and land speculation, their wastrel cousins, assigning the management of their fields to overseers, would gamble on races and with cards, or simply loaf. Prime evidences of dissipation among the gentry were the repeated attempts by the legislature to tax or outlaw gaming tables. The successful passage of such laws suggests that the confirmed gamblers were in a minority. Their repeated enactment, however, suggests that none of them proved effective. La Rochefoucauld-Liancourt observed that the most widely invoked of the acts against gambling was that which absolved losers from paying their debts.[10]

The range of education was as wide as that of social accomplishment. Planters always gave their children at least an elementary education, sometimes by hiring a tutor, but more often by sending them to a local grammar school. These were usually ephemeral affairs, set up by migrant Englishmen or Scots with more education than capital. In 1796 La Rochefoucauld-Liancourt reported a good grammar school in Norfolk where boys received instruction for forty dollars per year. Only reading lessons were available for young ladies, who had to travel to Williamsburg or to Baltimore for a more thorough education.[11] Lewis G. Sowell advertised in Norfolk his intention of "pursuing the instruction of youth in an apartment of the house occupied by Mr. John Heath, near the Hay Market." He offered Latin, English taught "gramatically," arithmetic, history, and geography, including

---

[9] See Anburey's *Travels*, p. 191; Latrobe on the Petersburg races in his *Journal*, pp. 22–25; Schoepf, *Travels*, II, 95.

[10] La Rochefoucauld-Liancourt, *Voyage*, IV, 313.

[11] *Ibid.*, p. 271 .

"the use of globes." He asked ten pounds per year for tuition in Latin, and twenty-four dollars for the other subjects. He also announced his intention to accept no more than ten or twelve students.[12]

Elementary education was not entirely restricted to those wealthy enough to pay tuition. In 1790 John Mayo donated a "tenement" a mile and a half outside Richmond for use as a free school. A teacher named Samuel Coleman there offered instruction to thirty needy children, and the public was invited to assist: a newspaper notice declared that donations might be paid to the state treasurer to help with "the discharge of such expenses, as must necessarily be incurred in the execution of the design."[13]

This was an age in which somewhat more pretentious schools, designated as academies, were springing up all over Virginia. These might offer elementary instruction, but were mainly designed to offer courses we would designate as secondary. In most cases the academy would be the final stage of the young Virginian's formal education. Abner Waugh's academy at Bolling Green, Caroline County, offered English, Latin, Greek, mathematics, geography, history, and natural philosophy, and promised "Astronomy, as soon as the necessary apparatus can be procured."[14] The sponsorship of academies by the aristocracy may be traced through the various acts of incorporation and appointments of trustees for them. Listed to oversee the nascent Albemarle Academy in Jefferson's county were, among others, Wilson Cary Nicholas, John Nicholas, William D. Meriwether, Thomas W. Lewis, and several of Jefferson's closest relatives: Thomas Mann Randolph and John, Dabney, and Peter Carr.[15]

Though nothing came of Jefferson's general scheme for

---

[12] *Virginia Argus*, 22 February 1804.

[13] *Virginia Gazette and General Advertiser*, 29 December 1790.

[14] *Ibid.*

[15] Shepherd, II, 427.

public education, the government acted in behalf of learning where it could afford to do so. The General Assembly was pleased to use the native love of gambling for constructive ends by licensing lotteries, such as the one "for the benefit of the RANDOLPH ACADEMY . . . 1800 Tickets at 5 Dollars each are 9,000 dollars to be paid in . . . prizes, subject to a deduction of fifteen per cent for the use of said Academy."[16] The House of Delegates supported the Richmond academy of E. Harris by loaning it a building until the House might once more "have use for it." Harris was pleased to announce the addition of an assistant, Mr. John Urquhart, "liberally educated at the University of Aberdeen," who would teach mathematics.[17]

In the absence of statistics, one can only guess at the annual educational enrollment of Virginia during the Jeffersonian period, hoping to indicate orders of magnitude. The vigorous growth of the Methodist and Baptist denominations probably caused a proportional increase in literacy among the poorer whites, so that it is reasonable to assume that the majority of white Virginians were at least literate and capable of simple arithmetic. Academies, while numerous, were nevertheless quite small, and so probably offered secondary instruction to no more than a thousand scholars per year. There is little indication that more than a hundred Virginians were formally engaged in higher education in any year before 1800.

The College of William and Mary, sometimes designated as the University, was the only institution of higher learning existing throughout the period between the Revolution and the War of 1812, and it failed to expand. In 1783, in 1795, and again in 1802 the student body was reported as being between thirty and forty, with a faculty of six or seven instructors. This stagnation resulted from the transfer of the

---

[16] *Virginia Gazette and General Advertiser*, 30 March 1791.

[17] *Ibid.*, 29 December 1790.

capital from Williamsburg to Richmond, leaving the former town to dwindle into an insignificant village, and from the shift of population and political weight to the Piedmont, where the Presbyterians established Hampden-Sydney College and where, much later, Jefferson succeeded in establishing the University of Virginia. Instruction at William and Mary overlapped that of the academies, and even that of the grammar schools. Isaac Weld, Jr., observed that most of the students commanded so little Greek and Latin that those languages were dropped and replaced by modern ones.[18] In 1786 Peter Carr had been studying French, preparing for Italian, and might have undertaken Spanish, had he been able to find a dictionary.[19] Other subjects offered were law, medicine, natural and moral philosophy, and mathematics. "Half a dozen or more of the students," wrote Weld, "the eldest about twelve years old, dined at [the Bishop's] table one day that I was there; some were without shoes or stockings, others without coats. During dinner they constantly rose to help themselves at the sideboard. A couple of dishes of salted meat and some oyster soup formed the whole of the dinner."[20]

Older boys were absent from the Bishop's table because it was then the policy of the college to let its dormitory stand vacant and board students at private residences around town. This was to avoid the debauches, private quarrels, and rebellions to which Virginia youths were easily drawn. La Rochefoucauld-Liancourt suspected that the professors preferred this dispersion to the task of imposing an instructive discipline on their students.[21]

A few young Virginians journeyed each year beyond the

[18] Schoepf, *Travels*, I, 168.
[19] Peter Carr to Thomas Jefferson, 30 December 1786, Carr-Cary Papers, UVL.
[20] Weld, *Travels*, I, 168.
[21] La Rochefoucauld-Liancourt, *Voyage*, IV, 289–290.

borders of their state for instruction. One hears of their attending the colleges at Princeton, New York City, New Haven, and Cambridge, and especially the medical school of Dr. Benjamin Rush in Philadelphia. Finally, many young Virginians received instruction, both within the state and abroad, as either private students, apprentices, or clerks with doctors and lawyers. Thus John Randolph was sent by his stepfather, St. George Tucker, to read law in Philadelphia under the guidance of Edmund Randolph, then Attorney General of the United States. Private instruction of this kind, along with that provided by parents and guardians, accounted for much more learning in the early national period than did the struggling little colleges and universities.

Scholarship in Virginia was recommended as a means to personal and public profit, and not to foster what Veblen has called "idle curiosity." The practical strain may be admired in the following hortatory excerpts. The first is from St. George Tucker to another stepson, Theodorick Bland Randolph: "You are now, my dear Boy, turned of fifteen — it is now high time that you should begin to reflect on your future mode of life. At sixteen I shall demand your final determination, whether you will pursue a learned profession or a laborious occupation. Should the former be your choice, (and it appears to me you can not avoid giving it the preference) you must pursue your studies in the interim with great diligence."[22] A leading politician of Virginia, James Barbour, sent his son to Harvard with the following advice: "Mathematics [is] essential to excellence in every branch of art and science. . . . The law of nature, and the nations, the civil law, the common law of England, and the Statutes of the Federal and State Governments will eventually claim your attention."[23] Finally, James Minor, who later became a successful physician and planter in Louisa County, began his

---

[22] 10 July 1786, Item no. 3400, Bryan Family MSS, UVL.
[23] 7 July 1815, Barbour Family Papers, UVL.

education with these parental instructions: "Except as a necessary qualification for some professional pursuit, the knowledge of the dead languages is pernicious in the acquiring and unprofitable in the use. . . . I myself hardly ever take up a Latin book. . . . French you cannot pay too much attention to. It is a soft, easy, familiar language, and one very necessary to the citizens of this country. . . . I have already recommended history to you. This you must not by any means neglect. . . . We see heroes, patriots, villains, despots, conquerors, and man in every shape and circumstance. We may apply everything we read of to our own circumstances, or [to] those of our country."[24]

Only rarely did the spirit of inquiry invade a Virginian's study. A friend of James Minor named Watson was an experimenter; he dissected the eye of an ox and noted that its formation was different from that described in one of his textbooks.[25] James's brother Peter, when at William and Mary, described his enthusiasm over "that part of Natural Philosophy which treats of Electricity." Peter and three of his classmates "fitted up a small machine with which we repeat all the Bishop's experiments, some of which are highly beautiful."[26]

In brief, Virginians shared with other Americans the national trait of valuing knowledge for its practical uses. Wealthier Virginians maintained an agreeable provincial culture, having both the education and the leisure required to enjoy books, most of which came to them from England along with other manufactured articles. The Virginians most notable for wisdom and culture did not live in the petty cities of their commonwealth, preferring to remain on their scat-

---

[24] G. Minor to James Minor, 12 January 1802, James Minor Papers, UVL.

[25] G. Watson to James Minor, 6 April 1805, James Minor Papers, UVL.

[26] Undated letter in James Minor Papers, UVL.

tered estates. Vigorous interchanges of ideas were much scarcer and slower than in northern provinces where wealth and refinement were so much more concentrated in the towns. The diffuse and rural society of Virginia operated against concentrations of intellectual as well as of business capital. Therefore Virginians were characteristically only consumers, and not producers of painting, poetry, novels, histories, and political tracts.

Very few original publications came from Virginia between the defeat of Cornwallis and the Treaty of Ghent. Among these were Jefferson's *Notes*, a few tracts on political economy by John Taylor of Caroline, a number of legal studies and compilations by St. George Tucker and William Hening, Madison's contributions to *The Federalist*, Marshall's *Life of Washington*, and William Wirt's *Old Bachelor* and *British Spy*. All of these were written in a plain and forthright style, except the essays of Wirt, which represented an attempt to imitate the fashionable British essayists. As literature Wirt's efforts were modest, but they contain mildly interesting social criticism. Otherwise, Jefferson's *Notes* excepted, Virginia's authors worked exclusively in the fields of law and political economy.

If books were rarely made in Virginia, speeches were made frequently enough. Indebtedness, speculation, and the Virginia land system kept active a force of lawyers who prided themselves more on rhetorical than scholarly skill. Political crisis, stretching from the French and Indian War to the Era of Good Feelings, sent able Virginians to their legislature where they modeled their behavior on that of the Roman senate of republican times. Their skill with words often extended to state papers and private letters. The ease and fluency with which most leaders of Virginia conveyed ideas was not, however, attended by a like ability in creating or analyzing them. Madison and Jefferson were exceptional rather than representative of the ruling class of Virginia, whose ideas, political and otherwise, were relatively fixed, and whose genius was for political organization and leadership. It is not clear that this genius was much stronger in Virginia than in other states. Had her politicians been simply the equal of those of her neighbors, Virginia would have enjoyed a primary role in the politics of the new republic from the extent of her territory and from her population, which was then the largest in the union. Especially important was the preeminence of Virginia among the planting states. Even so, one is tempted to believe that the plantation society naturally produced more commanding leaders than came from the commercial cities of the North.

There is an old and valuable explanation for the quantity and quality of capable politicians in Virginia and the rest of the Old South. It holds that the plantation was a microcosm for learning the skills of human management, and that the county court, with its wide range of powers and virtual independence, was ideal for perfecting those skills. At her best, Virginia produced men who were independent, liberal, and generous. Each wanted to enjoy his private empire with a minimum of interference from others, and was willing to set an example in laissez-faire. But when it appeared that independence and liberty were threatened, Virginians could quickly and adroitly deduce their common interests, and act on them together. This was especially easy because the ruling class of Virginia was homogeneous, the planting interest being the only great interest within the state. Furthermore, the planter could always spare more time for public affairs than could the wealthy men of the North, who came increasingly to rely on the professional politician to represent their interests.

The independent planter and his cherished way of life loom behind all the firm axioms of Virginia politics during this period. The maintenance of power in the county courts was another necessity induced by that decentralization and sparseness of settlement already discussed. For all but the most serious offenses it was impractical to travel outside the county for judgment. It was especially desirable to bring swift judgment on criminal slaves, whose public punishment was felt to be an important restraint on the rest of the black population.

Reliance for defense on a militia rather than on a standing army was an important axiom also. This attitude had been imported from England and was common throughout the United States, but it survived with greater strength in Virginia than it did among any of her northern neighbors. Virginians quite sensibly wanted to avoid the expense of a professional army because they were already providing for a militia which was at all times partially mobilized. Some of Virginia's visitors made fun of the currency of military titles: the taverns seemed to be full of captains, majors, and colonels, and even generals were by no means rare.[27] But militia musters had their serious purpose in Virginia. The days of Indian warfare for the Virginia militia were about over, and no invasion by a foreign power threatened Virginia between 1783 and 1812. However, Virginians felt themselves always threatened by slave insurrections, especially after the successful slave revolt of Santo Domingo in 1791. Every night of the year, if the law were being obeyed, militia patrols were scouting their neighborhoods to make sure that peace prevailed. Only a careful vigilance could assure protection against the enemy within. Having met the expense of this, Virginians had no use for a national military establishment.[28]

In commercial policy Virginia consistently used political means, so far as she could, to mitigate the difficulty of being

---

[27] Latrobe, *Journal*, p. 24.

[28] See Henry H. Simms, *Life of John Taylor* (Richmond, 1932), p. 89, where Wilson Cary Nicholas is cited as arguing that Virginia, needing trained warriors at home, should not be taxed to defend other states. I first encountered the argument that militia policy was influenced by slavery in Shulim, *The Old Dominion and Napoleon Bonaparte*, p. 32 (note).

unable to control either the prices of her staple crops or those of her essential importations. Merrill Jensen notes that there was some enthusiasm for protective tariffs in the General Assembly in 1787. But such a policy was considered only for the support it might give to the growth of industries within Virginia herself. Once the new Constitution took effect, goods from the northern states could not be discriminated against, and Virginia assumed her classic low-tariff position. Although there was animosity against British traders, it remained sensible to allow them to compete with the Yankees, or else independence might have resulted only in exchanging one set of economic masters for another. Even this was far from being satisfactory, for the longer the Virginians contemplated them, the more the British and the Yankee capitalists looked alike, and during the political battles of the times it became common to charge that the one group was the tool of the other. Reflecting upon this as an old man, Madison thought that it would be proper to make more stringent naturalization acts against merchants, as if the whole economic class were tainted. Merchants, he wrote, were "less permanently tied to their new country by the nature of their property and pursuits. . . . It cannot be doubted that the naturalized citizens among us have found it more easy than native ones to practice certain frauds." [29]

Virginians looked to France for their economic salvation. Nothing had been so infuriating over the years as the British success in taking up the export crop of tobacco and then selling most of it on the continent of Europe, thereby gaining what seemed to the Virginians a gratuitous profit for the merchants and gratuitous revenue for the British Crown. Revolutionary France, however, should have offered a direct European market to the Virginians, and, of equal importance, should have opened the trade of the French West Indies on

---

[29] Letter to Richard Peters, 22 February 1819, Madison, *Letters and Other Writings*, III, 120.

a permanent basis. The strong Francophile bent of Virginia politics during this period reflects not only sympathy for the libertarian ideals of the Revolution, but also hope that British control of the Virginia trade might be destroyed and that a mutually profitable commerce might develop between the republicans of the old and new world.

There was some commercial activity to stimulate such a conviction. After Revolutionary France went to war with Britain, it opened its West Indies trade to the Americans and sent its ships to American harbors for equipment and provisions. In February of 1794 James Brown, a merchant of Richmond, wrote to Wilson Cary Nicholas that French ships abounded, seeking grain: "Prices have not advanced much, though the demand is brisk." [30] A few days later another Richmond merchant, Robert Pollard, asked Nicholas to rush all the flour he had at his Albemarle County mill. "The flour," he wrote, "is supposed to be wanted for the French fleet lately arrived at Norfolk with the New Minister. . . . Perhaps if you will forward down all the flour you have on hand it may get here in time to obtain the present prices." Two more letters followed, bearing the same message with increased urgency. [31]

In May of 1793 Daniel L. Hylton of Richmond wrote a letter to Thomas Jefferson, then Secretary of State under Washington. Hylton hoped to sell lumber to the French Navy:

In conjunction with Mr. Miles King, Doctor William Fourchee, and my brother, Mr. William Hylton, we [sic] have made purchase of Mr. Wilson Miles Cary for his plantation called Rich Neck situated on Warwick River to carry on the lumber business in its various branches. The French Minister, Citizen Genêt, as he passed through this place, had some conversation with my friend, Dr. Fourchee, on this subject, and at his request we have taken the

---

[30] Wilson Cary Nicholas Papers, UVL.
[31] *Ibid.*

51

liberty of forwarding to your care a cubic foot of the oak with the leaf of the tree for his inspection. Should he approve the texture of the wood and is willing to enter into contract with us for any quantity either cut or standing, I only wish you to give him such assurance of our abilities for the performance on our part he may think necessary. It is our wish not from interest alone, but gratitude we owe that nation whose friendly aid we are at this moment indebted to for the free enjoyment we now exercise of our property and liberty.[32]

As early as 1793 most Americans might still feel that France was the natural ally of the United States, both because of our good fortune in the treaty of 1778 and because of our common republicanism. But by the later 1790's and the 1800's, the profit motive must have sustained the Virginians' preference for France, because the rule of the Directory and that of Bonaparte left little basis for a feeling of political kinship. Agrarian Virginia sustained more interest in direct access to continental markets and to the West Indies than she did in the political purity of her friends. During the years when Napoleon ruled France and Thomas Jefferson was President of the United States, partiality toward France reflected territorial as well as commercial ambitions: the French, to put the matter bluntly, were to assist us in relieving Spain of Louisiana and Florida. By securing both banks of the Mississippi, along with its outlet to the sea, and by also securing the Gulf of Mexico coastline, the Virginia dynasty guaranteed to the rising generation of southwestern planters the same secure access to the highways of world trade that the old planting states along the Atlantic had enjoyed.

Nothing in orthodox Virginia politics threatened the plantation system, or the slave labor upon which it was based. On the contrary, Virginia politics in the age of Jefferson pointed consistently and forthrightly toward the prosperity and expansion of the plantation system. In opposing a policy

---

[32] Letter of 21 May 1793, Carr-Cary Papers, UVL.

of fostering manufacturers, in seeking new foreign markets for the planters' staples, and in securing new territories for the spreading of plantation society, the rulers of Virginia demonstrated their contentment with their own economic and social situation. The educational system of Virginia simply trained the leaders of the state to defend its values persuasively and to pursue its interests intelligently. The easy and gracious society of the plantation was something normally cherished by Virginians, and rarely abandoned by them willingly. Although Virginia planters did not always prosper at planting, they did not give up the notion that they could and should do so. The ideal of the plantation aristocrat was not only preserved during the Jeffersonian period, it was powerfully transmitted to the new states and territories of the South, all of which were, to some extent, frontiers of Virginia.

Professor Main has indicated that aristocracy was probably declining in Virginia after the Revolution. His evidence for this is the constant breaking up of the huge estates of the late colonial period. The underlying theory seems to be that aristocracy is directly proportional to the concentration of property, so that the more property is distributed, the less aristocracy there will be. Of course this view is cogent, but it admits of much qualification. In the old countries of Europe land had long since become so scarce that if an aristocrat divided his holdings among his children there would very soon be too little in any one portion to support the aristocratic way of life at all. In early America, on the other hand, the supply of available land seemed unlimited, and aristocratic planters early discovered that they could, by appropriate business and political acumen, form comfortable estates not for just one, but for all of their children. Long before Thomas Jefferson destroyed the legal forms of primogeniture and entail in Virginia their practice had dwindled, and the planter class had accepted the custom of endowing all children with land and slaves, if possible. This permitted the rapid growth of that class, for Virginia families were normally large, and the planter aristocracy allowed entry from below.

One may well ask at this point whether a class as expansive and accessible as the Virginia planters deserves to be called an aristocracy at all. It is certainly true that the quality of exclusiveness was lacking, and that the very idea of hereditary titles was repugnant to most Virginians. On the other hand, the planters continued many habits that are undeniably characteristic of aristocracies. They avoided manual and menial labor, they owned large landed estates, they sustained the romantic attitude toward their women, and they furnished their houses with such luxurious articles as silverware, china, crystal, musical instruments, and libraries. Furthermore, they cultivated military skills, participated in sports (with special attention to those involving blooded horses), and maintained a courtly sense of honor and an uncalculating generosity which made constant headaches for the merchants upon whose credit they often lived. They were receptive to the literary, decorative, and musical arts, but did not themselves normally produce authors, artists, and musicians.

The aristocratic habits of the planters simply could not be maintained without their Negro slaves. The very abundance of land which made the class open and growing precluded their commanding the services of a white peasantry, nor could they extend any meaningful degree of freedom to their Negroes without running the risk of the former slaves developing independent ambitions. The planter required a peasantry, but he could maintain one only by preserving the legal forms of chattel slavery. Still, in keeping with his aristocratic ideals, the planter would almost always think of his Negroes as peasants rather than as slaves, hence his customary habit of designating them as "my people."

By the end of the eighteenth century, of course, landed aristocracies were gravely threatened both by spiritual and by material forces. New humanitarianisms, sponsored both by pious Christians and enlightened secularists, deplored serfdom and despised slavery. The industrial and commercial revolutions were rapidly creating a new aristocracy of technical and entrepreneurial skill, which demanded a free and fluid labor market. Even Virginia, remote and isolated though it was, felt the impact of these forces. The impact of humanitarianism will be treated later, but it is proper here to mention the response of Virginia to the demands of modern capitalism.

These demands were embodied in the economic program of the early Federalists, who had the advantage of being led by the greatest of all Virginians, George Washington. It is a mistake to consider Washington as a figurehead for Hamilton in the matter of economic policies, for if Jefferson was possessed by dreams of freedom, education, and rustic tranquility, Washington was equally, if less poetically, possessed with visions of roads, canals, factories, and cities, all knitted together in a richly varied, self-supporting, and powerful America. Because many Americans have been concerned for almost a hundred years with curbing the political influence of massed capital and the social injustices of the industrial revolution, they are inclined to have more sympathy for those who opposed the economic modernization of America than for those who were its eager advocates. Yet it is no more relevant to associate the horrors of sweatshops and tenements with Federalist principles than it is to associate the prevalence of hookworm in the rural South with Jeffersonian ideals. In both cases there is a relationship, but not a necessary one, nor one envisioned by either party in the youth of the nation.

It is significant that Washington won the support of the Virginia legislature for one of his favorite projects, the development of the Potomac-Ohio transportation system. Because the planters of Virginia required access to world markets, they were always interested in improving the rivers which flowed into Chesapeake Bay. If, as Washington hoped, they could also divert the trade of the Ohio Valley through their territory, so much the better. But no support came from Virginia for the national policy of encouraging manufacturers, nor for a national system of banking.

Virginia rejected the alternatives offered by the Federalists, and in doing so practically endorsed her traditional economic system, including slave labor. It is interesting to speculate about what might have become of slavery if Virginia had chosen to exclude foreign goods and sponsor industrialization at home. Certain successful applications of slave labor in factories suggest that the status of the Negro need not have changed at all. On the other hand, had Virginia developed more like the states to the north, there might not have been that continual enhancement of differences between northern and southern society which checked the spread of emancipation at the southern boundary of Pennsylvania and eventually brought civil war. But what is important and demonstrable is that Virginia neither accepted the program of potential change offered by the Federalists nor developed another. Of the Virginians of 1800, Henry Adams wrote: "To escape the tyranny of Caesar by perpetuating the simple and isolated lives of their fathers was the sum of their political philosophy; to fix upon the national government the stamp of their own idyllic conservatism was the height of their ambition." [33]

Virginians were, as Adams so engagingly tells us, profoundly conservative in political and economic matters, but we must not accept Adams' implication of torpor and stagnation: the planting aristocracy of Virginia was vigorous and growing. Its way of life caused it to outgrow its native province, and in time the profits of cotton would bring a new and gaudier prosperity to many of its migrant members, but the social ideal of the plantation aristocrat, with his loyal host of dusky "people," remained constant and essential.

---

[33] Henry Adams, *History of the United States of America* (New York, 1931), I, 138.

CHAPTER

THREE

The Life of the Negroes

It is difficult to generalize about the treatment of slaves in Virginia between the Revolution and the War of 1812. The foreign travelers have supplied abundant testimony, for this was an American institution which fascinated them. Most of them agreed that in Virginia slavery existed in its mildest form, but this no longer helps us very much. If, as was sometimes said, the average survival of a slave introduced into the rice swamps of South Carolina was only three years, Virginia's slavery could be comparatively milder and still be grim. Spokesmen for Virginia often observed that slavery had become milder and more humane since the Revolution, but here, too, one must be cautious. In the Jeffersonian era southern

statesmen still identified themselves with the liberal and progressive people of the Western world. They were therefore
more apologetic than candid about slavery. Their testimony
is used sparingly here, but will receive due attention later.

Certain of the visiting foreigners emphasized the brutality
of the slave's existence. Thus, David Montague Erskine, later
the second Baron Erskine, wrote in a travel diary he kept
for his father, the first Baron: "One half or more of the inhabitants [of Norfolk] are black, and slaves, moreover, in a
country calling itself a free Republic. Out of ten thousand
inhabitants five thousand are slaves who work for the white
people, who think it beneath them to stir themselves, and it
is not at all uncommon for a white to keep blacks to let out
as horses are in England."[1]

J. F. D. Smith agreed that the Negroes had to work like
draft animals, but he added that the slaves enjoyed "such a
fund of contentment and resignation" that they seemed to
be "the happiest inhabitants in America."[2] Isaac Weld, Jr.,
thought that slaves were treated well, but only on the large
plantations: "The lot of such as are unfortunate enough to
fall into the hands of the lower class of white people, and of
hard task-masters in the towns, is very different."[3] La Rochefoucauld-Liancourt, on the other hand, thought that the
farmer who owned only one or two slaves, and therefore had
to work with them, usually provided for them more humane-
ly than did the great planter who employed an overseer. La
Rochefoucauld-Liancourt was the more expert observer of
the two, so that his generalization is probably more correct,
but it is likely that Weld had heard of particular cases to
support his position. Finally, the Abbé Robin maintained
that, far from being badly treated, the American Negroes

---

[1] Letter of 18 October 1798, in Erskine's Travel Diary, a copybook of
letters, UVL.

[2] Quoted in *JNH*, I, 104.

[3] Weld, *Travels*, I, 150.

were allowed to work in a casual and leisurely fashion. "The American," he wrote, "not at all industrious by nature, is considerate enough not to expect too much from his slave, who, in such circumstances, has fewer motives to be laborious for himself."[4]

It is one of the established principles of American Negro slavery that the overseer, working on an annual appointment for a percentage of the crop, would usually treat slaves more harshly than their owner, who might be bred to more humane behavior, and would certainly have a greater interest in maintaining the good health of his slaves. One can, of course, find exceptions to most rules. In 1793 John Nicholas was disappointed with the poor yield of one of his plantations, and blamed his overseer for working the slaves too lightly. "Although he has mistaken my wish, I believe he thought he should please me by his levity to the Negroes," Nicholas complained to his brother.[5]

John Tayloe owned so many plantations that he found it necessary to employ a secretary, William Holburne, who served, among other capacities, as an overseer of overseers. Some of Holburne's communications to George Gresham, the overseer at Tayloe's "Hopyard," supply evidence about relations among slaves, overseers, and owners. Holburne's letters tell of a twenty-two-year-old female slave, Nancy, who made an unauthorized trip to the main plantation, where she complained of Gresham's "ill treatment, and forcing her to go to work when Sick, and otherwise maltreating the slaves generally." Holburne sent Nancy back to the Hopyard, bearing instructions that she was not to be punished, pending an investigation of her complaints a few days later. Holburne also reminded Gresham that Mr. Tayloe wished his people "to be well taken care of in sickness and in health,

---

[4] Quoted in *JNH*, I, 404.
[5] Letter to Wilson Cary Nicholas, 23 August 1793, Wilson Cary Nicholas Papers, UVL.

particularly the former, but to be made to do their duties." If "correction" were required, it should be applied "with no other weapon than a hickory switch."[6]

Several days later a very angry Holburne wrote again, because Gresham had "whipped the wench contrary to my directions." Apparently Gresham replied that he understood his business, and might properly punish the slaves in his care when the occasion required, for Holburne's next letter was an assertion of his own authority: "There is no man more fond of *proper system* than I am, and strict obedience to orders, according to situation and agreement, which I must say *you* deviated from. . . ." Gresham obligingly sent his next unruly slave to Holburne, thereby removing cause of further complaint over punishments. Holburne administered "the necessary correction," and then when a Mr. Kelly arrived with more information about the slave's transgressions, Kelly was permitted "to give him a few more stripes."[7] Thus both discipline and proper system were maintained.

The normal hours of work for field hands were from sunrise to sunset, though they were sometimes obliged to work on tobacco in the sheds after dark. Negroes hired by the day normally worked ten hours in the summer and nine in the winter. Most planters were sufficiently Christian to require no labor on Sunday, apart from necessary domestic routine, and some observed the practice of excusing their slaves on Saturday afternoons so that they might work their own gardens. Where this was done, the rations supplied by the planter would be reduced proportionally. Children were kept busy at lighter chores, such as sowing grain.

Diet varied from plantation to plantation, but those places which encouraged slaves to raise vegetables and chickens seem to have been in the minority. La Rochefoucauld-Lian-

---

[6] Letter of 15 March 1809, Letterbook of John Tayloe and William Holburne, Tayloe Family Papers, VHS.

[7] Letters of 22 March and 31 March 1809.

court remarked that Negroes generally had meat less than six times a year, and otherwise lived only on Indian corn and, occasionally, buttermilk.[8] George Washington, who gave great attention to all questions of management, discussed his views on the feeding of slaves with Benjamin Latrobe in 1797. Corn was more nourishing than wheat, thought Washington, although his slaves "while the novelty lasted, seemed to prefer wheat bread as being the food of their masters." Were wheat or rye bread used instead of corn, Washington thought he must make "a considerable addition to their allowance of meat. But notwithstanding all this he thought the balance of advantage to be against the Indian corn."[9] This corn was normally ground into coarse meal and served up as hoecake, which had the advantage that it could be prepared out in the field. There the slaves would build one of those bonfires of which they were so fond — their love of fires sometimes worried their masters — and prepare a dough which they would affix to the blades of their hoes and roast.

John Breckinridge, a Virginian who moved to Kentucky in 1793, found that in addition to "the standard rations of bacon, bread, and molasses," he was obliged to supply his slaves with whiskey, apparently on a regular basis. John Tayloe may or may not have supplied a regular ration, but he appears to have given extra support to his hands at harvest time in 1805, for which he imported five barrels of whiskey.[10] Many other planters helped their slaves celebrate Christmas with whiskey and rum, and the enormous quantities of spirit listed in mercantile inventories of the time suggest that slaves were treated other times as well. However, a significant number of planters were giving up liquor for religious reasons in this period, and may well have been expected to withhold it from their slaves.

---

[8] La Rochefoucauld-Liancourt, *Voyage*, V, 12.

[9] Latrobe, *Journal*, p. 60.

[10] John Tayloe Minute Book, 1805, p. 97, Tayloe Family Papers, VHS.

The clothing of slaves was as crude as their diet, but at least there were no reports of slaves shivering through the winters for want of enough. If they went barefoot in warm weather, the frequent mention of "coarse shoes for slaves" in merchants' accounts suggests that their feet were protected from the cold. The frequent records of slaves skilled in the making of shoes is further evidence. An important trend in apparel after the Revolution resulted from the spread of cotton cultivation in lower Virginia, which permitted the use of inexpensive garments, locally manufactured. Unfortunately for Virginia, most of her territory had too short a growing season for competition with the deep-South areas then coming into the production of cotton.

John Davis, a traveler given to romance, wrote that the Negresses of Virginia possessed "garments of gladness . . . bracelets, and chains, rings, and earrings," with which, on the Sabbath, they would "deck themselves bravely to allure the eyes of the white men."[11] Slaves were continually buying gaudy trinkets from peddlers and trading them among themselves, a practice made possible in the first place by small gifts or bonuses of cash bestowed by some masters. A long series of worrisome laws attempted to forbid any buying or selling by slaves whatsoever, but the very frequency with which these laws were renewed attests, like the frequency of laws against gambling, to their futility.

Housing for slaves ranged from extra rooms tacked on to the main house through huts with dirt floors and heaps of straw for beds. Some planters, however, encouraged their slaves to build and furnish respectable cabins with wooden floors and furniture. Certainly this kind of housing, comparable to that enjoyed by the middling class of whites, was rare. But John Randolph, for one, provided it for those of his slaves who had proved themselves industrious.

---

[11] John Davis, *Travels of Four Years and a Half in the United States of America*, edited by A. J. Morrison (New York, 1909), p. 400.

Music, dancing, visiting, and worship were the social diversions of the slaves. Travelers often marveled at their disposition, after a hard day's labor, to sing and carouse by a campfire until midnight. Public policy demanded the strict regulation and even the discouragement of slaves who strolled from plantation to plantation for their Sunday visits, but in most parts of Virginia the laws on this subject seem to have failed to alter local practice. Occasional petitions to the legislature protested the sinister potential of large groups of Negroes coming together for worship, and indeed, there were laws against any unauthorized and unsupervised meetings of Negroes. But there was an even stronger sentiment in favor of exposing slaves to the benefits of the Christian religion, so that proposals for the outlawing of their services were always attenuated to requirements that white men be present.[12]

Some planters took an active interest in the spiritual welfare of their human property. John Randolph, when visiting his plantations, would occasionally favor his slaves with a sermon. Archibald McCall, the planter-merchant whose hospitality Robert Hunter, Jr., enjoyed during the winter of 1785, summoned his slaves into his dining room every Sunday night and read them prayers.[13] Harry Toulmin attended a service in 1793 at which a slave was the preacher to some two hundred other slaves. Along with "the duties of religion," the preacher urged "that those who did the will of God, whatever were their color or their station, were as the Brother, or Sister, or Mother of Christ," an idea which he developed "with peculiar pleasure." As the sermon progressed, "he worked his audience to a wonderful pitch of enthusiasm. Yet some white people who were there could stand by with the most perfect unconcern and some white

---

[12] The laws restraining the movements of slaves are fully discussed in Chapter Five.

[13] Hunter, *Quebec to Carolina*, pp. 206, 211, 220.

children were permitted to be playing about in the middle of the assembly."[14]

Primary responsibility for preserving good order among slaves fell on their owners, but there were also established procedures for the application of public justice. The justices of the county courts were empowered to sit in final judgment on slaves charged with felony or treason. Such slaves were granted counsel, whose prescribed fee of five dollars was paid by the owners. A slave convicted of crimes outside benefit of clergy was hanged after thirty days, except in cases of treason, where speedier execution was encouraged. The owners of convicted slaves received the market value of their property out of public funds. This prudent measure relieved the danger of an owner concealing the crime of his slave for fear of losing his investment. Another precaution against the owner's interest was the rule that no man might sit in judgment on his own slave. The considerable public expense of executing a slave probably encouraged mercy in passing sentence. In the case of many of the lesser conspirators in Gabriel's Rebellion, economic as well as humane motives caused the death sentences to be commuted to sale outside the state.[15]

Where felonies were within benefit of clergy, offenders were to be "burnt in the hand by the jailor in open court," and should "suffer such other corporeal punishment as the court shall think fit to inflict," always provided that no one should receive benefit of clergy twice. The most common punishment was whipping, for which the upper limit was normally thirty-nine lashes. Burning, maiming, and whipping were all public spectacles, intended to edify the slave population generally. It was unlawful, however, "for any county or corporation court, to order and direct castration of any

---

[14] Toulmin, *Western Country*, pp. 29–30.
[15] Shepherd, I, 125–127. This is an omnibus act outlining a penal code for slaves. On Gabriel's Rebellion, see Chapter Five.

slave, except such slave shall be convicted of an attempt to ravish a white woman, in which case they may inflict such punishment." In such cases, the owner would be compensated if his slave were killed, or died "through negligence of the surgeon undertaking to dismember or cure him."[16]

The evidence of one credible white man was sufficient to convict a slave, though of course no Negro, slave or free, could be a witness against a white. Negro testimony was admissible only in cases where Negroes alone were concerned. Any Negro or mulatto who should "lift his or her hand in opposition" to a white person, might receive up to thirty lashes on the order of a justice of the peace, unless it could be shown that such Negro or mulatto had been "wantonly assaulted."[17]

The only law which offered special protection to colored Virginians was that which made a capital offense either of the stealing of slaves or of the kidnaping of free Negroes.[18] Slave-stealing was a profitable and widely practiced crime, and it was often easier to seize a free Negro than a slave, run him a few hundred miles south, and find a buyer who would ask no questions. Slave or free, a Negro so abducted was likely to be much worse off after his relocation. One of the best domestic markets for slaves in those days was South Carolina, where the British had carried off many slaves during the war, the mortality rate was high, and the cultivation of cotton was rapidly being introduced in the uplands.

The laws of Virginia were fairly administered to protect whites from Negroes and to protect Negroes from each other, but, as might be expected, they were not notably successful in protecting Negroes from whites. It is true that in 1788 a law was repealed which had virtually permitted the master

---

[16] Shepherd, I, 125–127; David J. Mays, *Edmund Pendleton, 1721–1803* (Cambridge, 1952), I, 44.

[17] Shepherd, I, 125, 127.

[18] *Ibid.*, p. 126.

to kill his own slave if he saw fit.[19] Also there was weighty testimony that public opinion, as well as economic interest, operated against needless brutality toward slaves. La Rochefoucauld-Liancourt, visiting Monticello in 1796, saw the neighboring planters distressed and outraged by one of their number who beat his slave nearly to death.[20] But certain cases on record suggest that public opinion was only partially successful in this area. St. George Tucker, in 1786 a court reporter, thought that Thomas Sorrell, charged with the murder of a Negro whose labor he had hired, had been acquitted "directly contrary to the evidence."[21] In 1808 a man named Kennedy was found guilty of shooting a slave, and his punishment consisted of paying the owners $450.[22] Except in the case of upholding property rights, it was difficult then, as later, to bring a white jury to convict a peer for injuring a Negro.

Virginians developed many methods for protecting their slaves from passing into the hands of doubtful or unknown masters, or from being removed far from their friends and relatives. One of these was to find a respectable purchaser for a slave already committed to sale. For example, John Callaway wrote to his son, Dr. Henry G. Callaway, on behalf of a Negro girl, Sarah, who was to be sold at Lynchburg for a debt due a merchant. "I've no doubt," wrote the elder Callaway, "you would be well pleased with her, if you was to buy her. She is very young, well grown, of good temper, very handy, and . . . entirely honest." Callaway further advised his son that, should he wish to buy a slave, he would do well to "get one that is well known. For it is hazardous buying strange Negroes."[23] Littleton Savage, of Northampton Coun-

---

[19] Hening, XII, 681.

[20] La Rochefoucauld-Liancourt, *Voyage*, V, 35.

[21] Catterall, I, 94.

[22] *Ibid.*, p. 118.

[23] Letter of 16 January, 1809, Pocket Plantation Papers, UVL.

ty, foresaw the possibility that the sale of his livestock might not meet all the demands on his estate, in which case slaves not already assigned to his heirs would have to be sold. But he directed his executors to dispose of them only by private sale, not by public auction, and to "good masters."[24]

An unusual case was Hinde vs. Pendleton. The Hindes had retained a female slave for many years, during which time she had borne four children. Then it was discovered that she had been legally conveyed many years earlier to John Robinson, whose heirs successfully sued for the possession of her. As there was no equitable way to divide the mother and her children, the heirs arranged to have her sold at public auction, so that they could divide the cash proceeds. "The plaintiff . . . attended with his wife, who manifested a tender affection for the slaves, and such anxiety to retain them, which was increased by a reciprocal abhorrence in them from a separation, that she seemed resolved to buy them at any price." Mindful of Mrs. Hinde's feelings, and fearful that sympathy would prevent anyone from bidding against her, the Robinson heirs instructed the auctioneer to make sure that the slaves were not sold for a pittance. The auctioneer complied by employing a by-bidder, a method, the court noted, which had not specifically been recommended by the defendants, and this by-bidder forced the price up to 52,000 pounds of tobacco, "confessed to be enormous." Fortunately the deception was discovered, and the court ordered the sale to be altered so that only the market value of the slaves should be paid.[25]

Even where an unavoidable sale was made to an honorable buyer, conscience might continue to trouble the Virginian. "I have sold Nelly and her two children to Mr. Rothwell for six hundred dollars," wrote Peter Carr in 1806. "I think it a very good price, and should feel quite happy, but that the poor

---

[24] Northampton County Will Book no. 32, 1802–07, p. 252, VSL.
[25] Catterall, II, 96–97.

creature is so distressed as very much to damp my satisfaction. I hope, however, that time will wear it off — I believe him to be a good man." [26]

John Hedges, Sr., made a number of curious provisions for slaves in his codicil of April 2, 1804. His slave Henson was to receive five pounds each year "from the person who by any means may hereafter possess him, paid each 20 September." A female slave, Jane, was similarly to be paid fifteen pounds. A child, Aggy, should belong to his son, Robert Hedges, until her twenty-fifth birthday, after which she should either be freed or paid an annual salary of ten dollars. Any children she might have should be treated in the same way.[27] Wills of this kind were practically impossible to enforce unless the heirs were themselves disposed to follow the peculiar instructions contained in them. However, the mere occurrence of such wills is evidence of some incidence of personal attachment to slaves.

Even where slaves were sold at public auction there would normally be an effort made to keep families intact. In 1793 Wilson Cary Nicholas sold thirty-one of his slaves by auction at Warren Court House. Of these, twenty-two were sold in groups suggesting families, such as "Rippin and Camelia," "Dise and three children," and "Cambridge, Moll, and Esther." The entire sale raised £1571.11.0 for Nicholas, or, roughly, $5,029.[28]

Unfortunately, every one of these methods for mitigating the personal insecurity of the slave affords insights into just how insecure the slave could be. If the Hinde family demonstrated unusual generosity in protecting a group of Negroes, the heirs of Robinson showed relative indifference to the matter. Their concern was to realize all the money they could from property that was legally theirs. And so it often had to

---

[26] Letter to Mary Carr, 31 December 1806, Carr-Cary Papers, UVL.
[27] Prince William County Will Book no. 1, 22–23, VSL.
[28] Receipt of 20 December 1793, Wilson Cary Nicholas Papers, UVL.

be. A single slave devised to more than one person could not be divided; therefore he had to be sold, and the money divided instead. If a man defaulted on his debts, and had no other property of liquid value, the law must foreclose on his slaves and scatter them asunder from the sheriff's auction block.

Furthermore, the solicitude for placing slaves with good masters strongly suggests that there were masters who were not so good. The danger of falling into the hands of a positively cruel master was slight, but callous or indifferent masters were probably numerous enough. Such masters would be undesirable mainly for what they omitted, neither reading prayers nor taking their subjects to church, failing to supply anything above the meanest necessities in the way of food, shelter, and clothing, and giving no presents, no allowances, no special privileges. Finally, there were always plantations directed by transient overseers, whose characteristics, as a class, have already been discussed. But as a further reflection on them, here are the words of a high Virginia court, considering the subject of the mistreatment of Negro children: "If Negro children do perish, by cruelty of those with whom their mothers live, as is supposed, it is believed to be in cases where they are hired out, or are under the direction of overseers at places far distant from the habitations of their owners." [29]

Even if a family of slaves were kept intact when relocated by sale or inheritance, bonds with friends and more distant relatives were unavoidably broken. And forced separations were only the most obvious of the insecurities which were the lot of slaves. Bills of sale and inventories hint at another enduring tragedy of slavery when they often list family groups as consisting only of mothers and their children, a phenomenon which occurs so often that it is quite unlikely that the father would, in every case, be deceased. More often the

---

[29] Catterall, I, 97.

absence of a father would mean that the male parent was simply not intimately bound to the mother and their children. The normal functions of a father, such as maintaining discipline, providing the necessities of life, and supplying the family with its name and social position, were all precluded by slavery, where these functions were assumed by the master. Masters often encouraged their slaves to regular marriages, sanctified by preachers, although slave marriages had no legal status in Virginia. But a father had little enough to do with his children, either in training or providing for them. Himself a slave, he could hardly command their respect. The failure of the institution of slavery to develop stable and self-sufficient family units created an enduring problem for American Negroes when they were freed.[30]

In the thirty years preceding the Civil War public policy in the South forbade the instruction of slaves in reading and writing, in the interest of public safety. In the Jeffersonian period there were no laws against such instruction, but very few masters found it profitable or desirable to teach their slaves anything beyond the plantation and household skills that made them valuable. Slaves might occasionally move about from plantation to plantation, but only the favored few who served as valets, teamsters, and coachmen gained much experience of the world. The majority were kept innocent of worldly affairs beyond their immediate environment, and were accordingly narrow-minded and superstitious. The ra-

---

[30] James Madison wrote the following observations in 1823: "The remarkable increase of slaves, as shown by the census, results from the defect of moral and prudential restraint on the sexual connection; and from the absence, at the same time, of that counteracting licentiousness of intercourse, of which the worst examples are to be traced where the African trade, as in the West Indies, kept the number of females less than the males." Madison, *Letters and Other Writings*, III, 314–315. A striking record of slave families sold without fathers is a bill of sale dated 9 November 1807, from Cornelius B. Thomas to William Hare and Reuben Patterson; W. C. Rives Papers, Box I, LC.

tionalist Moreau de St. Méry remarked that slaves were "quick to believe in sorcerers," and that "their superstitious weakness of mind [made] them a ready prey to the Methodists. . . . Alas that human reasoning can fall so low!"[31]

Another effect of slavery has always seemed deplorable enough outside of the South. The path of preferment in the way of interesting work, rewards, and comforts was for the slave one of subservience and accommodation. If he could fulfill, or even better, anticipate his master's will, and his master was discerning and grateful, the slave might lead a comfortable life. But only rarely could a slave win a position of relative responsibility and independence while still within formal bondage, and even if he were ultimately given his freedom as a reward for faithful service, his opportunities remained severely limited. Possibly the role of servant can be, as D. H. Lawrence argues, a valuable and fulfilling one, if one chooses to serve an admirable master. The slaves of Virginia, however, rarely had the choice of their masters, and all too often they cultivated the practical hypocrisy of serving and outwardly honoring men for whom they inwardly felt contempt.

Some Negroes were free; enough, in fact, to give Virginia the largest free Negro population in the Union. In 1783 there had been only about 3,000 in this situation, but by 1790, when the law permitting emancipation had been operating for eight years, the number had swelled to over 12,000. At the same time there were 292,000 slaves, so that the proportion of freedmen remained small. By 1810 there were over 30,269 freedmen and over 392,000 slaves. The free Negro population had grown much more rapidly.

The free population had a higher rate of growth between 1790 and 1810 for several reasons. Very few free Negroes left Virginia, while, in the words of Madison, "it is notorious that very many [slaves] have been carried from the state by ex-

---

[31] Moreau de Saint-Méry, *American Journey*, p. 59.

ternal purchases and migrating masters."[32] Furthermore, the free population was steadily augmented until the law of 1782 was abridged in 1806, while there was no external supply of slaves. The law against bringing slaves into Virginia was successfully enforced.

Freedom was the greatest gift a master could bestow upon his slave, but whatever might have been the intentions and hopes of particular masters, the weight of public opinion bore down so hard upon the free Negro that his situation was only a little better than that of the slave, and some thought that it was worse. An act of December, 1793, declared it a crime for anyone to import a free Negro into Virginia, punishable by a fine of £100, and further declared that any free Negro blundering into the state by himself should be sent back the way he had come.[33] Then, in January of 1806, the General Assembly passed a law which provided that "if any slave hereafter emancipated shall remain within this commonwealth more than twelve months after his or her right to freedom shall have accrued, he or she shall forfeit all such right, and may be apprehended and sold by the overseers of the poor of any county or corporation in which he or she shall be found."[34] The effect of this law was to reduce the number of emancipations, for few Negroes had much taste for wandering off to unknown territories, leaving behind the friends and familiar scenes of a lifetime. And they would have to wander far to find a place where they would be welcome, or even tolerated.

Those free Negroes who were entitled to stay within the commonwealth were discouraged by a host of regulations which pronounced their inferiority. They could not vote, they were bound to register every three years and to pay for their

---

[32] Letter to "Mr. Rush," 21 April 1821, Madison, *Letters and Other Writings*, III, 213–214.
[33] Shepherd, I, 239.
[34] *Ibid.*, III, 252.

certificates of freedom, they had to pay a special tax in addition to their property taxes, and if they failed to meet these obligations they were liable not only to seizure of property, but also, this proving insufficient, to being taken by the sheriff for hiring out. They were not permitted to bear arms, except that each householder might own one weapon.[35] By an act of 1801 any free Negro going into a county other than the one in which he was registered might be arrested as a vagrant.[36]

Free Negro orphans were to be bound out as apprentices under the same general law that applied to white orphans, but an act of January, 1805, set aside the requirement of an elementary education for the Negro orphans.[37] Worse than this, it was unlawful for the free Negroes to organize their own schools.[38]

Although the free Negro population was considered undesirable, the Virginians could not bring themselves to reassign this minority to owners. Instead, a status was evolved in which free Negroes served as a special addition to the slave labor force, supplying hired hands during the seasons of peak activity, and other services. Of 128 "free Negroes and mulattoes" registered in the lower district of Lunenberg County in 1814, only 19 appear to have lived on their own land. The rest, presumably, were tenants or squatters. They were classified according to occupation as follows: [39]

Hirelings	5	Shoemakers	4
Apprentices	17	Shoemakers and	
Spinners	9	farmers	4

---

[35] *Ibid.*, I, 123. By an act of 1806 it was necessary for such householders to obtain special licenses for their weapons. See John H. Russell, *The Free Negro in Virginia, 1619–1865* (Baltimore, 1913), p. 96.

[36] *Ibid.*, p. 107.

[37] Shepherd, III, 124.

[38] Russell, *Free Negro*, p. 141.

[39] Free Negro List, Lower Lunenberg County, 1814, UVL.

Weaver	1	Farmers	13
Planters	34	Ditchers	2
Spinners, weavers,		Turner	1
and planters	7	Coopers	2

With all of the liabilities under which they lived, a few free Negroes in Virginia managed to prosper. They were not prevented from owning land, nor from buying slaves, until after the Nat Turner rebellion of 1831. They were positively encouraged in the service professions, and many Negro craftsmen in the towns prospered. As with the slave, the pattern of success for the free Negro usually involved honestly and industriously serving the upper classes of whites, who were often generous in their appreciation. Thomas Field, for example, was a free Negro living on land rented from William Lovell, who obliged his tenant by issuing a certificate which would "enable him to travel to Greenbrier without molestation." Lovell was careful to note that Field owned his "gray stud horse."[40]

Another apparently prosperous free Negro was James Hammond of Alexandria, who advertised his intention to open an oyster house in that city in 1805. His newspaper notice contained some curious verse, including:

> He hopes the color of his face
> Will his calling never disgrace,
> But that his conduct and attention
> Will be a means to gain him custom.[41]

In a similar line of work was Samuel Johnston, of Fauquier Court House. In December of 1811 thirty-eight of the leading men of his neighborhood petitioned the General Assembly to permit Samuel, who had worked out his freedom for $500, to remain in Virginia with "his wife and children, who are

---

[40] Box I, Philip Pendleton Barbour Papers, VHS.
[41] Quoted in Janson, *Stranger in America*, p. 359.

slaves" and with the petitioners themselves, who clearly hated the thought of his leaving.

We have known him for a long time, in the situation of principal servant in a considerable tavern at this place, in which situation he has been constantly and uniformly diligent, sober, accommodating, faithful, and honest; possessed of those qualities essential to form a valuable citizen. If he succeeds in the application which is made for him, he wishes to remain amongst us. We wish it also, and it is for these reasons . . . that we recommend him to the general assembly as one on whom might profitably be exercised that generosity which would afford a wise encouragement to others to behave as he has behaved, and by a like fidelity and honesty to deserve as he deserves.[42]

Sam's customers won their petition, and he continued to serve them food and drink through many prosperous years. He was eventually able to purchase his wife and children, and, with the aid of another friendly petition, he secured them the privilege of residence, as free persons, in Virginia. By 1820 he owned an estate valued at $3,600. Service to the white gentry could earn rich rewards.

But it must be emphasized that the overwhelming majority of Negroes in Virginia continued to labor in the fields and in the tobacco sheds, without property, education, or the right to determine their own activities. Apologists for slavery once argued that this was, after all, a pleasant enough life, for the slaves were generally well treated, and need never worry about where their next meal was coming from, or who would provide for them in their old age. So long as one assumed, as most of the apologists did, that the character of the Negro race precluded any more responsible situations in society, this view was reasonable enough. In recent times, however, we have seen white men reduced to slavery, while black men, in America and abroad, have many of them achieved brilliant

___

[42] *JNH*, XIII, 91–93.

careers. The current consensus in America seems to favor opportunity for all citizens to support and advance themselves, rather than a paternalistic system guaranteeing cradle-to-the-grave security. To endorse the benefits of slavery is almost to endorse the benefits of any totalitarian system.

Furthermore, very few slaves lived long enough to enjoy the "retirement" which came when they were too feeble to work. Where ages were stated in inventories of slaves, it is striking how few slaves are listed as being over forty. In an era before the flowering of modern medical science, the life expectancy of all Americans was grievously short by present standards, but the life expectancy of slaves was still less than that of their masters. And if humane as well as economic motives inspired masters to provide medical care for their slaves, it does not follow that they received the consideration and care given to whites. To illustrate this point, here again are the instructions of John Tayloe's secretary, on the occasion of committing a thirty-seven-year-old slave back to the care of the overseer, George Gresham: "I send you up one of the hands named Patty, belonging to your plantation. She came down here in very ill health. She is now considerably better, and is anxious to return home. She is not fit for any outdoor business (and I doubt ever will be). I therefore think it's best to keep her spinning, shipping tobacco, or any indoor work you have to do. In fine weather I suppose she might do any *light* work outdoors."[43] Tobacco sheds and spinning rooms were typical sanatoriums for aging and invalid slaves.

---

[43] Letter of 11 February 1809, 1809 Letterbook, Tayloe Family Papers, VHS.

CHAPTER

FOUR

The Most Valuable Property

The principal proof of the value of slaves in Virginia derives from their essential role in production. But to demonstrate the economic value of the slave is not necessarily to prove that the Virginians appreciated his value. In addition to the relatively high market value of slaves, there are a number of other evidences, direct and indirect, of the attachment Virginians had to this species of property, their occasional moral and practical objections to slavery notwithstanding.

Because slaves were liquid assets, they could often be received in place of cash: "The Subscriber has for sale," declared an advertisement in a Richmond newspaper, "six hundred acres of Land, one third of it good for tobacco, and the other for corn and wheat. . . . I will take Negroes in payment and allow a good price for them."[1] Slaves could be devised in trust for the benefit of minors: "I bequeath to my granddaughter," read the will of a Virginia lady, "my Negro boy David, and I desire that the same boy may, by my Executor hereafter named, be bound out to such trade as . . . his genius and ability [are] best adapted to, and that when he acquires his trade he may be delivered to my said granddaughter."[2] Among the wealthier Virginians it was always good form to endow newlyweds with "servants," so, by way of example, Peter Carr wrote to his recently married stepson that, "Being our eldest, it is a privilege, which you ought to have, of making the first choice."[3]

Widowed and elderly women, minors, and professional men who were not able to manage plantations, and others who simply did not care for the responsibility, could, if they owned slaves to begin with, make a reasonable living by renting them out. Rents ran from seven to ten dollars for a month and from fifty to one hundred dollars per year, depending on the talents of the slave and the part of the country. A prime slave could earn his market value within four or five years, which makes it appear that the renting of slaves was an expensive business. Yet it had advantages. The lessee could get exactly the hand he wanted without making provision for slave families. Normally he was required only to feed and clothe the slave during the time of the rental, and

---

[1] *Virginia Gazette and Independent Chronicle*, 22 December 1787.

[2] Will of Mary Ann Harrison, 4 November 1803, Prince William County Will Book no. 1, VSL. Negroes owned by municipal bodies were sometimes hired out to support schools. See the account of the life of Willis H. Cromwell, 1792–1883, who worked as a ship-carpenter and wharf-builder on behalf of a school in Nansemond County. Carter G. Woodson Collection of Negro Papers, Box 2, LC.

[3] Peter Carr to George Stevenson, 24 May 1812, Carr-Cary Papers, UVL.

he bore no responsibility for the slave's health except in cases of demonstrable mistreatment. William Mayo, Jr., was an example of those Virginians who earned much of their income by renting out slaves. He advertised in a Richmond newspaper that he had "about thirty Negroes of different sexes and ages," to be hired out for the year at the January session of the Henrico Court. "All those who hired Negroes of the subscriber last year, [were] requested to return them with the hire by that day."[4]

Almost always, where a Virginian was wealthy, most of his wealth was contained in the value of his slaves. This is an evident and recurring pattern in the inventories which fill up the county will books of the period 1780–1815. Characteristic was the will of John M. Reynolds, of Campbell County. His five slaves were valued at £390, while all of his remaining personal property was worth but £70 more, and this included three horses, eleven cattle, eleven sheep, several geese and hogs, plows, other tools, and spinning equipment.[5] A much wealthier man, Charles Moorman, owned eighteen slaves valued at $3,267, and additional personal property valued at $1,589.[6] Only prime real estate, such as river bottoms and town lots, could compete with slaves for dependable high value, and land was a much less fluid asset.

Slave property was certainly an important source of public revenue. The case was well put by Richard Brent of Virginia, when he explained to the House of Representatives that apportioning taxes among the states strictly on the basis of land would work unfairly in the South. There, argued Brent, "slaves formed the most certain fund . . . for, whilst their wide and extensive waste lands would not command any price, slaves were always ready sale." Furthermore, taxes on slaves had always proved more productive of revenue

---

[4] *Virginia Gazette and General Advertiser*, 29 December 1790.
[5] Campbell County Will Book no. 1, 1782–1800, VSL, p. 341.
[6] *Ibid.*, pp. 362–364.

than taxes on land. If taxes were laid only on land, the people of the mountainous regions, owning few or no slaves, "would be extremely aggravated, and would murmur, and they would murmur with justice."[7] Because slaves were the most taxable resource in the South, their omission from any general scheme of taxation was unthinkable, and would be resented by those who did not themselves hold slaves.

Tax laws in Virginia followed the logic set forth by Richard Brent. The act of December, 1796, established a tax of twenty-five cents "on lands, for every hundred dollars value, agreeable to the equalizing law," which reduced the rates in western parts of the state. For each able slave above twelve years of age, the annual tax was set at twenty-eight cents.[8] Since assessments were likely to run below the already low market value of lands, and the "equalizing law" would reduce even further taxes on all lands above the Tidewater, it is understandable that slave property was the best source of revenue.

Because it was easier to dispose of slaves than other kinds of property, sheriffs were tempted to seize slaves in all cases of debt. A public reaction against this practice led to an act of November, 1792, which restrained sheriffs from taking slaves "if other sufficient distress" could be obtained, and permitted citizens to sue for damages if the restraint were violated.[9] Even this did not afford enough protection for slave property, so a year later another act forbade the seizure of slaves for debts amounting to less than thirty-three dollars or two thousand pounds of tobacco.[10]

But while it was desirable to protect people from losing valuable slaves for trifling debts, it was also necessary to

---

[7] Thomas Hart Benton, *Abridgement of the Debates of Congress* (New York, 1857), II, 55.

[8] Shepherd, II, 14–15.

[9] *Ibid.*, I, 47.

[10] Enacted 10 December 1793. Shepherd, I, 213.

make sure that greater obligations should not be avoided by trickery. As far back as 1757 it had been found expedient to pass a law forbidding "secret" gifts of slave property: a creditor, prepared to foreclose on his debtor's slaves, had sometimes found that the slaves had been given away, usually to a sympathetic relative or friend, who could be trusted to give them back at an appropriate time. Laws of 1757 and 1758 had therefore required that all gifts of slaves be executed by formal deeds or wills. An act of December, 1787, amended this by permitting informal gifts where the recipient had actual possession of the property, though possession must have lasted for three years to avoid liability for the donor's debts.[11] The texts of these laws conjure up a scene of planters hastily running their slaves from one plantation to another, just ahead of the sheriff.

The best example of the abiding attachment of Virginians to slave property may be seen in their behavior during and after the Revolutionary War, when that "species of property" was in various ways threatened, disrupted, lost, and even stolen. It is understandable that an individual planter would feel wronged by having his slaves swept away from growing crops which demanded their attention; such an immediate and practical concern need not reflect one way or another on the planter's deep and long-standing convictions about the justice and desirability of slavery. Yet it was entirely significant that during all the debates, pleas, and demands issued on account of kidnapped, confiscated, and escaped slaves, no Virginian ever paused to point out that the appreciable reduction in the number of slaves in Virginia, and the actual freeing of a few thousand of them, were, of themselves, desirable results. Instead, a strict and simple position prevailed: every slave removed from his master against the master's will and the laws of Virginia ought to be restored.

---

[11] Hening, XII, 505–506.

That slavery should have been a continuing concern during the war was inevitable, but even the fearful must have been surprised at how quickly the British used this vulnerable institution as a weapon against the patriots. As early as November, 1775, an embattled Lord Dunmore had declared all slaves of insubordinate Virginians free. "Is it possible," inquired Richard Henry Lee, "that his Majesty could authorize him thus to remedy evils which his Lordship himself had created?"[12] The Virginians responded to Dunmore's challenge, passing a law which provided that slaves found in arms against their masters should be sold for the credit of the colony in the West Indies, or, this proving inconvenient, they might either be punished for treason, or returned to their masters.[13] Thereafter the British were cautious about tampering with slavery. Attempts to turn the bondsmen of Virginia against their masters were dangerous to begin with, threatening to alienate neutral or Tory planters in the disturbed colonies, and there was the further risk that the sugar colonies of the West Indies would be distressed by an official policy of liberating slaves. Nevertheless, British commanders frequently offered asylum behind their lines to runaway slaves, and gave them jobs.

Virginians lost an estimated thirty thousand slaves to the British during the course of the war, of which most came from the Tidewater. It would probably be more accurate to say that Virginians lost thirty thousand slaves as a result of the chaos attending the military campaigns in lower Virginia, and from their point of view the British, as instigators and aggressors, should be held responsible. Actually, most of the slaves lost to their owners were seized as the plunder of war when patriots and Tories marched and countermarched across each others' plantations. Slave traders were pleased

---

[12] Letter to "Mrs. Macaulay," 29 November 1775; Richard Henry Lee, *Letters*, edited by J. C. Ballagh (New York, 1911 and 1914), I, 163.
[13] Hening, IX, 106.

to pick up contraband slaves along the shores of Virginia and take them to the Indies for ready sale. Furthermore, there was a brisk domestic trade in captured slaves. Both North and South Carolina applied to the governor of Virginia, Benjamin Harrison, for his help in recovering stolen slaves carried into his state. Writing to the governor of North Carolina, Harrison warned that, "If I should issue a proclamation, it would probably be the cause of their being sent immediately out of the country." Therefore he had determined to set the whole matter before the next General Assembly, so that it might enact a comprehensive law for the solution of the difficulty. Harrison concluded by writing his own request for assistance, "as I am informed the practice has taken place in the lower part of this country, from which very many Negroes have been taken and sold to the citizens of your State."[14] Within Virginia itself, the finders of slaves often appointed themselves keepers, even where the original owners had been on their own side. This led Governor Thomas Nelson to issue a proclamation in 1781: "The Governor has directed that all the Negroes taken from the enemy be returned to their former proprietors. The principle on which it is supposed men fight at present is to protect and secure to themselves and fellow citizens their liberties and property, and not to procure plunder."[15]

The French army turned out to be another threat to property. It accepted Negroes as servants and workmen without investigating their status in Virginia, and then sheltered them from the inquiries of Virginia authorities. This situation led Governor Harrison to protest to the very limits of propriety in a message to Count Rochambeau. Harrison was not content to declare that many of the Negroes with the

---

[14] The letter was dated 31 March 1782. H. R. McIlwaine, ed., *Official Letters of the Governors of the State of Virginia* (Richmond, 1929), III, 188.

[15] Robert Andrews to General Weedon, *ibid.*, p. 8.

French had lied about being free. He went further, charging that the French themselves had encouraged this deception: "The pretence that some make of their being free, and of their being the property of the British, is without foundation, and is inculcated into them to serve the purposes of detention." Harrison's remedy was thorough enough. He asked Rochambeau to gather "all the Negroes without distinction that are amongst your troops," and to deliver them to Virginia authorities, who would see that they were returned to their proper owners in Virginia and the Carolinas.[16]

For all its forcefulness, the appeal was futile. As Harrison remarked in a letter to Washington, "I have written on the subject till I am wearied out, without being able to procure [the Negroes]." Harrison went on to indicate an obstacle: the French were requiring proof of ownership before releasing any Negroes. In the absence of such proof they accepted the claims of the Negroes that they were free.[17] Harrison's request for "all the Negroes without distinction" followed the conventional Virginian attitude that a Negro must be considered a slave unless proven otherwise, for it was better policy to have Negroes endure the risks of false claims than to have planters do so. Nevertheless, the French, if only for their own convenience, refused to accept the practice of their Virginia allies.

The final difficulty over slaves came at the end of the war, when the withdrawing British armies permitted Negroes, perhaps between three and four thousand of them, to leave the country under their cover. In October, 1781, Governor Nelson wrote to Lord Cornwallis of a report that Negroes were "attempting to make their Escape by getting on the Bonnetta, sloop of war," and urged his lordship to "take measures to prevent the State and individuals from sustain-

---

[16] Letter of 26 June 1782, *ibid.*, p. 257.
[17] 11 July 1782, *ibid.*, p. 266.

ing an injury of this nature."[18] More distressing, because of the greater number involved, was the protection offered to Negroes by General Guy Carleton, who marched most of Cornwallis' army to New York, and departed only after the Treaty of Paris was proclaimed. Although many Virginians wanted to make direct application to the British general for their slaves, Governor Harrison and his House of Delegates thought the matter more properly the concern of the Continental Congress. The representatives of Congress responsible for the peace treaty tried to oblige the Virginians by securing a provision in the final draft which guaranteed the restoration of slave property. But General Carleton, while carrying out that part of the treaty which ordered his withdrawal, quite openly violated the part obliging him to give up the Negroes in his custody. Instead, he took them to Halifax.

William Grayson, one of the Virginia delegates to the Continental Congress, refused to be alarmed. "The affair of the Negroes," he wrote to Madison, "which has made so much noise in our house, is rather trifling." Carleton had carried off 1,386 men, 954 women, and 657 children, for a total of 2,997.[19] Nevertheless, this violation of the treaty became the initial justification for the refusal of the Virginia legislature to enforce the collection of debts contracted with British merchants before the war. In June, 1784, the Continental Congress received a copy of a resolution from the Virginia House of Delegates which advised, "That so soon as reparation is made for the aforesaid infraction, or Congress shall judge it indispensably necessary," the House ought to repeal those wartime laws which "inhibited the recovery of British debts," but that provision for their repayment should be consistent "with the exhausted situation of

---

[18] 20 October 1781, *ibid.*, p. 88.
[19] Letter of 28 November 1785, Burnett, VIII, 264.

this Commonwealth."[20] Later on, the issue of the military posts in the Northwest Territory was added, but the original refusal of Virginians to comply with the treaty was based entirely on the perfidy of General Carleton in carrying away their property.

Early in 1785 the Congress finally agreed on a diplomat to send to the Court of St. James. Elbridge Gerry wrote to the appointee, John Adams, that it had taken several days to achieve a majority for his selection. "It appeared," explained Gerry, "that the Southern States were impressed with the idea, that you being totally averse to the slave trade, would not exert yourself at the court of London to obtain restitution of the Negroes taken and detained from them in violation of the treaty."[21]

In October, 1786, John Jay submitted a comprehensive report to the Congress, which reviewed all the issues arising out of the peace treaty. In the case of the slaves, he submitted — and he was not challenged — that no one could reasonably expect the reparation of those who were captured during combat. Therefore, restitution should be made only for "Negroes kept as slaves within their lines and respecting whom the enemy had done no act which divested their masters of the property." If this meant anything, it meant that the British should be held responsible for runaway slaves whom they captured and pressed into their own service. But Jay went on to demonstrate that he thought most of the Negroes carried off by the British belonged to another class: those who fled to the British on the promise of freedom. He freely stated that he thought such people should not be returned, but that the British might be cajoled into returning cash as compensation for them. "In this way neither could have just cause to complain; for although no price can com-

---

[20] *Journal of the Continental Congress*, XXXI, 826.
[21] Letter of 24 February 1785, Burnett, VIII, 39.

pensate a man for bondage for life, yet every master may be compensated for a runaway slave." [22]

The British agreed with Jay's analysis, and early granted that Carleton's evacuation had been a clear violation of the treaty.[23] Other points at issue between the two countries, however, were less easy to solve, so that final adjustment was delayed for fifteen years. During that time the issue was kept alive in Virginia. For instance, Patrick Henry, while defending Dr. Thomas Walker of Albemarle County against collection of a prewar debt, charged the British with their failure to abide by the treaty, and Henry made their carrying off of the slaves the first part of his indictment.[24] Now it is perfectly clear that Virginians were happy, after the war, to find any excuse to avoid paying their heavy debts to British merchants. Nevertheless, their persistent and humorless demand for satisfaction in the matter of three thousand slaves demonstrates a fundamental attachment to property in slaves which was much less evident in theoretical discussions on the subject.

The subsequent career of Carleton's fugitives is interesting enough to deserve a swift summary. Most of them were settled in Nova Scotia, where they were at pains to decide which was chillier, the climate or the white Nova Scotians. Some petitioned the British government to transport them to Africa, and in March, 1792, over eleven hundred of them were landed in Sierra Leone. Under the direction of Lieutenant John Clarkson, brother of the famous abolitionist, Thomas Clarkson, they were absorbed into a prosperous colonial settlement, which served as a practical demonstra-

---

[22] *Journal of the Continental Congress*, XXXI, 863–866.

[23] Monroe to Madison, December 1785, Burnett, VIII, 278.

[24] William Wirt, *The Life of Patrick Henry*, 6th ed. (New York, 1833), p. 334.

tion to encourage the growing movements for emanicipation and colonization on both sides of the Atlantic.[25]

Apart from the inconsiderateness of the British, the French, and a few of their less honest fellow citizens, Virginians could be altogether proud of their slaves during the Revolution. Few took the opportunities created by civil disorder to rebel forcibly, and many of them made valuable contributions toward the winning of the war. The militia law of May, 1777, permitted the enrollment of free Negroes and mulattoes in the military forces of the state; "the free mulattoes in the said companies, or battalions, shall be employed as drummers, fifers, or pioneers." Later it was found that certain slaves were running away to enlist, so a supplementary act was framed which required recruiting officers to take only those Negroes or mulattoes who could produce a certificate of freedom issued by a justice of the peace.[26] Virginians who preferred to stay at home were allowed to send slaves in their place, so long as they agreed that such men, once enlisted, would be considered free at the end of their military service. The promise of freedom was necessary to avoid desertions, and possibly even sabotage. Unfortunately there existed some bad faith in these arrangements, for the General Assembly passed an act in October, 1783, which noted "that the former owners [who had sent slaves to war as their replacements] have attempted again to force them to return to a state of servitude, contrary to the principles of justice, and to their own solemn promise." The act went on to declare categorically that all slaves enlisted as substitutes were free men, who "should enjoy the blessings of freedom as a reward" for their service.[27]

The state itself owned Negroes, some of whom, perhaps,

---

[25] Earl Leslie Griggs, *Thomas Clarkson, the Friend of Slaves* (London, 1936), pp. 66–68.

[26] Hening, IX, 268.

[27] *Ibid.*, XI, 308.

were collected as payment for wartime taxes, but more likely were the confiscated property of Tories. These "public Negroes" were employed in manufacturing the supplies of war and in manning boats. An especially valuable service was performed by the slaves who worked the lead mines. During the years following the close of the war, a number of these slaves who had served the state were freed. This was still happening as late as November, 1789, when the legislature passed "An act for the purchase and manumitting Negro Caesar . . . in consideration of meritorious service on the armed vessels of the state during the late war." [28]

Like any other form of public property, the state's slaves were susceptible to graft. Governor Harrison was obliged to send a sharp remonstrance to Captain Charles Thomas in 1782. "Some time ago," wrote the Governor, "the Executive ordered all the Negroes belonging to the rope walk and tannery under your care to be delivered up to the Quarter Master," but it had since become apparent that Captain Thomas had retained several of them and had employed them for his "private business." Harrison demanded the immediate return of the Negroes, "or consequences will follow that will be disagreeable to you. . . ." [29]

The loyalty, peacefulness, and hard work of the great majority of the slaves during the war undoubtedly contributed to the generous atmosphere which permitted, in 1782, the passage of the act making it legal for owners to free their slaves. The loyal and self-sacrificing slaves were, in some cases, rewarded. But those slaves who took the opportunity afforded by war to escape to freedom were not admired. Freedom was not to be seized by the Negro on his own volition, but to be dispensed by the master at his own discretion. The unsettling of all institutions caused by the war afforded Virginians their greatest opportunity prior to the Civil War

---

[28] *Ibid.*, XIII, 102.
[29] McIlwaine, *Official Letters*, III, 243.

for dealing constructively with the problem of slavery. The famous committee for revising the laws of Virginia, Thomas Jefferson, George Wythe, and Edmund Pendleton, did indeed draft a scheme for a general, although extremely gradual, emancipation. But even in the days of Virginia's struggle for her own liberty, the three lawyer-statesmen decided that the public temper was not prepared to entertain such a proposal, so they refrained even from offering it.

CHAPTER

FIVE

Runaway and Rebel

It may be significant that the most effective Negro rebel in the history of Virginia was a preacher, Nat Turner. There were undoubtedly members of his race with harder lives than his who never dreamed of avenging themselves upon the whites. Turner knew enough to be dangerous, and justified the feeling of many slaveowners that their safety depended upon keeping their Negroes ignorant and under constant surveillance.

The frequent runaways of Jeffersonian Virginia might be regarded as evidence of mistreatment. This was explicit in the case of a slave named Jacob, who fled from John Ellis "for no other provocation than a small correction" applied to him "for neglecting his business."[1] However, many of the Negroes who ran away had benefited from that improving treatment noticed not only by Virginians, but by their critical visitors as well. The runaway, and especially the successful runaway, was likely to be an unusually clever slave, sometimes literate, and usually skilled in one or more crafts. He would also be informed enough about other parts of the world, and confident enough of his own talent, to hope that he could be better off elsewhere.

On the other hand, a slave whose imagination could hardly stretch beyond the limits of the next plantation, who could not spell his name, much less forge free papers, who had no skills other than those necessary for cultivating tobacco, wheat, and corn, who never tasted the pleasure of securing a personal possession in exchange for money, and who never had been told that slavery was wicked and that he had a natural right to freedom — such a slave was likely to stay on his plantation without making trouble, and if, in a fit of frustration, he happened to run away, he would be easy to capture. Public policy, as expressed in the laws of Virginia, encouraged the development of Negroes who would be docile and timid. The old theory that plantation life prepared Negroes for their eventual freedom runs aground on the patent fact that ignorance, dependence, and helplessness were encouraged by the planters' systematic policy of preventing their slaves from running away, or, even worse, starting a revolution.

The laws for controlling and preventing runaways and rebellions are a special kind of historical evidence. Most certainly they do not always reflect what was actually done in Virginia, but they do reflect what a legislative body made up of wealthy planters thought should have been done, which

---

[1] John Ellis to Charles Ellis, Jr., 1 December 1793, Ellis-Allan Papers, I, 67, LC.

is in itself important. Furthermore, the passage of laws, many of which contained lengthy explanatory preambles, indicated the problems which were pressing urgently on the minds of Virginia's rulers, as opposed to the problems which historians, with the benefit of hindsight, take to have been their "real" problems.

The control of runaway slaves was the purpose of those laws, mentioned in Chapter Three, which required free Negroes to stay within their own counties, and to show their certificates of freedom to anyone hiring them. If any unfamiliar Negro should appear in town or at a plantation without such papers, it was the duty of citizens to detain him, pending an inquiry into his background. In Virginia a Negro was always considered a slave until proven free, an axiom that was clearly embodied in a law of December, 1792. This act encouraged the apprehension of runaway Negroes by directing that anyone capturing a fugitive should receive a reward for doing so. It further held that any Negro unable to prove himself free should be confined in jail for as much as a year, during which time advertisements could circulate throughout the state. During this year, the sheriff might hire his captive out to recover the costs of keeping him. If, at the end of a year, no owner should have claimed his slave, the Negro would be sold for the benefit of the state. On the other hand, if a slave should perish in jail before his master could reach him, the public would pay his cost to the master.[2]

Significantly, the act contained no special safeguards to protect free Negroes from unwarranted seizure. Especially striking was the rule that a Negro, though he declare himself free, and remain a full year without being claimed, should nevertheless be sold as a slave. Nor was the principle that a Negro must be considered a slave until proven free first introduced into law by this act. Almost two years earlier the sheriff

---

[2] Shepherd, I, 178–179.

93

of New Kent was advertising that he "should be obliged to any person" who could identify three Negroes he was holding in his jail, all claiming to be free, and two of them man and wife. The sheriff hoped either to be informed his charges were free, or to have their owners collect them, and pay the costs of their visit.[3]

Advertisements that were circulated for the recovery of runaways often supplied excellent descriptions of them. Physical appearance, clothing, and unusual personal traits were included for purposes of identification, and sometimes an owner would also dwell on the circumstances of escape, the slave's motives, and the possible courses that might be followed. It is these advertisements that demonstrate the unusual quality of most runaway slaves. One refugee was "much accustomed to driving a wagon," was "good at any kind of plantation business," and was "tolerably ingenious." Of another, his master said, "He beats a drum pretty well, is artful and plausible, and well acquainted in most parts of Virginia, having formerly waited upon me." Another was described as "a most excellent house servant." Yet another was "artful," could "both read and write," and was "a good fiddler." His owner, Carter Beverley, warned, "It is therefore probable that he may attempt a forgery and pass as a free man." The advertisers repeatedly describe slaves as skillful dissemblers. The Negro, unable to defeat the white man in a direct confrontation, developed the protective art of confusing and misrepresenting things. He would rarely look a white man in the eye. For example, a runaway named Will was "round shouldered," had "a down look," and "when spoken to [was] apt to grin." Runaway Dick had "a very roguish down look." Runaway Isaac had "rather a hoarse and lazy kind of voice and speech," and was "apt to compel

---

[3] *Virginia Gazette and General Advertiser*, 12 January 1791.

you to repeat before he [would] give an answer." And another fugitive named Will was "a very dissembling fellow."[4]

Occasionally an advertisement would appear containing an extraordinary story, such as the following, published in 1803:

RUNAWAY from the subscriber in the forks of Hanover, about the middle of September last, a Negro man named JACOB. He is about five feet ten inches high, twenty-five years old, and rather spare made. I expect he will attempt to pass for a free man, being informed that he has in [his] possession a free pass. He went off with a white woman by name of Sally Davis, with whom he was intimate for some time before their departure, and it is probable she may aid him in imposing on the public with his pass, or may claim him as her slave. Sally Davis is between forty and fifty years of age, tall and spare made, very brown skin, [and] has taken with her three children, two sons and a daughter. The two boys are sons by her first husband, whose name was Cooper. Henry, the oldest, is tall and spare made, very dark skin, about twenty-one years old . . . Henry Cooper and Jacob are shoe-makers, and it is probable they will undertake work on the road, as I believe they are making for Georgia. . . .[5]

The runaway had three principal alternatives. He might seek a hiding place in the wilderness near his own neighborhood, he might attempt to reach a town and lose himself in its free Negro population, or he might try to escape from Virginia altogether. The second and third choices were more difficult to accomplish, but also offered more opportunity for permanent freedom. It was quite easy simply to run away and hide in the woods, but it was also uncomfortable, and if one lingered close enough to plantations to sneak occasional visits and supplies, eventual recapture was almost certain.

---

[4] The examples in this paragraph were drawn from *The Virginia Argus*, 11 February 1804, from the Richmond *Examiner*, 18 January 1794, and from Carter G. Woodson, ed., "Eighteenth Century Slaves as Advertised by Their Masters," JNH, I (April, 1916), 163–216.

[5] *Virginia Gazette and Independent Chronicle*, 9 April 1803.

Only a special wilderness surrounded by civilization, such as the Great Dismal Swamp of southeastern Virginia, could afford a permanent haven for the local runaway. Dr. Johan Schoepf told of runaway slaves who had lived in the Dismal Swamp for many years, because their masters were afraid to pursue them there. "So these Negro fugitives lived in security and plenty, building themselves cabins, planting corn, raising hogs and fowls which they stole from their neighbors, and naturally the hunting was free where they were."[6]

Escaping to a town was more difficult, for it could not safely be the town nearest to one's original plantation. The largest towns were safest: Alexandria, Fredericksburg, Richmond, Petersburg, and Norfolk. All of these had large free Negro populations, among which might be found those who could supply certificates of freedom, genuine or forged, and perhaps a job. The towns also offered opportunity to smuggle oneself aboard a ship, if the goal should be to leave Virginia altogether.

Many slaves ran away when proceedings for debt or for inheritance were tearing them away from their familiar surroundings. Such was the case with the runaways Jack, Batt, Kate, and Polly, "slaves belonging to the estate of Colonel Richard Anderson," seized by the sheriff of Hanover County "to satisfy an execution at the suit of Mr. Robert Hart."[7] Another slave named Jack was sold by the estate of Thomas Stone, in Charles County, Maryland, to a citizen of Stafford County, Virginia. Jack, however, believed that it had been the intention of his late master to free him, and deserted his new owner. That gentleman advertised that the fugitive might "pass himself for one of the Thomas family of Negroes belonging to the [Thomas Stone] estate, who make pretention to their freedom." Jack might also be "lurking about Balti-

---

[6] Schoepf, *Travels*, II, 99–100.

[7] *Virginia Gazette and Independent Chronicle*, 22 December 1787.

more" where lived his mother, "also a runaway, named Rachel."[8]

One of the first acts of the Virginia legislature after its assertion of independence was the passing of a law to discourage people from assisting debtors, servants, and slaves to leave the commonwealth. This made captains of ships and operators of coaches responsible for knowing the status of their passengers. If it turned out that they had transported a fugitive slave, their ignorance of his condition could not be offered as an excuse. The fine for abetting the escape of a debtor, servant, or slave, wittingly or not, was set at fifty pounds.[9] During the next thirty years the laws on this subject became increasingly complex and severe. But throughout this development, the increased severity was directed not against the fugitive himself, but toward anyone else who might make it easier for him to escape. It was basic to the social contract in Virginia that, although primary responsibility for the management of slaves fell on their owners, it was the responsibility of everyone to make sure that all slave property remained secure. Those who refused to cooperate, either for profit or for conscience, were liable to punishment.

A section of the omnibus slavery act of 1792 undertook to strengthen the safeguards against slaves leaving the state by water. "No master of any ship, or any other vessel," it declared, "shall transport or carry any servant or any Negro, mulatto, or other slave out of this commonwealth, without the consent or permission of [the owner]." The fine was now $150 in the case of servants, and $300 in the case of slaves. Moreover, after paying $300 in fines to the state for each slave illegally transported, an offender could be sued at common law by the owner, and find himself paying the recovery costs of the runaway, or his market value, and, of course, the

---

[8] Woodson, "Eighteenth Century Slaves," p. 185.
[9] Act of October, 1776, Hening, IX, 187.

legal costs. Then came a final severity: "In any action which shall be brought against the master of a ship . . . under this act, the court . . . may rule the defendant to give special bail, if they see cause, and shall not allow him to plead in bar, or give in evidence any act or statute of limitation; any former or other law to the contrary notwithstanding." [10]

A comprehensive act of January, 1798, supplied several devices intended to inhibit runaways. Any free persons guilty of harboring slaves without their masters' permission had to pay fines of ten dollars, which, significantly, would not go to the state, but to the informer. If free Negroes or mulattoes were found harboring slaves, and could not pay the fine, they should receive "corporal chastisement, not exceeding thirty-nine lashes." Another section of this act moved against free Negroes and mulattoes who, having properly registered themselves according to law, then gave their certificates of freedom to slaves. The slaves, "by virtue thereof have passed for free men, and have under sanction prevailed on masters of vessels to transport them out of this commonwealth," observed the legislators, in justifying the severity of their law. Any free person of color caught giving papers to any slave was to "be judged a felon and suffer accordingly." There being no disqualification from benefit of clergy in the act, a first offender presumably might get off with being burned in the hand and "such other corporeal punishment as the court shall think fit to inflict." A felon for the second time would hang.[11]

Still another section of this law of 1798 returned to the subject of shipmasters in Virginia waters. Now, in order for a master to take on any colored passenger, he must produce that person before a magistrate of the county adjoining the river in which his ship was docked. He must register his passenger's name and full description, his intended destination, and either evidence of freedom or certified instructions

---

[10] Shepherd, I, 129.

[11] *Ibid.*, II, 177, and, for the punishment of Negro felons, I, 127.

from an owner. The shipmaster must then obtain a document from the magistrate to prove that he had filled all of these requirements. Failure to follow this procedure made him liable to a fine of $500, collectable by the state, and responsible for the cost of any slave he might help to escape.[12]

About a year before the passage of this act, John Nicholas of Virginia was speaking in the House of Representatives in support of a national act for the registration and certification of all Negroes on the high seas. He dwelt on the advantages the act would have for free Negroes, who were in danger of being kidnapped and carried away by sea. William Vans Murray of Maryland was puzzled by this, and inquired whether the purpose of the bill was to prevent "the taking of free Negroes and selling them as slaves, or the taking of slaves to make them free?" John Swanwick of Pennsylvania, who had originally introduced the bill as a measure to protect slaveholders, replied that "it was intended to prevent both evils." A representative of South Carolina then remarked that he wished the question had never been raised, for he preferred the federal government to have no concern with slavery whatever. Swanwick's bill might be "a kind of entering-wedge."[13]

Although Nicholas was sincere enough in his desire to protect free Negroes, his argument was surely contrived to make more palatable to northern representatives an act whose main function would be to increase federal responsibility for slaves. This construction is made more plausible in view of the powerful Virginia support which developed for a new federal fugitive slave law in 1802. This proposed act anticipated the celebrated Fugitive Slave Act of 1850 in its provisions for extending responsibility for the security of slavery to the entire nation. Citizens of states where slavery was prohibited would not be allowed to hire Negro laborers unless they could produce legal certificates of freedom "with a county seal" or

---

[12] *Ibid.*, II, 177.
[13] Benton, *Abridgement of the Debates of Congress*, II, 46–47.

the signature of a justice of the peace. Anyone hiring a Negro without such proof of his freedom would be liable to pay a fine of $500.

Representatives from New England and the middle states gave predictable objections. The requirement for certification would work hardships on free Negroes, and the fine seemed out of all proportion to the negligible offense. Several southern sponsors of the bill, including Thomas Claiborne of Virginia, answered the northerners vigorously. Their reasoning was condensed into a single statement for the *Annals of Congress*:

They considered it a great injury, to owners of that species of property, that runaways were employed in the middle and northern states, and even assisted in procuring a living. They stated that when slaves ran away and were not recovered it excited discontent among the rest. When they were caught and brought home they informed their comrades how well they were received and assisted, which excited a disposition in others to attempt escaping, and obliged their masters to use greater severity than they otherwise would. It was, they said, even on the score of humanity, good policy in those opposed to slavery to agree to this law.

The strong fugitive slave act came up for a vote on January 18, 1802, and was defeated, 43 to 46. All New Englanders were opposed except Lewis Morris of Vermont. Fourteen representatives of Virginia voted in favor of the measure, and none was opposed. In fact, only two votes were cast in opposition from slaveholding states, and both were from North Carolina.[14]

In 1805 Virginia once again refined her penalties for those found guilty of assisting runaways. The fine due the state was now flexible, between the limits of $100 and $500, and a term of from two to four years in the new state penitentiary was added. Also the abettor of the fugitive slave should now pay to the owner twice the value of his property, and twice the cost of its recovery. Captains and masters of vessels retained

---

[14] *Annals of the Seventh Congress, First Session*, pp. 423, 425.

their special status in this series of laws by being subject to all the foregoing penalties and an extra fine of $200.[15]

Given the fundamental objective of freedom, the slave was most likely to run away, but there was an alternative course open to him: he might disarm or destroy his master. This possibility was painfully evident to Virginians. A stern policing of runaways was important for the protection of valuable property. But insuring against slave insurrections was necessary for the preservation of life itself.

Naturally there were firm laws against any kind of conspiracy. More interesting than these were the various regulations which aimed to prevent the slaves from ever even thinking about a conspiracy. A dangerous plot would necessarily involve slaves from many plantations, and its success would require considerable knowledge of terrain, and of the availability of weapons and horses. Without a good measure of planned cooperation, no rebellion could be attempted. Therefore, it was prudent to see that slaves, and especially clever and enterprising slaves, had no opportunity to plan and plot.

With this in mind, it is possible for one to understand a series of laws against "persons permitting their slaves to go at large and hire themselves out, under a promise of paying their masters or owners a certain sum of money in lieu of their services." A lazy owner of an ambitious slave might find it profitable to enter into such an arrangement, but the state could not permit it. A slave given free license by his master would, in the absence of this law, have much wider opportunities to travel than the free Negroes. But the state required that the owners of slaves be responsible for their behavior, either supervising it themselves, or hiring an overseer to provide the direct supervision. An owner shirking this responsibility by allowing his slave to wander at will must lose his

---

[15] Shepherd, III, 123.

property. He would receive three-fourths of the value, after the county court had seized and sold his chattel, and had kept a fourth of the proceeds for its trouble.[16]

The comprehensive law of 1792 extended the prohibition to cover masters licensing their slaves to trade. Under this act, punishment consisted of a fine of $30 for each offense, payable to the overseers of the poor.[17] Another section of the law declared that "No person whatsoever shall buy, sell, or receive of, to, or from a slave, any commodity whatsoever." The punishments prescribed were either fines or whippings, depending upon the color of the offender.[18] Finally, an act of January, 1798, forbade any person receiving a "hawker's and pedlar's" license to "authorize any Negro or mulatto, bond or free, to vend any goods, wares, or merchandise."[19]

Operators of vessels in Chesapeake Bay had found it profitable to use their slaves as sailors, but the opportunities for mischief that this allowed caused a cautious legislature to order, in May, 1784, that no more than one-third of a boat's crew could consist of slaves.[20] An act of January, 1802, reaffirmed this principle, and added, "That in case the skipper of any vessel be a slave, he shall receive for every such offense, thirty-nine lashes on his bare back."[21] These laws, more than most, are of interest particularly for their intent. The practice of favoring slaves with gifts of money continued throughout this period. Obviously, then, some of these slaves were using their money to buy merchandise in violation of the act of 1792. And foreign visitors mentioned boats whose crews were made up entirely of slaves, well after the passage of the act of 1784.

---

[16] Hening, XI, 59.
[17] Shepherd, I, 126.
[18] *Ibid.*, 124.
[19] *Ibid.*, II, 94.
[20] Hening, XI, 404.
[21] Shepherd, II, 326.

The legislators of Virginia, keeping foremost in their minds the safety of the whole commonwealth, tried to create a system of laws which forced owners to use their slaves only in jobs which permitted close supervision, and either allowed no risky contacts, or only those which could be carefully guarded. Similarly, the social life of slaves was to be policed to prevent the establishment of wide and private communication. No slave could stray from his master's property without a pass; it was the duty of any citizen who should catch him doing so to deliver the miscreant to a justice of the peace for a sound whipping. An owner or overseer catching a slave trespassing on his property was encouraged to give him ten lashes on the spot. A lenient owner who permitted an unauthorized slave to linger on his land for more than four hours could be fined three dollars for each offense, and permitting more than five Negroes to visit at the same time could cost him one dollar per excess Negro. To encourage the enforcement of these regulations, the fines were payable to informers.[22]

Anyone found "harboring or entertaining" a slave without his owner's consent could be fined three dollars or twenty lashes, whether he be "white person, free Negro, mulatto, or Indian." The same fine applied for attending any unlawful meeting of slaves. If, on information, any justice of the peace or subordinate officer should fail to punish those present at an unlawful assembly, he himself should be fined.[23]

The prevention of unlawful assemblies of slaves was complicated by the growing force of religion in the years following the Revolution. The evangelical and pietistic sects all believed in saving the souls of Negroes, whatever they thought of slavery. In their zeal, they could not be content with routine Sunday observances, but must build their campfires and exhort lost souls to salvation at every opportunity.

[22] *Ibid.*, I, 123–124.
[23] *Ibid.*, p. 124.

Some planters were themselves swept up in the enthusiasm, but most remained attached to the Anglican faith, and so were impatient with Methodists, Baptists, Presbyterians, and Quakers on religious grounds. When it appeared that these denominations were tampering with slaves, or affording them opportunities to meet secretly, without proper supervision, the politically dominant planters began to appeal for legislation. Here, for example, is the petition of "sundry of the inhabitants of Cumberland County," forwarded to the House of Delegates in 1778:

Your petitioners are greatly alarmed at the progress which some of the dissenters from the Church by Law established are daily making in various parts of this country by seducing the ignorant and unwary to embrace their erroneous tenets. . . . We, or some of us, have seen meetings in the night of our slaves to receive the instructions of teachers without our consent, which we apprehend could produce nothing but deeds of darkness and which have already produced their proper fruits of disobedience and insolence to masters, and glorying in what they are taught to believe to be persecution for conscience's sake. Your petitioners are not actuated by the narrow and blood-thirsty spirit of persecution. They wish to see a well regulated toleration established by which all those weak and conscientious brethren who from principle cannot join with the established Church may be permitted to serve God in their own way without molestation. But we wish also that those nightly meetings may be prohibited under severe penalties and that those only who, after a due examination of their morals, shall be found worthy may be authorized to preach, and only in such public meeting houses as it may be found proper to license for that purpose.[24]

Finally, in January of 1804, the General Assembly passed a law forbidding the "common practice in many places" whereby slaves would gather at night "in considerable numbers at meeting houses and places of religious worship." The practice was forbidden because it might "be productive of considerable evil to the community." Any justice or officer of

---

[24] Photostat, Virginia Legislative Petitions, VSL.

the peace was required to move against such a meeting, and any citizen asked to assist could refuse only on pain of paying a fine. However, the provisions of the act were not declared in force west of the Blue Ridge, where the evangelical Christians were in a majority, and probably would not have obeyed the law anyway.[25]

Even east of the Blue Ridge the law came under attack. Shortly after its enactment a letter appeared in the *Virginia Argus*. It contained no explicit protest but rather simply presented the terms of the law in terse summary, and asked that "printers on this side of the Blue Ridge will please give this a place in their papers." The sentiment of the writer was revealed by his signature, "a Friend to Religious Freedom."[26] Most annoyed were those devout planters who customarily took their slaves with them to evening prayer meetings. Their protests were answered by the next General Assembly, which allowed any master, or member of his white family, to escort his slaves "to any places whatever for the purpose of religious worship," so long as that worship was conducted by "a regularly ordained, or licensed, white minister."[27] By requiring that religious exercises be supervised and conducted by white men, Virginians minimized the danger of religion serving as a cloak for conspiracy. By requiring the presence of those who actually owned the slaves, they guarded against the meetings being used to criticize the institution of slavery itself. And by requiring the leadership of an ordained minister, they were able to maintain their blanket prohibition of Quaker meetings for the benefit of slaves, for the antislavery Quakers had no ministers.

Another measure might be construed as revealing the Virginians' abiding desire to prevent the circumstances in which conspiracies might grow. If a single slave should run off,

---

[25] Shepherd, III, 108.

[26] *Virginia Argus*, 15 February 1804.

[27] Shepherd, III, 124.

and be suspected of "lying out" in the vicinity, the master had to rely on his own resources, or on the slave's giving up voluntarily, for his recovery. But if two or more slaves were known to be hiding together in the wilderness, they constituted a public menace and could be hunted by a sheriff's posse. An order signed by two justices of the peace — counties normally had six to ten justices — would oblige the sheriff to organize his search.[28]

The slave code of 1792 did not go so far as to admit the possibility of an actual insurrection, but merely insisted on an inflexible death penalty for any slave who should be caught "consulting, plotting, or conspiring," to make insurrection, or to murder "any person or persons whatsoever."[29] Such a provision requires no explanation, but a supplementary act, passed in January of 1798, was somewhat more complex in its origins. This act decreed death "without benefit of clergy" to "free persons" who might be guilty of "advising or conspiring with any slave, to rebel or make insurrection, or who shall be guilty of plotting with a slave the murder of any person whatsoever." In this act the lawmaking planters of Virginia revealed their growing concern over the rapidly increasing class of free Negroes within the commonwealth. Furthermore, they betrayed how powerfully the notion of race worked on their imaginations, for to them it seemed that the free blacks were natural allies of the enslaved Negroes, and likely at any time to act in their interest. As a matter of fact, the free Negro population of Virginia was always remarkably docile, but their mild and amiable behavior could not prevent the continuing expansion of their rulers' fears. The planter who claimed that he, of all people in the world, understood the Negro best, never understood

---

[28] *Ibid.*, I, 125.

[29] *Ibid.*, pp. 125–126. In treason cases, the death penalty was to be inflicted immediately following conviction, instead of after the thirty days customary in punishing capital criminals.

that the Negro who enjoyed a limited degree of freedom and privacy earnestly hoped to avoid doing anything that might cause him to lose his precariously held advantages.

Whereas the danger of attack from the free Negroes was a morbid fantasy, Virginians had good enough cause to fear their slaves. Between the Revolutionary War and the War of 1812, Herbert Aptheker has found eleven cases of servile violence in the Old Dominion. Some of these involved only rumors and fright, and groundless or wildly exaggerated fears may even have been involved in several other cases where slaves were actually convicted of treason and hung. But certain events stand out clearly as rebellion. In 1781 a number of slaves in Williamsburg set fire to some buildings, including the recently abandoned' seat of government, and they killed one white man.[30] In 1792 a gang of slaves who had been lying out raided a plantation in Charles City County, and killed an overseer. In 1797 a battle in Prince William County resulted in the death of four whites and six slaves. And then, in 1800, though no white men lost their lives, there was good cause to believe that hundreds, or even thousands, had come dangerously close to doing so.[31]

Near Richmond on August 30, 1800, Tom and Pharoah, two slaves owned by Mosby Shepherd, told their master of a huge uprising which was to take place that day. Shepherd believed them, and promptly warned the authorities. While Governor James Monroe hastily summoned the militia, a tremendous thunderstorm made impassable the various paths which the rebels had expected to follow to their rendezvous. Efficient police work rounded up fifty conspirators within the next couple of days, and Gabriel himself, the supposed strategist of the uprising, was finally caught. For several

---

[30] Herbert Aptheker, *The Negro in the American Revolution* (New York, 1940), p. 27.

[31] Herbert Aptheker, *American Negro Slave Revolts* (New York, 1943), Chapter 9.

weeks thereafter, the highest officials of Virginia were busy inspecting the evidence and listening to the testimony of the captured slaves. The effect of this investigation on their imaginations was deep and lasting.

They saw swords, bayonets, and even bullets, which slaves had fashioned out of crude materials and hidden away. They heard of a daring plan for attacking the city of Richmond. The wooden dwellings at one end of town were to be set on fire by a few of the conspirators. While the white population was drawn to the conflagration, the main body of slaves would attack the state buildings at the other end of town, seize weapons from the armory, and then shoot down the white citizens on their return from the fires. The city captured, its white inhabitants slaughtered, and a supply of weapons gained, the conspirators would then spread their uprising in all directions, from plantation to plantation.[32]

Unfortunately, the man who knew most about the conspiracy, the ringleader Gabriel, refused to say anything at all, so that its full extent and aims were never discovered. Different notions emerged from the various accounts of those slaves who would testify. They seemed to agree that Methodists, Quakers, and Frenchmen were not to be molested, but there was conflicting testimony over the proposed fate of white women who fell outside these favored categories. One of the captives testified that he understood the younger white women were to have been spared.

John Randolph, who had attended some of the interrogations, thought that the slaves "exhibited a spirit, which, if it becomes general, must deluge the Southern country in blood. They manifested a sense of their rights, and contempt of danger, and a thirst for revenge which portend the most un-

---

[32] The account of Gabriel's Rebellion is mainly drawn from a report of Governor James Monroe to the Speaker of the General Assembly, 5 December 1800. James Monroe, *Writings*, edited by Stanislaus Hamilton (New York, 1898–1903), III, 238–243. Also valuable is Aptheker, *American Negro Slave Revolts*, pp. 220–226.

happy consequences."[33] He went on to add that such spirit had so far not been detected beyond the neighborhood of Richmond, and certainly not in his own part of Virginia. Nevertheless, like most leading Virginians, Randolph was thereafter possessed by the idea of a slave rebellion. In 1813 he protested against the withdrawal of militia from his neighborhood for service against the British, because of "the danger from *an internal foe,* augmented by the removal of so large a portion of our force."[34]

Governor Monroe wrote on September 15, 1800, that ten slaves had already been tried and executed, and that from twenty to forty more were still awaiting trial. He was distressed by the increasing number of executions, but hesitated to issue any pardons. "It is hardly to be presumed," he wrote, "a rebel who avows it was his intention to assassinate his master, etc., if pardoned will ever become a useful servant." Monroe further lamented that he had no authority to deport criminal slaves.[35]

By the middle of January, 1801, the Virginia legislature had granted him the authority he wanted. The governor was now empowered to sell "slaves under sentence of death for conspiracy" to purchasers outside the commonwealth. If such a slave should ever return to Virginia, he would be seized and executed. The owners whose slaves had been arrested were to receive public compensation "in the same manner as for slaves executed."[36]

Along with a personal revulsion against hanging every last slave who was discovered to have had anything to do with

---

[33] Quoted in William Cabell Bruce, *John Randolph of Roanoke* (New York, 1922), II, 250.

[34] Letter to Josiah Quincy, 28 June 1813, Bruce, *Randolph,* I, 394.

[35] Letter to Jefferson, Monroe, *Writings,* III, 208–209. Aptheker states that thirty-five slaves were eventually hanged; *American Negro Slave Revolts,* p. 222.

[36] Monroe to Jefferson: letters of 13 February 1802 and 11 June 1802, Monroe, *Writings,* III, 336–338, 351–352.

Gabriel's conspiracy, Monroe had a public motive for wanting to deport the slaves. According to statute, the state was obliged to repay the market value of every slave it arrested. Since the slaves involved with Gabriel were the most vigorous and talented sort of men, their punishment would cost the state over $20,000, quite apart from the costs of militia musters, of holding them prisoners, and of trials and executions. After executing the ringleaders, then, it was in keeping with republican ideals of frugality as well as humanity to try to sell the remaining rebels abroad.

The polite consideration which states within the Union usually felt for one another ruled out the possibility of selling the convict-slaves in South Carolina, Georgia, or any other province of the United States. Jefferson suggested that they might be sent to Sierra Leone, but Monroe objected that since no slavery existed there, criminals would enjoy a better status than they deserved, and besides, they could not be sold to defer costs of transportation. The General Assembly eventually recommended that convicts be sold in other parts of Africa, or in the Spanish or Portuguese dominions of South America.

Pondering over the desirability of deporting criminal slaves, the governor and the legislators of Virginia soon began thinking about exporting Negroes who might in the future cause inconvenience or danger. The idea took hold of their imaginations of transplanting Negroes, especially free Negroes, but also those whose masters voluntarily chose to send them out of the country. This eventually led to the enrollment of many eminent Virginians as charter members of the American Colonization Society, an organization which placed so much emphasis on the removal of free persons of color as to be best considered an anti-Negro, rather than an antislavery organization. Anyway, back in 1801, Governor Monroe wrote, on instructions from the General Assembly, to President Jefferson, asking if the federal government might arrange for lands, either in the territories of the United

States, or in foreign parts, where Negroes might be resettled. Monroe obviously thought the American territories the poorer alternative, and Jefferson rejected them altogether. He remained willing, however, to consider other locations in the Western Hemisphere. One of Jefferson's interesting notions was that transported Negroes should only be sent into territories controlled by governments unlikely to threaten the United States militarily. This would preclude their knowledge of American terrain being used against us.[37]

No free Negroes were involved in Gabriel's scheme, yet almost all of the restrictive laws which came in the years following were aimed against that class.[38] These included the provision that Negroes newly freed must leave Virginia within one year, and could return only on pain of being seized and sold into slavery. Also there was the removal of mandatory education for apprenticed Negro orphans. Some schools for free Negroes were closed.[39] The conspiracy, which had been a fruit of slavery itself, became the justification for further tightening the hold of slavery on Virginia and choking off the small, but promising, progress of gradual, voluntary emancipation.

Gabriel's conspiracy brought home and justified an apprehension which had been growing in Virginia ever since the first Santo Domingo rebellion in 1791. The series of bloody wars which marked the history of that island might have offered some satisfaction to the friends of liberty, for the slaves who first rose up in 1791 succeeded in preserving their turbulent independence after 1803. But though Virginians honored the right of revolution in theory, they could

---

[37] Monroe to Jefferson, 15 June 1801. Monroe to the General Assembly of Virginia, 21 December 1801, Monroe, *Writings*, III, 292–295, 321–322. Jefferson to Monroe, 2 June 1802, Jefferson, *Works*, VIII, 153–154.
[38] Russell, *Free Negro*, p. 167.
[39] Carter G. Woodson, *The Education of the Negro Prior to 1861* (New York, 1915), pp. 110–111.

not extend it where it meant Negro slaves slaughtering their white masters.

In 1806 Napoleon, still not reconciled to his loss of Santo Domingo, asked the American government to cut off all its trade with the rebel island. A bill was duly introduced, forbidding commerce for one year. While arguing in its favor, John Eppes, a representative of Virginia, observed:

We are called on by a nation friendly to us to put a stop to this infamous and nefarious traffic. It is time to do it; let us pass the bill at once. . . .

Some gentlemen would declare St. Domingo free; if any gentleman harbors such sentiments let him come forward boldly and declare it. In such case, he would cover himself with detestation. [This is] a system that would bring immediate and horrible destruction on the fairest portion of America.

Running the risk of seeing himself covered with detestation, William Ely of Massachusetts protested, for his state profited from the Santo Domingo trade and had nothing to fear from a servile insurrection. Had France, he inquired, "any right to call on us to starve" former subjects whom she could no longer control? The House apparently thought France could, for the nonintercourse act passed by a vote of 93 to 26, with twenty-four New Englanders and two New Yorkers supplying the opposition.[40]

It should be remembered that this was a measure strongly commended to Congress by President Jefferson, although his influence was applied in the usual indirect way. It appears to have been his hope that our cooperation in Napoleon's recapture of Santo Domingo would help persuade the French dictator to apply his influence over Spain in behalf of our acquisition of the Floridas. But Jefferson was all the more willing to sacrifice the freedom of Santo Domingo because it threatened, in a way curiously analogous to Fidel

---

[40] Debates of 24 and 25 February 1806, *Annals of the 9th Congress, First Session*, pp. 513–516.

Castro's Cuba of our own times, to export its wicked revolution to other parts of the hemisphere. At the same time, John Randolph, Jefferson's most dangerous political enemy in 1806, refrained from bringing his customary charge of subservience to the villain Napoleon, even though this was the most flagrant case of it. Instead, Randolph avoided the debates and failed to appear in the House on the day of the vote.[41]

With Santo Domingo and Gabriel preying on their imaginations, Virginians did what they felt must be done to reduce the threat of race war to an absolute minimum. If this meant depriving a few Negroes of marginal opportunities, and the curtailing of emancipations, it did not mean, except in the vicinity of Richmond, a more regimented and severe life for the average slave. It did, however, mean a strengthening and stabilizing of the institution of slavery, of a kind which many books tell us did not occur in the South until the 1820's or '30's.

It remained as true as ever, though, that Virginians could show their appreciation to Negroes who behaved as their masters thought good Negroes should. In fact, within five months of the Gabriel conspiracy, two slaves were handsomely rewarded for their good behavior, and at considerable expense to the taxpayers of Virginia. On January 14, 1801, the legislature directed Governor Monroe to pay Mosby Shepherd his price for the slaves Tom and Pharoah, and bestow upon them their freedom. The preamble of the act observed, "Sound policy dictates, that rewards should be held out to those who have rendered essential service to our country." Gabriel's rebellion at least freed a couple of slaves.[42]

---

[41] Charles C. Tansill, *The United States and Santo Domingo, 1798–1873* (Baltimore, 1938), pp. 108–109; Adams, *History of the United States*, III, 142.

[42] Shepherd, II, 273.

CHAPTER

SIX

Gentlemen's Opinions on Race and Freedom

The crowd of notable statesmen who represented Virginia in the early republic wrote and spoke against slavery with vigor and feeling. Their sentiments have often been cited as evidence that they were as antislavery as any Americans of their time, and that they were clear headed and secure in their belief that slavery would soon cease to exist. A close examination of the things they said about slavery, and where and when they said them, produces more complex conclusions. Virginians were most often defending slavery while denouncing it, for unlike southerners of later generations, they could command the sympathy of outsiders simply by showing the right attitudes.

During the Revolutionary War, Virginians were obliged to cooperate as closely and amicably as possible with soldiers and statesmen from the northern states and from France, almost all of whom found slavery distasteful. Again, in the two decades following the drafting of the federal constitution, Virginians were pleased to collaborate with northerners in the formation of national parties, and whether they avowed Federalism or Republicanism, they were certain to meet many enemies of slavery. Further exposure to foes of slavery came from the enthusiastic support of the French Revolution given by Virginians, and from partisanship for France in her wars against Britain.

This is not to say that Virginians cynically adopted a mask of antislavery for the benefit of outsiders whose esteem they hoped to win. Rather, they found themselves partners in the liberal vanguard of their times, and were properly embarrassed at a stigma from which their other partners were free. Accepting with pleasure, and sometimes with fervor, most of the assumptions of the Enlightenment, Virginia's leaders must necessarily denounce slavery as an evil institution. From their frequent statements in this vein, these statesmen have caused their constituents to enjoy the reputation of being antislavery, as if the statesmen were voicing the convictions of their society and class. But if one looks closely, it appears that attacks on slavery usually occurred in the relations of Virginia with the outside world. In private correspondence, in the Congress of the United States, and in foreign capitals, Virginians typically indicted slavery whenever the subject arose. But among the class of wealthy planters whom they chiefly represented not one Virginia statesman of the Jeffersonian era ever advanced a practical proposal for the elimination of slavery, or for the systematic amelioration of the Negro's condition, with the single exception of St. George Tucker, a jurist and pedagogue. Schemes were, indeed, discussed in private. But, Tucker

excepted, no politically prominent man came forward publicly to advocate the end of slavery. As there is practically
no evidence to suggest that the dominant planters would
have responded to such initiative, one must conclude that
those leaders who genuinely hated slavery refrained from
acting because they were convinced that their leadership
would be rejected. Under a system of frequent elections, the
Virginia statesman who came out publicly against slavery
would very quickly be retired to private life.

The Virginia statesman saved himself from the charge of
hypocrisy by acknowledging certain "truths" about Negroes,
slavery, and society. He developed a set of logical propositions which made it natural and consistent for him to denounce slavery in principle, yet satisfy his constituents in
practice that he would do nothing to injure their interests.
Some of the axioms which were used to support these
propositions were reasonable enough for the times. To entertain others must have required considerable mental effort.

One of the more dubious notions was that Virginians
could not be held responsible for the existence of slavery
among them, because it had been forced upon their ancestors
by the tyranny of the English crown. The Virginia Constitution of 1776 mentioned how the King of England, "by an
inhuman use of his negative," had prevented the colony
from excluding slaves.[1] Only the intervention of gentlemen
from the Deep South kept Jefferson from including this
count in his indictment of George III contained in the Declaration of Independence. But, of course, neither the Crown
nor anybody else had ever forced a Virginian to buy a single
slave. For over twenty years before the Revolution the British government had prevented Virginia from barring the
further introduction of slaves, but this hardly represented
either renunciation of slavery on the part of Virginia or a

---

[1] F. N. Thorpe, ed., *The Federal and State Constitutions, Colonial Charters, and Other Organic Laws* (Washington, D.C., 1909), VII, 3815.

systematic policy of the Crown to force slavery into areas where it was not wanted. By the time colonial Virginia tried to prevent slave importation, her leading planters were faced with the problem of perennial overproduction, and of course owned more than enough slaves, who were a large majority in the Tidewater area. Also, given this problem of overproduction, the value of slaves was likely to fall if slave traders were permitted to dump unlimited quantities of their merchandise into a Virginia market which had a limited capacity to absorb them. As a rule Virginians did not like to sell their slaves, at least not in the open market. But neither were they happy when the market value of their slaves declined.

Another important reason for prohibiting the importing of slaves, even in colonial days, was an apprehension of slave rebellions. If the slave population should be permitted to grow more rapidly than the white population, the danger of successful insurrection would be markedly increased. Virginians had enough imagination to foresee the possibility of living under garrison conditions, and the prospect was repugnant to them. They further felt, probably with justification, that imported slaves were likely to be less docile than those bred to their proper station in the Old Dominion.

Therefore, the ruling class of colonial Virginia tried to control the size of their slave population. The British government, on the other hand, could argue that as long as there were people in Virginia who wanted to import Negroes, they should have the right to do so. Such a policy had the advantage of keeping content the British interests in the slave trade, and those British merchants who were pleased at the abundance and low cost of Virginia tobacco. All of these complexities were kept out of mind, however, or at least out of public utterance, and Virginians after the Revolution stuck to their dogma that the evil of slavery dwelt among them because of the diabolical commercial policy of the Old Empire. Given this notion of inherited evil without inherited guilt, they often represented themselves as laboring under a burden. The wretched class of unfortunates residing among them, they claimed, depended for its mere survival on their stewardship and careful management.

Turning these unfortunates free, on the other hand, would be a disaster for both the Negroes and the whites. The former race had not the moral fiber, intelligence, and industry necessary for citizenship in the society of the latter. Hostility and jealousy were bound to result from a coequal existence within the same territory, until one race must enslave or destroy the other. On the other hand, if the races should not destroy one another in civil war, the black must eventually interbreed with the white, destroying the intelligence and beauty of the superior race.

Even a careful, gradual emancipation would be dangerous (here again the argument strains the bounds of rationality) because the free Negro, bound by culture and complexion to his brothers still within slavery, must be regarded as a continual threat to the public safety. A more cogent reason for the slaveholding Virginian to retain his burden was that the liberated Negroes might wander into northern states in great number. Would they be welcome there? Northern statesmen who remained skeptical of other points in the Virginian apology, must feel the weight of this one. For whereas their own constituents might criticize the existence of slavery, few of them had any love for the Negro or desire for his company.

It is doubtful whether the majority of Virginians who owned slaves found it necessary to embrace the foregoing propositions. Those who were not involved in public affairs seem, in what letters and diaries they have left, to have accepted slavery as a normal feature of life, excepting the abolitionists of certain religious persuasions. Obsessions with guilt over the holding of slaves are, with the exception noted, extremely difficult to find. There were occasional anxieties, but such exist in any sphere of life. Anyway, it was bad form to dwell on the evils of slavery in public. Such ideas might reach the slaves themselves, making them unruly and discontented. This would force the masters to apply a stricter, harsher discipline. Therefore the net result of public protest against slavery would be to make the life of the slave more miserable, which was surely an effect not desired by those who deplored the evil effects of slavery in the first place.

Discussions of the evils of slavery were confined to private drawing rooms in Virginia, except for an occasional outburst in the legislature, or from an evangelical pulpit. The newspapers of the times avoided so delicate an issue, and there were no other forms of journalism practiced. Jefferson thought in 1785 that "the bulk of the people" favored some kind of emancipation "in theory," and that a distinguished minority was prepared to act immediately. The majority, however, had not "the courage to divest" themselves "of a property which, however, keeps their consciences inquiet."[2] This was written from Paris to a liberal Englishman, Dr. Richard Price, who was actively interested in British and American emancipation. Jefferson was then in liberal company, and could look with satisfaction on the small but significant gains made by Negroes since the American Revolution. He was then more optimistic than he was to be after returning to America.

On the other hand, a man who had not seen the subtle changes occurring in Virginia in the seventies and eighties immediately reached a pessimistic conclusion. Brissot de Warville, after commenting with satisfaction on the measures under way in northern states to liberate Negroes, deplored the absence of such developments in the South. Here he found "another world," where no one spoke "of projects for freeing the Negroes." He added that "the indolent masters behold with uneasiness, the efforts that are making to render freedom universal," withholding their praise from the efforts of the English and American emancipation societies

---

[2] Letter of 7 August 1785, Jefferson, *Works*, IV, 82.

and authors.[3] Brissot then outlined the terms of the predicament with which Virginians considered themselves stalemated. He thought it consisted of so many excuses, and he concluded that slavery was fundamentally endorsed by the protesting masters. His was the simple point of view that genuine antislavery thought must necessarily lead to antislavery action.

With regard to slavery, Virginia statesmen were in the peculiar position of repeatedly describing an evil and then proceeding to insist that nothing could be done about it. Thus, said John Nicholas to the House of Representatives in 1797, "On inquiry . . . it would not be found the fault of the southern states that slavery was tolerated, but their misfortune; but to liberate their slaves would be to act like madmen; it would be to injure all parts of the United States as well as those who possess slaves."[4] Nor had the general government any business tampering with Virginia's slaves, or even thinking about them except in one respect. Another representative of Virginia explained this to Congress: "Mr. Lee observed that gentlemen were sent to that House to protect the rights of the people and the rights of property. That property which the people of the southern states possess consisted of slaves, and therefore Congress had no authority but to protect it, and not take measures to deprive the citizens of it. . . ."[5] This was said after a petition of free Negroes came before the House of Representatives, praying that it might consider means of bringing more people out of bondage. General Henry Lee answered, in effect, that Congress might properly act only to continue the holding of people in bondage.

John Randolph joined the debate to "hope that the conduct of the House would be so decided as to deter the peti-

---

[3] Brissot de Warville, *New Travels*, pp. 280–281.

[4] *Annals of the 5th Congress*, III, 664.

[5] *Annals of the 6th Congress, 2nd Session*, p. 231.

tioners," or anyone else, "from ever presenting [a petition] of a similar nature. The effects must be extremely injurious." [6] Finally, a less celebrated representative of Virginia, Samuel Goode, submitted an amendment to the House resolution denying the petition, which denounced the petitioners themselves. He argued, quite in the fashion of the southerners of the 1830's, that emancipation was a subject "from which the general government is precluded by the Constitution," and that petitions advocating it had "a tendency to create disquiet and jealousy, and ought therefore to receive the pointed disapprobation of this house." [7] As a matter of fact, southerners, including Virginians, were fully as eager to choke off antislavery petitions to Congress in the Jeffersonian era as they were in the days of Garrison and Weld. When a petition drawn by Benjamin Franklin was submitted in 1790, suggesting with characteristic mildness that Congress might consider some means of uplifting Negroes held in bondage, Congress was embroiled in a week of acrimony. Fisher Ames of Massachusetts described the scene: "The Quakers have been abused, the eastern states inveighed against, the chairman rudely charged with partiality. Language low, indecent, and profane has been used; wit equally stale and wretched has been attempted; in short we have sunk below the General Court [of Massachusetts] in the disorderly moment of a brawling nomination of a committee, or even of a country town-meeting." [8]

It was not the attitude of the representatives of slaveholders that changed between the 1790's and the 1830's, but rather the attitude of the North. In the earlier period northern Congressmen acquiesced, somewhat grudgingly, in the refusal to consider such petitions, and accepted the southern

---

[6] *Ibid.*, p. 233.

[7] *Ibid.*, p. 240.

[8] Quoted in John Bach McMaster, *History of the People of the United States* (New York, 1883–95), I, 579.

contention that they probably caused more harm than good. Because the refusal to consider petitions was not followed by widespread public indignation and a flood of further petitions, the southerners had no cause, as they later did, to try to prevent such petitions even being brought into the halls of Congress.

But even in the Jeffersonian era northern disapproval of slavery was more suppressed than suspended, and it could erupt in moments of anger. Thus, when John Randolph was attacking Matthew Lyon for his support of the Yazoo claimants, the Vermonter protested that "these charges have been brought against me by a person nursed in the bosom of opulence, inheriting the life services of a numerous train of the human species . . . the original proprietors of which property, in all probability, came no honester by it" than the Yazoo claimants. To be consistent, then, Randolph ought to "give up the stolen men in his possession."[9] On another occasion, William Branch Giles of Virginia moved that an amendment be added to a naturalization law which would force foreign noblemen to renounce their titles when seeking American citizenship. Samuel Dexter, Jr., of Massachusetts then moved that such foreigners should be obliged to give up any slaves they might own, and George Thatcher, also of Massachusetts, added a further requirement that these immigrants might permanently be barred from holding slaves. In this way the New England Federalists parried the Republican charge of fondness for titled aristocracies. Giles responded that "he was sorry to see slavery made a jest of in that House," for the motion of the New Englanders "was calculated to injure the property of gentlemen." Our course he "lamented and detested" slavery, but, "from the existing state of the country, it was impossible at present to help it." James Madison joined the debate to urge that "the operation of re-

---

[9] Quoted in William Cabell Bruce, *John Randolph of Roanoke: 1773–1833* (New York, 1922), I, 219.

ducing the number of slaves was going on as quickly as possible," but that the discussion of the subject by Congress "had, in the meantime, a very bad effect on that species of property." Were it not for this "bad effect" he might himself vote for Dexter's amendment.[10]

The Virginians were put to another test in Congress when, in 1806, the House was working on legislation to prohibit the international slave trade, to go into effect as soon as the Constitution should allow. The act before the House specified that contraband slaves seized by the federal government should be sold for the profit of the government. To this James Sloan of New Jersey submitted the amendment that contraband slaves should be set free. John Eppes of Virginia then moved an amendment to the amendment providing that contraband Negroes should be set free only "in one of the States of the Union, where slavery is not by law permitted." But Eppes and all of the other Virginia representatives, with one exception, voted against Sloan's amendment, and the act passed with the original provision that contraband Negroes should be sold into slavery.[11] It is hardly necessary to point out that the Virginia votes were not those of men morally aroused *against* slavery.

The prosperous slaveholder, John Page, comforted himself in 1795 with Biblical speculations. "May not the difference between Europeans, Asiatics, and Africans," he asked himself, "be attributable to the Punishment of Ham as to the blacks?" This was an hypothesis warmly advanced by proslavery preachers in later years. Comparably suggestive of complacency over slavery in Virginia were some reflections of the Scotch agent, William McKean. No abolitionist zeal colored the views of this hard-working trader and plantation manager. But he did believe that more and better work could be exacted from the slaves of Virginia had they been

---

[10] *Annals of the Third Congress*, pp. 1039–40.
[11] *Annals of the Ninth Congress, Second Session*, pp. 168, 264–265.

given some education while young, and he was perplexed at the unwillingness of the planters to provide such education: "numerous indeed are the arguments used against it."[12]

In brief, the antislavery pronouncements of Virginia's statesmen were so rarely accompanied by any positive efforts against slavery as to cast doubt on their sincerity, and when initiative against slavery was proposed by others they normally resisted it. This makes still more doubtful the proposition that their constituents were agreeable to antislavery sentiments. The indirect evidence available to us on the position of the Virginia planters suggests that most of them were for all practical purposes proslavery. But even if the average planter held views on the Negro question identical to those of Thomas Jefferson, slavery would have remained fixed in Virginia, for the most liberal of all Virginia statesmen was himself unable to find a practical means to dismantle the institution he freely acknowledged as a curse. He was effectively prevented from doing so because, on the one hand, he shared too many of the traditional southern ideas about the character and potentialities of the Negro, and, on the other hand, he was unwilling to risk the certain loss of political influence that outspoken opposition to slavery must have caused.

Jefferson attained an important station in public life at a fairly early age, and continued to command the serious attention of many Americans until his death in 1826. Over a period of six decades his hopes about slavery changed significantly, so that the possibility and the imminence of emancipation seemed much stronger to him at one time than at others. In the years just following the Declaration of Independence he worked out an elaborate law for the gradual emancipation *and removal* of the Negroes of Virginia but he, along with his colleagues in revising the laws, refrained from submitting this to the legislature. At that time Jefferson

---

[12] William McKean Letterbook, p. 27, VSL.

thought that the people of Virginia would very likely be more receptive to his scheme after the passage of years brought an increase in liberal and humanitarian sentiment. But the occasion never arose, and it seems clear that by the time of his presidency, Jefferson had entirely dismissed the notion of doing anything himself in behalf of emancipation. In 1891 Moncure D. Conway, a native Virginian who had suffered immense odium by being an abolitionist before the Civil War, ruminated in a private letter about Jefferson's reputed opposition to slavery. "Bancroft has given him a world-wide reputation," Conway wrote, "as having tried to pass an antislavery act in Virginia. Never did man achieve more fame for what he did not do." [13]

Jefferson did indeed recommend in 1784 that the western territories should be closed to the introduction of slavery, and this recommendation, unlike the celebrated sixth article of the final Ordinance for the Northwest Territory, applied equally to the Southwest. As president, however, he guaranteed the protection of Spanish and French slavery in Louisiana, and helped open that territory to American slavery as well. Nor does he seem to have used his influence as president to discourage the attempt, led by William Henry Harrison, to suspend the operation of Article Six in Indiana and Illinois. Jefferson's reputation has indeed been fortunate, when one considers that he has been recognized universally as the father of exclusion in the Old Northwest, but has never been labeled as the father of slavery in Louisiana, except by a few seething Federalists in his own day, who have long since been discredited.

In the company of liberal intellectuals abroad, Jefferson freely expressed, in the 1780's, the antislavery thoughts that he had developed in association with his former teacher, George Wythe, before the American Revolution. This was

---

[13] Letter to William Wirt Henry, 23 December 1891, W. W. Henry Papers, Box 2, VSL.

so well known that certain Federalists in South Carolina tried to ruin Jefferson's reputation in the South by urging their countrymen to believe that Jefferson was, in fact, committed to an early and complete emancipation.[14] They also pointed to Jefferson's letter to Benjamin Bannaker, a free Negro who had an unusual gift for mathematics and worked out the astronomical predictions for a popular almanac. But this letter, written when Jefferson was Secretary of State under Washington, was his last public gesture of any kind on behalf of the Negroes of America.

In 1796 William Loughton Smith of South Carolina and Oliver Wolcott of Connecticut published *The Pretension of Thomas Jefferson to the Presidency Examined*,[15] which, among other things, described Jefferson as brutal and callous toward Negroes for the benefit of northern readers, and as an advocate of precipitate emancipation, for the benefit of southerners. The Federalist pamphleteers exposed Jefferson's contradictions and equivocations on slavery with vigor and skill. Unfortunately for their own position, they far surpassed Jefferson in trying to take all sides of the question, charging him on one page with a "very ridiculous and elaborate attempt to prove that the Negroes are an inferior race of animals,"[16] and then on another charging him with holding "the delusive and visionary principles which he has imbibed on that subject [of emancipation] by his residence in France."[17] This attack on Jefferson was so obviously opportunistic and, on the subject of slavery, irresponsible, that it probably did him no harm during the years of his political

---

[14] William S. Jenkins, *Pro-Slavery Thought in the Old South* (Chapel Hill, 1935), p. 62.

[15] Published in Philadelphia. The authors, after the fashion of the times, did not identify themselves.

[16] [William Loughton Smith and Oliver Wolcott], *The Pretension of Thomas Jefferson* . . . (Philadelphia, 1796), p. 6.

[17] *Ibid.*, p. 13.

ascendency. Perhaps, however, it demonstrated to him the wisdom of leaving the whole subject alone.

Wolcott and Smith gathered their ammunition mainly from Jefferson's book, *Notes on Virginia*, which contained extensive discussions about the character and situation of the Negro slave. Jefferson began his remarks on the biological attributes of the Negro with the suggestion that his supposed inferiority might have been caused by degrading environment rather than by biological endowment. Nevertheless, Jefferson proceeded to speculate on the peculiar characteristics that he supposed the Negro to have. Some of his observations are more than a little embarrassing to recount, but they are essential to the understanding of his conflicting and often confused reasoning on the Negro question. For instance, he found it a flaw in Negroes that their dark pigmentation allowed no expressive quality in their faces, asking: "Are not the fine mixtures of red and white, the expressions of every passion by greater or less suffusions of color in the [white race] preferable to that eternal monotony, which reigns in the countenances, that immoveable veil of black which covers all the emotions of the other race?"[18]

Pursuing his demonstration of the superior beauty of the Caucasian, Jefferson cited his "more elegant symmetry of form," and held up the advantage of "flowing" hair over the kinky, woolly kind. He capped his argument by stating that the Negro himself showed a preference for whites, which occurred "as uniformly as . . . the preference of the Oranootan [*sic*] for the black women over those of his own species."

After citing a few more physical distinctions, Jefferson considered some aspects of the Negro's behavior. He believed

---

[18] There are so many editions of Jefferson's *Notes on Virginia* that I omit page references to quotations borrowed from it. I have mainly used the London edition of 1786, but William Peden's modern edition is the one students are most likely to encounter.

that Negroes needed less sleep than whites, for "a black, after hard labour through the day, will be induced by the slightest amusements to sit up till midnight, or later, though knowing he must be out with the first dawn of the morning." Then, on the more important question of intelligence, he submitted that the existence of Negroes "appears to participate more of sensation than reflection. To this must be ascribed their disposition to sleep when abstracted from their diversions, and unemployed in labour. An animal whose body is at rest, and who does not reflect, must be disposed to sleep, of course." As to the faculties of memory, reason, and imagination, Jefferson thought "that in memory [Negroes] are equal to the whites; in reason much inferior, as I think one could scarcely be found capable of tracing and comprehending the investigations of Euclid; and that in imagination they are dull, tasteless, and anomolous. . . ."

Most of the genuine abolitionists of the nineteenth century, and the late eighteenth as well, were concerned with the condition of the Negro and the means of improving it, but Jefferson was most concerned with the evil effect of slavery on white Virginians. He wrote eloquently but abstractly about the injustice of slavery for the Negro. On the subject of the white slaveholder, however, his views were penetrating and sympathetic:

The whole commerce between master and slave is a perpetual exercise of the most boisterous passions, the most unremitting despotism on the one part, and degrading submissions on the other. Our children see this, and learn to imitate it; for man is an imitative animal. . . . The parent storms, the child looks on, catches the lineaments of wrath, puts on the same airs in the circle of smaller slaves, gives a loose to his worst of passions, and thus nursed, educated, and daily exercised in tyranny, cannot but be stamped by it with odious peculiarities.

Besides deforming the character of Virginians, Jefferson feared that slavery might eventually result in their destruction, a catastrophe in which the wrath of God might well vent itself. Were there a war of races, he reasoned, "The Almighty has no attribute which can take side with us in such a contest."

In another section of his *Notes*, Jefferson confronted the issue of what should be done about slavery. Here he reached the conclusion, typical among Virginia statesmen, that though emancipation should have been the goal of enlightened policy, it had to be attended by the complete withdrawal of the Negroes:

This unfortunate difference of colour, and perhaps of faculty, is a powerful obstacle to the emanicipation of these people. Many of their advocates, while they wish to vindicate the liberty of human nature, are anxious also to preserve its dignity and beauty. Some of these, embarrassed by the question, "What further is to be done with them?" join themselves in opposition with those who are actuated by sordid avarice only. Among the Romans emancipation required but one effort. The slave, when made free, might mix with, without staining the blood of his master. But with us a second is necessary, unknown to history. When freed he is to be removed beyond the reach of mixture.

Years later, in his generous letter to the Negro Bannaker, Jefferson wrote that this mathematician had proved the capabilities of his race, and that he wished to see Negroes emancipated "as soon as the imbecility of your present existence will admit."[19] But, as the Federalist pamphleteers gleefully and justly pointed out, Jefferson had posited that slavery must itself have been the cause of that imbecility, so that "if the appearance of their want of talents was owning merely to their condition, the sooner they emerged from that condition the better."[20] Furthermore, it is clear in the correspondence between Jefferson and Monroe following Gabriel's rebellion that Jefferson persisted in his theory that Negroes, once freed, must be transported beyond the continental ter-

---

[19] [Wolcott and Smith], *The Pretension of Thomas Jefferson*, p. 11.
[20] *Ibid.*

ritories of the United States. Considering that in Virginia alone the Negroes numbered almost half the population, and were increasing rapidly, such a migration would be hopelessly expensive in the first place, an enormous hardship on the Negroes in the second, and, in the third, the cause of a catastrophic shortage of labor on the farms and plantations of Virginia. Indeed, in making emancipation entirely dependent on the quixotic scheme of relocation, Jefferson effectively ruled out the possibility of any general emancipation at all.

Even in his boldest undertaking, the plan for general emancipation that was indefinitely withheld, Jefferson proposed an emancipation so gradual that it would guarantee the planters of Virginia slave labor for several generations, and the entire project was dependent on a federally subsidized removal of all free Negroes.[21] And by the time of his presidency, Jefferson was unwilling to be associated with any projects for the reduction of slavery. In 1805 Thomas Brannagan of Philadelphia wrote Jefferson asking him to subscribe to (which meant also to endorse) his poem, "Avenia; or, a Tragical Poem on the Oppression of the Human Species." With respect to this, Jefferson wrote to Dr. George Logan that he had "most carefully avoided every public act or manifestation" on the subject of slavery.[22] Jefferson continued:

Should an occasion ever occur in which I can interpose with decisive effect, I shall certainly know, and do my duty with promptitude and zeal. But in the meantime it would only be disarming myself of influence to be taking small means. The subscription to a book on this subject is one of those little irritating measures, which, without advancing its end at all, would by lessening the confidence and good will of a description of friends composing a large

---

[21] Mary S. Locke, *Anti-Slavery in America . . . 1619–1808* (Boston, 1901), p. 76.
[22] Jefferson, *Works*, VIII, 352.

body, only lessen my powers of doing them good in the other great relations in which I stand to the public.

A legion of general historians and biographers have endowed Jefferson with the most exalted reputation in American history among intellectuals. Reflecting on Jefferson's experience with and attitudes toward slavery, they have cited Jefferson's attacks on the institution with commendable thoroughness, but have been much less conscientious both in tracing his provincial views of the character and capacity of the Negro and in acknowledging the degree to which Jeffersonian politics tended to promote and extend the planting interests of the South. They have suggested that, considering his birth and upbringing in a slaveholding society, his opinions were still surprisingly liberal and in advance of his times.

It is certainly true that there were Europeans and American northerners who shared the belief that the Negro race was genetically inferior in moral and intellectual endowment, and who would fully sympathize with Jefferson's horror at the prospect of miscegenation. But from the 1770's onward there were also serious and dedicated men in Europe, the northern states, and even in Virginia who demonstrated in practice as well as in theory that the Negro slave could be educated, emancipated, and civilized. Jefferson was not ahead, but rather far behind, such public advocates of emancipation as John Jay and Alexander Hamilton of New York, Anthony Benezet and Benjamin Franklin of Philadelphia, and Robert Pleasants and Warner Mifflin of Virginia.

Yet it is certainly true that Jefferson went as far, in attacking and limiting slavery, as an elected representative of Virginia could go, while retaining the suffrage and confidence of the effective majority in that state. Like the Congress of the United States, an elected representative of Virginia was free, not to attack the property of gentlemen, but only to protect it. But Jefferson accepted the limitations of being a Virginia statesmen with good grace, for he was quite as bound to slavery in his private life as he was obliged to be publicly. The labor of his slaves created and sustained the modest splendors of Monticello, and the crops they grew purchased (though they never quite covered the cost) the fine wines and books that made his life at home seem so attractive. Jefferson was not one of those southern Founding Fathers who freed his slaves. The claims of creditors would, under Virginia law, have precluded or at least postponed such an emancipation, but even without these he had so many relatives committed to the plantation way of life that such an act would have amounted to a disinheritance. George Washington, a much more acute business manager than Jefferson, and a man with no direct heirs, helped his various relations in Virginia develop fine estates in their own names, and was still able to relieve his conscience and embellish his reputation by freeing those slaves he owned in his own right. But apart from freeing a couple of typical old "faithful retainers," Jefferson was obliged by his own way of life to leave his Negroes indefinitely bound to servitude.

Much bolder than Jefferson in advocating emancipation was St. George Tucker, who, like Jefferson, had studied law with George Wythe, and in 1796 held Wythe's old job of teaching law at William and Mary. Tucker was also a judge of the general court of Virginia and the stepfather of John Randolph of Roanoke. Obviously Tucker could afford to be more outspoken on the subject of slavery than men who ran directly for public office, and especially men in national politics who wanted to keep the confidence of South Carolina and Georgia. Anyway, it was Tucker who revived and modified the old plan of Jefferson and Wythe, and published it to the world in 1796 in his pamphlet, *A Dissertation on Slavery with a Proposal for the Gradual Abolition of It in the State of Virginia.*[23]

---

[23] Published at Philadelphia.

In this treatise, Tucker swept over world history to discuss slavery in all its forms, and invoked the doctrine of natural law to demonstrate that slavery in any form was wrong. He then proceeded to outline the history of slavery in Virginia, emphasizing all the laws passed on the subject from 1662 until his own time. In this entire body of legislation he could cite with pride only the post-Revolutionary acts ending the importation of Negroes and permitting their emancipation by the voluntary acts of owners. Otherwise, Tucker felt that the laws governing slavery were growing stricter, in spite of an increased disposition to treat slaves well. The institution was obviously out of step with the times, and might justly be brought down by violent revolution if not terminated soon by more sensible methods.

Tucker held the typical belief that "marked physical and intellectual inferiority" made the transportation of freed Negroes beyond the United States desirable, and therefore came very close to defeating his scheme with the customary impossible conditions. But he wanted results enough to compromise on the principle of removal. He noted that shipping Negroes to some distant wilderness would either destroy the Negroes, or cost a fortune, for few of them had the training for pioneering, and none had the capital. Therefore he proposed a scheme which would get Negroes out of Virginia, but not at risk to their lives, and not at a burdensome cost to their former masters. And his scheme would be so gradual that no slaveholder need fear the sudden loss of his labor force.

This was Tucker's plan. All slave females born after a certain day would be scheduled for freedom, but not until their twenty-eighth birthday. Masters would then be compensated for the cost of their support in childhood. All descendants of these females should also be free, but if born on the plantation, they, too, must remain through their twenty-eighth year. This plan guaranteed Virginians a labor supply for at least three generations, and probably more, for no slaves then living would be freed at all, nor would any of their male children. Slave girls kept on plantations until their twenty-eighth birthday were almost certain to bear children before they left. But, after the first generation of males was passed, all slaves would be able to look forward to their eventual freedom.

Tucker's idea for getting the Negroes out of Virginia was simplicity itself. Laws discriminating against free Negroes were to be strengthened until that class should find it intolerable to remain in the state. Free Negroes would then scatter into the new territories of the West and Southwest, where there seemed, in those days, to be an endless supply of land.

Only a gradual scheme had any hope of winning the approval of Virginia planters, and in trying to supply a method for easy gradualism, Tucker invited practical difficulties. Girls born before the starting date, and therefore destined to a lifetime of slavery, might have younger sisters entitled to freedom. The male children of the older sisters must be slaves, those of the younger might be free, and all of the brothers of these girls must be slaves for life. Again, most of the girls destined for freedom in the first generation would be likely to take husbands before their twenty-eighth birthday, and most of these husbands could not look forward to emancipation. Trouble also loomed for the scheme of dissipating unwanted Negroes into the American wilderness: most frontier communities were likely to discriminate against Negroes quite as effectively as Virginia, and they were especially likely to do so if it appeared that gentlemen were trying to dump unwanted population on them. Should the Negroes undertake to start frontier communities entirely their own, where would they secure the necessary capital, or the judges, lawyers, ministers, teachers, and doctors so necessary to the success of a new settlement?

Serious as they are, objections of this kind could not refute the broad ideas of Tucker's plan. He was, after all, interested in securing a gradual but eventually thorough emancipation, and an eventual sharp decline in the number of Negroes in Virginia. His plan, itself a variation on the older one of Jefferson and Wythe, was carefully considered and suggested many opportunities for revision of details. But when Tucker sent a copy of his *Dissertation* and a respectful letter commending it to the Virginia House of Delegates, that public body would not even discuss his ideas, much less put them into practice. Tucker's friend, G. K. Taylor, wrote to him, after failing to introduce the plan for emancipation, that, "Such is the force of prejudice, that in the House of Delegates, characters were found who voted against the letter and its inclosure lying on the table. . . . I despair of being able to obtain leave to bring it in." [24]

Tucker's disappointment was further evidence of the unwillingness of most Virginians to consider emancipation seriously. Antislavery feeling existed in the state, even east of the Blue Ridge, but it failed to impress the politically significant majority. The enlightened leaders of the state had to defer to the majority by avoiding a direct challenge; what remained permissible was a declaration of general principles, a safe step removed from a plan for immediate action. A Virginian could say, as the elderly Madison did in 1819, that the removal of slavery would be desirable, that it should be gradual, that it should only be undertaken with compensation for the owners, and that freed slaves should leave Virginia, with Africa the most likely place for their resettlement. [25]

Or, one might dwell on possibilities, showing while doing so a proper respect for obstacles and difficulties. Such was the case when Governor James Monroe wrote to President Thomas Jefferson on the topic of colonization. He was not sure it would be "practicable," but thought "it would certainly be a very fortunate attainment if we could make [the

---

[24] Quoted in Jenkins, *Pro-Slavery Thought*, p. 53.
[25] Madison, *Letters and Other Writings*, III, 133–134.

Negroes] instrumental to their own emancipation, by a process gradual and certain, on principles consistent with humanity, without expense or inconvenience to ourselves."[26] Monroe gave away the perfect hopelessness of his position by holding that benefits for the Negroes should be without expense or inconvenience to their white masters. One might dwell on the rights of Negroes, but these must always be subordinate to the vested interests of whites. Of course as a politician Monroe realized that an inconvenient and costly scheme could make no headway in the legislature. But he gave no indication that he wished one could.

Among the eminent Virginians of the time, only George Wythe seemed to take the position that Negroes held the full attributes of humanity, and therefore possessed rights which were anterior to any claims that white men might have. Like the Quakers, Wythe entertained a direct concern for the Negroes which took precedence over the safety, convenience, or profit of their masters. Just before he died in 1806, Wythe submitted, in one of his legal opinions, that "whenever one person claims to hold another in slavery, the *onus probandi* lies on the claimant."[27] In other words, he held that the Negro must be considered free until proven a slave. He derived this position from the general proposition, contained in the Virginia Bill of Rights, that the birthright of every human being is freedom. It was ironic that Wythe died of arsenic poisoning, administered by a wastrel grandnephew who was jealous of sharing the old man's legacy with free Negro servants, and who was acquitted of murder because these Negroes were prevented by law from testifying against him.[28]

---

[26] Monroe, *Writings*, III, 353.

[27] Catterall, I, 112.

[28] The best account of Wythe's murder is by Julian P. Boyd, *The Murder of George Wythe* (privately printed, Philadelphia, 1949). A contemporary account is in Catterall, I, 109. There is a cautious summary of the case in the article, "George Wythe," by Theodore S. Cox, *DAB*, XX, 586–589.

The case in which Wythe had set forth his opinion on Negro freedom was finally settled after his death. The final decree was written by St. George Tucker, who held that Wythe had been wrong "in his reasoning on the first clause of the Bill of Rights," which had been "notoriously framed with a cautious eye" to exclude Negroes, and "not by a side wind to overturn the rights of property." The conclusion was still more firm: "This court [does not approve] of the Chancellor's principles and reasoning in his decree . . . entirely disapproving thereof, so far as the same relates to native Africans and their descendants." [29]

It is one of the many curiosities of American history that Abraham Lincoln and many other members of the later Republican Party both believed and asserted that the Declaration of Independence had been intended by the Founding Fathers to apply in principle to all races of men, and not simply to white Americans. Roger Taney, on the other hand, argued (with more impressive historical evidence) in the Dred Scott decision that the Fathers consciously excluded Negroes. Lincoln held that the promise of "life, liberty, and the pursuit of happiness" had not been possible of immediate fulfillment, but was established as a national ideal and goal, while Taney held that the Fathers must have been dreadful hypocrites to hold out such an ideal to American Negroes while continuing slavery as usual. Actually there was no consensus whatever among the Founding Fathers or among their constituents. In Massachusetts slavery fell before the assertion of natural law, while in the South most aristocrats would have agreed with St. George Tucker that any organic laws guaranteeing liberty did not apply to Negroes. The conflict of views between Taney and Lincoln also existed during Revolutionary times.

Whether it was racism, with its horror of miscegenation, or plain economic interest that was more important in prevent-

---

[29] Catterall, I, 112.

ing the spread of emancipation in Virginia, it is clear that both of these were fixed limitations on the thinking of Virginia statesmen who agreed, in the abstract, that slavery was evil and ought to be eliminated. The two strands were powerfully intertwined: if Negroes were freed, they might still be kept as a laboring class, as eventually they were after the Civil War, but the Virginians' racism ruled out this solution. On the other hand, economic interest ruled out the transporting and resettling of significant numbers of Negroes in foreign parts.

In conclusion, a suggestive approach to the Virginians' thinking on race is to compare their attitudes toward Negroes with those they held toward American Indians. Any Virginian with eyes to see could observe countless Negroes who had learned the agriculture and crafts of their masters, and who, with proper encouragement, also adopted their masters' familial institutions and religion. The Indians, on the other hand, were strikingly reluctant to give up their ancient barbarism and melt into the culture of the conquering white man. Yet with available evidence demonstrating that Negroes were far more capable of absorption into normal American society, Virginians continued to hold that they were not. On the other hand, they actually took pride in carrying the blood of distinguished Indians, as in the case of the numerous descendants of Powhatan, and seriously urged as a matter of policy that the Indian problem be solved by interbreeding and acculturation. An extreme example of this was a bill introduced into the House of Delegates in 1784 by Patrick Henry, which proposed that the state should subsidize people marrying Indians with public education, relief from taxes, and bounties for children.[30] In formulating his Indian policy for the Northwest Territory, President Jefferson did not go so far as to subsidize intermarriages, but he looked forward with equanimity to the time when Indians would "incorporate

---

[30] Wirt, *Patrick Henry*, pp. 258–260.

with us as citizens of the United States or remove beyond the Mississippi. The former is certainly the termination of their history most happy for themselves."[31]

During colonial times warfare of the most savage kind raged intermittently between Virginians and Indians within the Old Dominion. During the early national period the migrants and soldiers of Virginia continued to endure the cruelties of Indian warfare and to return them with interest along the spreading frontiers of the Old Southwest. But while willing to avenge Indian raids, to seize and exploit Indian lands, and to drive Indians to the deserts beyond the Mississippi, Virginians, or at least those of the ruling class, rarely regarded the Indian as congenitally inferior to the white. In his *Notes on Virginia*, in fact, Jefferson argued with poetic vigor that cultural circumstances alone were responsible for the backward condition of the American Indians, and that they were altogether a splendid race.

In the early years of tobacco culture in Virginia there was a distinct shortage of labor, for the use of Negro slaves did not become general until the end of the seventeenth century. From time to time Virginians attempted to keep Indians captured in wars as slaves, but found them recalcitrant and unreliable. The Negro slave, on the other hand, was usually pliant enough. What seemed to the Virginians a racial difference here was merely a difference of circumstance. The Negro slave, if he were a native of Africa, would typically have been captured by a coastal tribe of Africa from his native territory, and then transported to the West Indies. By the time he reached Virginia he would have long since been separated from any familiar lands or people, and could only look to his master for some degree of safety and security in his new situation. The Indian, on the other hand, would himself be a native of Virginia, familiar with the country, and,

---

[31] Logan Esarey, ed., *Messages and Letters of William Henry Harrison* (Indianapolis, 1922), I, 71.

unless his tribe had been entirely exterminated, sure of a familiar welcome if he made his escape. In brief, the enslaved Indian had somewhere to go; the Negro did not.

The main reason that Virginians advocated intermarriage with Indians while denouncing it with Negroes was that the Negroes were vastly more numerous, and, because of their very intimacy with their masters, likely to intermarry extensively. Indian blood could be absorbed, while Negro blood would perennially assert itself. More interesting, however, is that high respect which Virginians held for their ancient and savage Indian enemies, compared to the patronizing contempt they held for the Negroes. Proud of their own military traditions, the Virginians positively honored the Indians for their fortitude and bravery in combat, however much they deplored the ungentlemanly arts of stealth, surprise, and mutilation which the Indians cultivated. Indians were proud, and the proud Virginians sympathized with this, also. The Negroes of Virginia, on the other hand, were perpetually prevented from developing military skill of any kind, and were systematically punished for any assertion of recalcitrant pride. Virginians made sure that their Negroes were subordinate and dependent, and then held them in contempt as a race because, after all, they were slaves.

CHAPTER

SEVEN

The True Emancipators

A greater number of slaves were freed in Virginia between the Revolution and the War of 1812 than were freed at any other time until the Civil War. The free Negro population increased from 3,000 to 30,000 between 1780 and 1810. However, at the same time the slave population increased from about 250,000 to almost 400,000, not including the numbers of slaves exported to Kentucky and other places. The increase in the size of the free Negro population was remarkable, but the total number of freed persons remained less than 8 percent of the slave population. Far from being commonplace, emancipation was quite exceptional during this period. It never became so common as to indicate a trend toward full emancipation. The limited manumission of the 1780's and 1790's led, not to wider manumission in the 1800's, but rather to legal curtailment of the practice.

Clearly most Virginians found it expedient to keep their slaves during their lifetimes, bequeathing them to their children. Most of them probably did this as a matter of course, not even bothering to debate the question of emancipation with themselves. It is extremely difficult to find critical discussions of slavery in the papers of average well-to-do Virginia planters. The exceptions were either men of high affairs who were continually being required to explain slavery to curious foreigners, or members of evangelical sects.

But most planters were surely like Randolph Jefferson, the "unknown" brother of Thomas, who divided his slaves equally among five sons.[1] So far as can be told from his letters, Randolph Jefferson was barely literate and concerned only with the management of his plantation and the happiness of his family.[2] Yet he was of the upper class, owning more than ten slaves and more than a thousand acres of land. He was an officer in the militia. If he ever had doubts about slavery, there remain no records to demonstrate it. In practice, he accepted and sustained the institution.

Then there were Virginians who, after considering emancipation, decided that it must bring the Negro greater hardships than the state of slavery itself. A certain John Cooper held this belief so firmly that he bequeathed his Negroes only to persons he trusted to keep them in bondage: "I should have made a more equal and general division among the Negroes . . . but to some it would be but burthening their conscience to hold them as slaves, or they must liberate them, which in my opinion would be a very great disadvantage to the slaves."[3]

---

[1] Will of Randolph Jefferson, 28 May 1808, Carr-Cary Papers.

[2] Bernard Mayo, ed., *Thomas Jefferson and His Unknown Brother Randolph* (Charlottesville, 1942), *passim*.

[3] Catterall, I, 109.

Among Virginians who actually did emancipate slaves, the most generous were elderly people who had no close relatives and had depended for many years on the labor and care of their servants. George Wythe offered one example of this. Another was Micajah Chiles of Charlottesville, who decreed freedom for his slaves Frank, Mark, Fanny, and Bridget, on account of their "faithful services." Chiles's only heir was a man named Henry Fleming West Alberty, whom he called "my reputed son."[4]

It more often happened that the owner of many slaves would free one or two favorites rather than the whole lot. For example, John Stratton of Northampton County freed his slave, Caleb, "in consideration of [his] faithful services and good behavior." However, he also directed his executors "to sell all or any of my Negroes whenever they may deem it necessary from their behavior or the interest of my Estate."[5]

Many owners seemed to be willing that their slaves go free, but left various kinds of conditions to be fulfilled, or gave wide options to their heirs or executors. Since the living were significantly more eager to retain slave property than the dead, slaves sometimes never did gain freedom, and where they did, it might be only after many years' delay. For instance, Angora, slave of James Jones of Albemarle, might go free, or have a new master of her choice, but only "at the expiration of my beloved wife's life."[6] Even more doubtful was the future of Fanny, Wilkinson Barzey's slave, who must wait for the death of her master's wife, and then be turned over to his friend, James Pross, who might "either set her free, or otherwise dispose of her, as he may think proper."[7]

---

[4] Will of Micajah Chiles, 9 January 1799, Albemarle County Will Book no. 4, VSL.

[5] Will signed in 1801 and entered 1804, Northampton County Will Book no. 32, pp. 236–237, VSL.

[6] Albemarle County Will Book no. 4, 15 August 1800, VSL.

[7] Will dated 1792, Middlesex County Will Book, 1675–1798, Part 2, p. 549.

Obed Calvert of Prince William County wanted his slave Frank to remain on his plantation "to keep things together for the purpose of Preasment [i.e., appraisal] and sale . . . as my executors may not be so well acquainted as to the number of stock, and so he will be of peculiar use to them." Then, if Frank proved to have been "serviceable and trusty" in the settlement of the estate, the executors might give him "a small acknowledgement . . . and pronounce Frank free at their own discretion."[8]

Thomas Bell of Albemarle wished that his slave Armistead be freed at the age of thirty-one, until which time he should not be sold, except by his own choice. Bell's elderly slave Derby was not to be sold at all.[9] Sophia C. M. Bullit, either a spinster or a childless widow, wanted her four slaves to be free, but had not the legal power to free them because of indebtedness. Therefore she instructed her executors to hire out the slaves until they had earned enough to satisfy the creditors of her estate. After this the slaves should be free, and one of them, "the boy Frederick," was to receive "fifty acres of Kentucky land to supply him three years' schooling, after which he should be bound to a trade."[10] A similar trust was set up by Joseph Mayo, who died in 1785. After two years his slaves had worked enough to pay all claims against his estate, but it took the executors two years more to prove, in the courts, that they had done so. Thus the slaves were freed four years after their master's death.[11]

Not even George Washington found it possible to free his slaves directly and immediately. Instead they must wait for the death of his wife, as Washington explained in his will:

Upon the decease of my wife, it is my will and desire that all the slaves which I hold in my own right shall receive their free-

---

[8] September, 1804, Prince William County Will Book no. 1, p. 53.

[9] Late 1800, Albemarle County Will Book no. 4.

[10] 27 May 1803, Prince William County Will Book no. 1, pp. 14–15.

[11] Catterall, I, 98.

dom. To emancipate them during her life, would, though earnestly wished by me, be attended with such insuperable difficulties on account of their intermixture by marriage with the Dower Negroes, as to excite the most painful sensations, if not disagreeable consequences from the latter, while both descriptions are in the occupancy of the same proprietor, it not being in my power, under the tenure by which the Dower Negroes are held, to manumit them.[12]

Unless heirs and executors were sympathetic toward the idea of manumission, the wish that slaves be freed might easily be thwarted. Gloister Hunnicutt, a Quaker, had wanted to emancipate his slaves, but it was still difficult to do so at the time of his death in 1781. Therefore he bequeathed them to the monthly meeting of which he was a member, confident that, as soon as it became practical, the slaves would be freed. A year later private emancipation was made legal, and two representatives of the meeting drew up papers to release the slaves. However, Pleasant Hunnicutt, the son and heir of Gloister, refused to give up the Negroes, and, when challenged to do so at law, was sustained in his tenure by a district court. Eventually this judgment was reversed on appeal, but not until 1804. Thus Gloister Hunnicutt's Negroes were detained in slavery twenty-two years longer than they should have been, according to the clear instruction of his will.[13]

The twenty-four slaves of "a certain Miss Mary Robinson" were even less fortunate. Just before her death, she altered her will so that slaves "previously deeded to her nephew Whiting" should be free. "I cannot satisfy my conscience to have my Negro slaves separated from each other, and from their husbands and wives," she wrote. Whiting, already in possession of the slaves, decided to carry them off to Georgia, "to prevent the machinations of those who inspired them with

---

[12] Quoted in Helen Hill, *George Mason, Constitutionalist* (Cambridge, 1938), p. 287.
[13] Catterall, I, 109.

a belief that they were free." This flight was frustrated when, at Norfolk, Whiting was arrested on suspicion of being a slave stealer. This gave the slaves an opportunity to appeal in court for their freedom, but the court was obliged to rule that Whiting was their proper owner, Miss Robinson's will having no power to free slaves she had already deeded away.[14]

In the two cases just mentioned, the closest heirs wanted to retain Negroes as slaves, contrary to the wishes of their late owners. Didier Colin, on the other hand, managed to obtain slaves for himself merely by taking advantage of his discretionary powers as executor of the estate of Frances Timberlake. That lady had specified in her will that her slaves should be freed and her land sold to answer the debts against her estate. Colin, however, sold the land to himself, "at less than half its value, after inadequate advertisement." The trifling sum thereby credited to the estate was not adequate to meet the charges against it, and Virginia law required that slaves could not be freed by a man, or by an estate, with outstanding and otherwise unsecured debts. Therefore, Colin had a right to sell the slaves, and he proceeded to sell them, also, to himself, at an absurdly low price. His chicanery remained unchallenged for twelve years, and he himself died before the slaves finally succeeded in obtaining a court order for a new and fair administration of the Timberlake Estate.[15]

A mean and mercenary streak, supposedly alien to the climate of Virginia, appeared in those heirs and executors who ignored instructions to free slaves. However, the younger men who seized Negroes in violation of final testaments had a rational grievance: had not their elders enjoyed the profits and convenience of slaveholding so long as they were alive? Was not this emancipation after death a way of win-

---

[14] *Ibid.*, p. 114.
[15] *Ibid.*, p. 115.

ning a benefit for their consciences at no cost to themselves, but at considerable cost to the younger generation? Freeing slaves, it was generally held, was a profitless and risky business, increasing the number of shiftless loafers who must be a burden to society, and increasing the danger of Negro rebellion. Keeping slaves, on the other hand, permitted a choice among working, renting, or selling them, any of which might be profitable, and at least one of which was bound to be.

The man who must wait until death to free his slaves was not, after all, a striking witness against the institution of slavery. For by keeping his chattels during his natural life he was conceding that he could find no attractive way of living without them. Furthermore, if a man lived for many years after his decision to free slaves in this way, he might see many of them pass their best years, or even die without experiencing the promised state of freedom. At least a disposition to free slaves after death, to the limited extent that it existed, revealed a degree of uneasiness about the justice of slavery, or else it demonstrated a fear that slaves, treated fairly enough by a kind owner, might suffer if they fell into the hands of a callous or cruel one. And the promise of freedom could be made dependent on good behavior, making slaves more pliant and productive.

But if a man were really concerned to free his slaves, he should have set about it within his own lifetime, making sure that no financial claims could be raised to undo his work, and being careful to obey the laws controlling the freeing of Negroes. And if he wanted freedom to be meaningful and enduring, he should have made sure that his slaves were properly educated and skilled to meet its obligations. The leading statesmen of Virginia were able to contemplate such training only in a vague and theoretical way, because of their conviction that the Negro could not safely live in freedom among whites. How could they plan the training of Negroes to live respectably among whites when they ruled out such an arrangement at the outset? Only the fabulous scheme of a mass migration of Negroes away from Virginia justified for them a program of education.

Not from the enlightened aristocrats, not from refined theories of republicanism and natural law, perhaps not even from the increased zeal for freedom fostered by the Revolution did the genuine spirit of emancipation in Virginia derive. Instead it came from the pious and primitive religious zeal of the dissenting sects, most notably the Quakers and Methodists. During the 1780's and 1790's these groups were officially pledged against slavery and rallied their membership to accomplish a complete emancipation, started immediately. American Methodists were warned against slavery by John Wesley, who wrote a tract denouncing it. The most important emissaries sent to organize American Methodism, Thomas Coke and Francis Asbury, held Wesley's views and spread them the length of the country. But there was also a native revulsion against slavery, an example of which can be seen in the career of the Reverend Freeborn Garrettson.

Garrettson was a native of Maryland, but the society in which he was raised was, so far as the slavery issue was concerned, practically identical to Virginia. Around 1775 Garrettson, then in his early twenties and recently converted in the Great Awakening, found his soul sorely troubled and his mind disturbed. After a day or two of agony and prayer he was possessed by the conviction that slaveholding was causing his torment of soul. From this oppression he escaped by executing a prompt and complete emancipation for his Negroes. His experience of dark guilt followed by joyous release convinced him that all other men who held slaves must suffer a similar taint on their immortal souls, and when he decided to spend his life as a circuit-preacher for the Methodists, the freeing of other men's souls from taints became his foremost concern. Much of Garrettson's preaching was accomplished in Virginia, where he urged his abolitionist doctrine widely, if "privately," among fellow Methodists.[16]

Relieving masters from a burden of sin was the initial impulse of Methodist emancipation. But there was also a growing recognition of the religious capacity of the Negro, which made Methodists solicitous on his behalf. Indeed, the richly emotional worship of the Methodists offered the benighted slaves something they could understand and join with enthusiasm. Garrettson wrote of his tour on the Brunswick circuit of Virginia in 1777: "I there met with a black boy who was happy in the Lord; and I thought he exceeded all the youths I had ever seen for a gift and power of prayer."[17] Summarizing his experiences in Virginia and the Carolinas, Garrettson wrote: "I would often set apart times to preach to the blacks, and adapt my discourse to them alone; and precious moments have I had. While many of their sable faces were bedewed with tears, their withered hands of faith were stretched out, and their precious souls made white in the blood of the lamb. The suffering of these poor outcasts of men, through the blessing of God, drove them near to the Lord, and many of them were truly happy."[18] But while Garrettson was more than satisfied with the spiritual capacities of Negroes, he ran into difficulties with their masters: "I endeavoured frequently to inculcate the doctrine of freedom in a private way, and this procured me the ill will of some who were in that unmerciful practice [of holding slaves]."[19]

Francis Asbury, touring Virginia in 1781, noted with satisfaction that Negroes were attending his services. After one

[16] Nathan Bangs, *The Life of the Reverend Freeborn Garrettson*, 2nd ed. (New York, 1830), pp. 33–34.
[17] *Ibid.*, p. 54.
[18] *Ibid.*, p. 59.
[19] *Ibid.*

of his sermons, "Harry, a black man, spoke on the barren fig-tree. This circumstance was new, and the white people looked on with attention."[20] In 1783 Asbury attended a conference at Petersburg, where "all agreed in the spirit of African liberty."[21] In April, 1785, however, the Reverend Thomas Coke, preaching on the Virginia circuits for the first time, undertook to speak out against slavery in a sermon, and saw a number of his audience withdraw in anger. The group waited for Coke outside the building, exhorted by "a lady, whose fashionable appearance was more conspicuous than either her politeness or her humanity." She offered fifty pounds to anyone who "would seize the preacher, and give him one hundred lashes."[22]

Fortunately champions stepped forward to challenge those who were laying hands on Dr. Coke, and he suffered no injury. Further, he was rewarded by seeing two of these champions promptly liberate sixteen and eight slaves respectively. When Coke preached the next day, however, he noted that a large proportion of his audience stood by in gloomy hostility, "armed with staves and clubs." Again he escaped harm, this time by simply avoiding the subject of slavery altogether: "His discourse . . . not leading him towards this forbidden ground . . . he seemed to be protected from the mob."[23]

Meditating upon these experiences, Coke decided that the hostility of slaveholders toward his ideas derived from their great fear of a slave revolt. Thereafter he was careful to impress on slaves, whenever he preached to them, their Christian duty of obedience to their masters, so long as the laws retaining them in slavery had not been repealed. This policy

---

[20] Francis Asbury, *Journal and Letters* edited by J. Manning Potts, Elmer T. Clark and Jacob S. Payton (London and Nashville, 1958), I, 403.

[21] *Ibid.*, p. 441.

[22] Samuel Drew, *The Life of the Reverend Thomas Coke, Ll.D.* (New York, 1818), p. 133.

[23] *Ibid.*, p. 134.

allowed him to escape violence, although his views still aroused enough hostility to get him indicted in certain counties. [24]

Coke joined Asbury in circulating petitions among Virginia Methodists, praying the General Assembly to legislate a gradual emancipation. On May 26, 1785, the two churchmen traveled to Mount Vernon, hoping to secure for their petition the most distinguished signature in the land. General Washington received them cordially, and said that he shared their sentiments on the subject of slavery. But he declined to put his name to their petition. Instead, he promised that "if the Assembly took the subject into consideration, he would signify his sentiments by a letter." [25]

The following autumn the antislavery petitions were presented to the House of Delegates, which determined, unanimously, not to take them into consideration. Washington was thereby saved the task of writing a letter. One member, in fact, moved that an antislavery petition, rather than merely being laid on the table, be thrown under it. This was regarded, according to Madison, "with as much indignation on one side as the petition itself was on the other." [26] Furthermore, though no one would actually vote even to consider the question of emancipation, Madison at least noted "an avowed patronage of its principle by sundry respectable members." [27]

At the same session of the House of Delegates, other petitions arrived demanding repeal of the act permitting the private emancipation of slaves. These prayers not only gained a hearing, but also produced a motion for a bill to be drawn containing their principles. This motion passed by the casting

---

[24] Wesley H. Gewehr, *The Great Awakening in Virginia, 1740–1790* (Durham, 1930).

[25] Coke's Journal, quoted in Drew, *Life of Coke*, p. 138.

[26] Letter to George Washington, 11 November 1785, Madison, *Letters and Other Writings*, I, 200.

[27] *Ibid.*

vote of the speaker, but the subsequent bill "was thrown out on the first reading by a considerable majority." [28]

Thus Methodists found Virginia politicians uniformly unwilling to advance the cause of emancipation, and a fair number of them prepared to push it back. All that remained to the clergymen, then, was to exert moral persuasion through their own expanding denomination, hoping to bring about a broad change in public opinion which politicians would be bound to heed.

The first half of the 1780's were promising enough. A Methodist conference in 1780 had ruled that traveling preachers could own no slaves, and had further passed a resolution condemning slavery and urging emancipation. In 1783 the General Conference extended the rule against holding slaves to local preachers; wherever it was legal to do so, they must free their slaves within a year, or risk suspension. In 1784 all Methodists were enjoined from selling slaves, nor could they buy them, except where they might do so for the purpose of emancipation. Later in 1784, at a special Christmas conference, the Methodists of America decided that wherever it was legal, all Methodists should liberate their slaves within a year, although Virginians might take two years because of special difficulties they might encounter. [29]

From this pinnacle of antislavery zeal, there was a precipitate decline. A general conference of 1785, confronted with the probable loss of thousands of members in the slave states, suspended the emancipation rule. In 1800 the strictures on traveling preachers were relaxed: they were now to free their slaves only "if practicable." In 1804 the remaining requirements about buying and selling and a general exhortation to exert influence, moral and political, against

---

[28] Letter to Jefferson, 22 January 1786, Madison, *Letters and Other Writings*, I, 217.

[29] Gewehr, *Great Awakening*, pp. 243–246.

slavery were dropped. In 1808 the Methodist Church decided to hold no position on slavery whatever.[30]

For the Methodists to hold so advanced a position, and retreat so far from it, should not be blamed entirely on organizational expediency. Important though emancipation was, they must have felt it considerably less important than salvation. If, by becoming militant abolitionists, they were prevented any access to slaves, they would have been defeating their own main purpose, which was to get all men, black and white, into Heaven. By tempering their hostility to slavery the Methodists of Virginia were able, in 1803, successfully to oppose a law which interfered with their right to preach to slaves. Finally, a number of Virginia Methodists never became convinced that emancipation was as essential as Coke and Asbury had taught them. Here are the words of Devereux Jarratt, an earnest Virginia Methodist, who had angered Dr. Coke by challenging the absolute position against slavery: "I told [Dr. Coke] I was no friend of slavery; but, however, I did not think the minutes [opposing slavery] proper, for two reasons. First, the disturbance it would make and the opposition it would meet with in the societies. Second, he ought not to make a disputable matter a positive term of communion. And as he was a stranger in the land, I told him the spirit of Virginia would not brook force. . . ."[31]

The Quakers were, in their own way, as eager to avoid giving offense as the Methodists, yet there was no backsliding from their abolitionism. They had been moving toward it for a much longer time, having resolved to stay out of the slave trade as far back as 1722, and having entertained John Woolman, an abolitionist Friend from Philadelphia, in 1757. In

---

[30] *Ibid.*, pp. 243–248.
[31] Devereux Jarratt to Rev. John Coleman, 15 April 1790, quoted in Asbury, *Journal*, II, 82.

1772 the Quakers of Virginia were petitioning the legislature to relax the strictures against manumission. Failing to secure this, they nevertheless voted in their meeting of 1773 to try freeing their slaves anyway. In 1782 the Friends were powerful lobbyists in behalf of the act permitting private manumissions, and in 1784 the yearly meeting decreed that Friends should no longer hold slaves in Virginia. This decree remained in force, and was generally obeyed.[32]

There were several reasons why the Quakers should remain faithful to abolitionism while Methodists, Baptists, and Presbyterians faltered. The Quakers had grown accustomed to being a people apart, and, having been persecuted during the Revolution for their pacifism, they were freshly trained to accept hostile pressures for the sake of conscience. Furthermore, though they were never very numerous in Virginia, their modest numbers were a positive advantage for enforcing discipline, and they received encouragement and moral strength from their coreligionists throughout the rest of the United States and across the Atlantic. Again, scruples against luxury made it easier for the Virginia Quaker than for the high-living Virginia aristocrat to give up his slaves. Finally, because of their growing preoccupation with practical ethics, the Quakers were more capable of solving the problems of abolition than the other-worldly Methodists.

Although they lived amidst slaveholders who were often hostile to them for their hostility to slavery, and on other counts as well, the Quakers of Virginia gained immense support and inspiration from living so close to Philadelphia, the center of North American Quakerdom. In the city of brotherly love the Quaker Anthony Benezet had achieved such great success with his evening classes for young Negroes that he secured the endowment of America's first full-time school for

---

[32] Thomas Edward Drake, *Quakers and Slavery in America* (New Haven, 1950), pp. 48, 59, 83.

that race. Benezet's practical demonstration that Negroes were indeed capable of education both prompted the teacher to become an ardent abolitionist and disarmed those of his critics who would plead racist theories. Prodded by Benezet and Woolman, the Pennsylvania Friends voted in 1776 that none of their members should hold slaves, and they secured in 1780 a state law for the gradual emancipation of all Pennsylvania Negroes. In 1785 the Quakers were addressing a petition to the Continental Congress, praying that it consider means to abolish Negro slavery throughout the United States.[33]

Toward the end of the eighteenth century, Virginia Quakerdom produced two outstanding champions of the Negro. One of these was Warner Mifflin, of Accomac County on the Eastern Shore. He dated his conversion to abolitionism from the time when one of his father's slaves stopped him in the fields to inquire by what right the one of them was free to do as he pleased while the other must forever be a slave. Being unable to find an acceptable answer to this question, Mifflin became thereafter a foe of slavery. By 1775, when he was already married and established on his own plantation, Mifflin had freed all his slaves.[34] During the Revolution he gained an international reputation for his conciliatory efforts on behalf of Quaker neutrality and a general armistice. In 1782 he lobbied at the Virginia legislature for the act permitting private manumissions, and in 1790 he helped a Congressional committee draft a law against American participation in the foreign slave trade.

After the war Mifflin moved from Virginia to Delaware, but his father, Daniel Mifflin, remained in Accomac until

---

[33] Alice Felt Tyler, *Freedom's Ferment* (Minneapolis, 1944), p. 465. There is an excellent biography of Benezet by George S. Brookes, *Friend Anthony Benezet* (Philadelphia and London, 1937). For the petition, see *Journal of the Continental Congress*, XXVIII, p. 19.

[34] Mary S. Locke, *Anti-Slavery in America*, pp. 37–38.

his death in 1795. Daniel, according to his son, "was not long behind me, in espousing the cause of liberty."[35] He freed a hundred slaves and also "became a zealous advocate" for other slaves in the neighborhood. "He often appeared alone in courts of law, amidst surrounding opponents, to plead the cause of individuals of the African race, who had a claim to freedom."[36]

The Mifflins antagonized many of their neighbors in Virginia, both by their neutrality in the war and by their abolitionist principles. Warner Mifflin gave the following description of the troubles he encountered when he emancipated his slaves:

On setting my blacks free, I thought it best to put them from me, in order to manifest that they were free. It was then circulated, that Mifflin had set free a parcel of lazy, worthless Negroes, that he could make nothing by them, and therefore had set them at liberty. This reflection, however unjust, had some weight with me; and regarding that scripture injunction, "let not then your good be evil spoken of," I thought it expedient to propose their having land, and teams; and in return, they should give me half their produce. This was put in execution with those who chose to accept the terms. Immediately the tune was turned, and it was reported, that Mifflin was making more money by his Negroes now, than ever, and keeping them in more abject slavery, under the pretence of their being free. . . .[37]

Robert Pleasants, the other leading Quaker abolitionist of Jeffersonian Virginia, inherited his principles from his father, John Pleasants, who had tried to free his hundreds of slaves in 1771, but was prevented from doing so by the prevailing laws. Eventually Robert Pleasants was able to secure the

---

[35] From Warner Mifflin's *Defence*, originally published in 1796 and reprinted in Hilda Justice, *The Life and Ancestry of Warner Mifflin* (Philadelphia, 1905), p. 81.

[36] *Ibid.*

[37] *Ibid.*, p. 85.

emancipation of all his father's slaves, and also that of eighty more whom he owned in his own right.[38]

John Pleasants had specified in his will that his younger slaves be taught reading, and that all of his slaves should, after reaching the age of thirty, be given "the full benefit of their labor in a manner most likely to answer the intention of relieving [them] from bondage."[39] Thus, if the law were to require that the Negroes be kept technically in slavery, they could still be prepared, so far as was possible within the limits of the plantation, for the life of free men. Robert Pleasants gave land and money for the construction of a school for Negroes in Henrico County.[40] This was typical of the Quaker approach to emancipation.

It is interesting to compare the advocacy of emancipation of Jefferson, Madison, Tucker, Washington, and the rest of the great statesmen with the abolitionism of the Quakers. It is particularly significant that on point after point, the Quakers had faith in the power of moral energy to create beneficial change, while the statesmen, supposedly some of the most liberal in American history, held to a gloomy set of immutable principles which man, it appeared, could have no power to alter. The statesmen believed that the Negroes must naturally be enemies to the whites; the Quakers held that the Negroes were capable of learning their own benevolent pacifism. The statesmen believed the intelligence of the Negro inferior; the Quakers employed their meetinghouses for the evening instruction of slaves. The statesmen argued that emancipation must be accompanied with immediate removal, and that a mongrelization of the races was to be

---

[38] Locke, *Anti-Slavery in America*, p. 37; Drake, *Quakers and Slavery*, p. 83.

[39] Will of John Pleasants, printed in Catterall, I, 105.

[40] Carter G. Woodson, *The Education of the Negro Prior to 1861* (New York, 1915), pp. 111–112.

feared; the Quakers held that emancipation must take precedence over any other consideration, and were willing to consider a variety of plans for resettling the Negro once he was freed. If the Quakers had any fear of miscegenation, it was feeble compared to their fear of violating the golden rule in so wanton a way as the enslaving of another human being.

The emancipation schemes of the great statesmen invariably called for some kind of compensation for the slaveowner; the Quakers denied that there could be any property right in men, but rather emphasized that wages were due Negroes who had been forced to labor for others. And most important of all, the Quakers were willing to avow their principles, quietly but firmly, wherever they went, and were eager to start the process of freedom at once. The statesmen had to be politic, either waiting, like Washington, for a considerable spirit of emancipation to show itself before publicly joining, or making an advocacy so conditional that no slaveholder could fear his property was menaced.

No one was more acutely aware than Robert Pleasants of the difference between cautious and theoretical antislavery as opposed to a practical and immediate concern for the rights of Negroes. For two decades he issued a series of appeals to the great leaders of Virginia in the hope of winning their support for a general emancipation. In 1777 he appealed to Patrick Henry, then governor of the state, for Henry's support against "meddling people, who have threatened to put in force the former most unjust and unreasonable law" permitting church wardens to seize Negroes who had been freed without specific authorization from the government. Then Pleasants added the proposal "that all children of slaves to be born in future, be absolutely free at the usual ages of 18 and 21."[41] Henry supported the act to permit

---

[41] Letter of 28 March 1777, from transcript in the William Wirt Henry Papers, VHS, Box I.

voluntary emancipations, but not the more sweeping proposal.

In 1785 Pleasants addressed himself to George Washington, reminding the general of the sacrifice that he had undergone to win liberty for the United States. Why not, then, submit to the much slighter inconvenience that would be caused by freeing the general's slaves?[42] As president for the Virginia Society for the Abolition of Slavery, Pleasants also drafted petitions to both the Virginia General Assembly and the Congress of the United States, while continuing privately to solicit the support of Henry, Jefferson, Madison, and St. George Tucker. He was especially vigorous in protesting some of the ideas set forth in Tucker's pamphlet of 1796. "I much disapprove," he wrote to the jurist, "of thy proposition of prohibiting free Negroes and Mulattoes from holding estates in land, or other property, or to be restrained by *law* from contracting marriages with whites, disposing of property by will, or enjoying other rights of citizens." Indeed, measures designed by Tucker to drive the Negroes away were ill-advised both because they would maintain prejudices against them and because it would be better for all concerned if the Negroes did not leave at all. For, Pleasants argued, "labouring people are not only the riches of every country, but . . . with suitable encouragement and proper instruction" they might "act so as to contribute to the peace, happiness, and prosperity of the country, as well as other citizens."[43]

The government of Virginia at least took notice of the antislavery activities of the Quakers. It took official cognizance of that Quaker practice of diligently investigating the legal titles by which Negroes were held, and suing for freedom

---

[42] Letter of 2 December 1785, in transcript of the Letterbook of Robert Pleasants of Curles, 1754–97; Quaker Records, IV, 144–145, Valentine Museum, Richmond.

[43] Letter of 30 May 1797, Robert Pleasants Letterbook, p. 328.

wherever such titles were doubtful. The result was an act of December, 1795, whose preamble explained its purpose:

Great and alarming mischiefs have arisen in other states of this Union, and are likely to arise in this by voluntary associations of individuals, who, under cover of effecting that justice towards persons unwarrantably held in slavery, which the sovereignty and duty of society alone ought to afford; have in many instances been the means of depriving masters of their property in slaves, and in others occasioned them heavy expenses in tedious and unfounded law-suits. . . .[44]

To avoid such mischief, the act laid down a procedure by which slaves might sue for their freedom: the slave should appeal to a magistrate, who might, at his discretion, require the master to post bond until the next session of court. Then came an unusual provision: "The petitioner shall obtain counsel, to be assigned by the said court, who, without fee or reward, shall prosecute the suit of such complainant."[45] In other words, the only advocate to be permitted the slave suing for his freedom would be one appointed by the court, and, even worse, one who could expect no reward whatever for winning his case. On the other hand, such a lawyer might very well lose the business of local slaveowners, which is to say the wealthy patrons on whose business he depended for his livelihood, if he undertook to press as strenuously as possible a suit for freedom.

Worst of all, the act positively attacked the Quakers and other friends of the slaves: "If any person or persons shall be found aiding, or abetting, or maintaining any person in the prosecution of a suit upon a petition as aforesaid, and such person shall fail to establish his or their claim to freedom, every person so found . . . shall forfeit . . . to the owner . . . the sum of one hundred dollars, for every person

---

[44] Shepherd, I, 363–364.
[45] *Ibid.*, p. 364.

so complaining."[46] So general was this act that it could be extended to cover cases where simple advice was given a Negro concerning his own rights. It made a crime of an activity which, in most cases, was generous and humane. Such a warping by the slave interest of traditional legal rights was supposed to have started only after the violent abolitionists of the Garrison school forced southern slaveholders into a defensive position. But this law was passed before Garrison was born.

In 1798 the Virginia legislature devised another law to restrict the emancipating tendencies of Quakers and Methodists. This provided that "in all cases wherein the property of a person held as a slave demanding freedom, shall come before a court for trial, no person who shall be proved to be a member of any society instituted for the purpose of emancipating Negroes from the possession of their masters, shall be admitted to serve as a juror."[47]

The implication borne by this act was that abolitionists were biased men who could not be trusted to judge a case on its legal merits, but would vote, no matter what the evidence might be, for freedom. Yet the pious abolitionists of those days were notably law-abiding, desiring only to change laws they felt wicked, and going to court on behalf of Negroes only when they felt such Negroes were entitled, by laws already standing, to rights of which they were being deprived. What this act chiefly proved was that the effective majority in Virginia considered emancipation, even in its mildest eighteenth-century forms, to be a radical doctrine, the holders of which were not to be trusted in a court of law.

To say that Virginia was, in the age of Jefferson, disposed toward emancipation, or tending toward it, is badly over-

---

[46] *Ibid.*
[47] *Ibid.*, II, 77.

stating the case. Even the famous law of 1782 (whose repeal was considered in 1785–86) has been given more weight than it deserves. Usually it has been cited as a distinct turning point, as if it had been illegal to free any slaves whatever prior to its passage.

Actually, the rights of masters in their slaves had always been sufficiently paramount to permit them to practice emancipation, so long as they removed their slaves from Virginia. Nothing prevented a man from taking his slaves out of Virginia if he cared to, and, once he reached territory where free Negroes could settle, he might emancipate them on the spot. Furthermore, before the Revolution a man might obtain permission from the governor and council to liberate his slaves within Virginia herself, where they could then live as free Negroes. Under the first state constitution this right was no longer vested in the governor, but, like so many others, was given to the legislature.[48]

The Act of 1782 made emancipation much easier, though even without it the proportion of manumissions doubtless would have increased during the peak years of Quaker and Methodist agitation. And this act did not itself survive the age of Jefferson, for in January of 1806 it was modified by the requirement that thereafter all Negroes freed in Virginia must leave the state within a year. Otherwise, they were to be "apprehended and sold by the overseers of the poor."[49]

---

[48] Hening, IX, 320, shows an act of 1777 which reviews the colonial law, and then invokes the new procedure of freeing Negroes by special permission of the General Assembly.

[49] Shepherd, III, 252.

CHAPTER

EIGHT

Slavery and the Union

The planters of Virginia forbade the importation of slaves into their own state shortly after declaring their independence of the British tyrant. As the United States strengthened its national organization, first by drawing the Constitution of 1787, and then by making it work, the Virginians continued to discourage the international slave trade. At the Constitutional Convention Virginia's delegates joined with gentlemen from the northern states in support of a firm prohibition of that evil commerce. Along with northerners, Virginians agreed to compromise this measure so as to keep South Carolina and Georgia in the Union. The constitution prohibited any interference with the trade for twenty years from the time of its writing, but so soon as that limitation expired the Virginia-dominated Congress outlawed it. Still, hostility to the slave trade was not at all the equivalent of hostility to slavery.

In fact, there is no evidence to suggest that the planters opposed the domestic slave trade. In their private capacities they would, in the traditional southern fashion, look with disfavor on professional traders of slaves, and try to avoid public sales of their "people." As servants of the public, however, Virginians adhered to a practical formula on the subject of the slave trade, which served to keep it flourishing. Neither foreign slaves nor slaves from other states were to be brought into Virginia for purposes of sale, but bona fide immigrants from others of the United States might bring in slaves who were their own property and whose services were wanted on their Virginia lands. At the same time the sale and migration of slaves out of Virginia should be greatly encouraged. As soon as the Constitution would permit, the foreign sources of slaves should be shut off, but the domestic slave trade ought to be preserved. By removing foreign competition, Virginia could hope to maintain attractive prices for slaves, and could also expect enough of them to be carried out of the state to maintain a safe proportion between the races in the Old Dominion. From this it naturally followed that Virginians would oppose any effort to close western territories to slavery, for such a measure would reduce the market for Virginia slaves.

The export slave trade benefited Virginians in the first instance as a further device for maintaining good discipline on their plantations. Unruly slaves could be threatened with being sold down the river, and if unruliness persisted they could, indeed, be sold. In 1787 Moses Austin was trading in Richmond, and advertised that he wanted "One Hundred Negroes, from 20 to 30 years old, for which a good price will be given. They are to be sent out of the state, therefore we shall not be particular respecting the character of any of them — Hearty and well made is all that is necessary."[1]

Virginia first exercised her sovereignty against slave imports in October, 1778. The resulting act levied fines of £1,000 against the importer of any slave, and of £500 against the purchaser.[2] These fines were nominally much higher than those of succeeding laws, but they were figured in the inflated Virginia currency of the war which, after the treaty of peace, was called in at one thousand to one.[3] This act contained the provision permitting outsiders desiring to settle within Virginia to bring in slaves for their own use, and specified that such slaves must be registered.

In May, 1780, a special exception was made. Refugees from Georgia and South Carolina were allowed to bring their slaves into Virginia, where they might remain until one year after the close of hostilities. If they tried to keep them in Virginia, they had to forfeit them, the slaves going free.[4] In 1789 and 1790 acts were passed giving immigrants extra time to register their slaves and to take their oaths that the slaves were not brought in for sale. Apparently a significant number of people, "being strangers to the laws of this state," had come in with slaves, kept them on their own acres, and completely ignored the registration law.[5] The desire of the government to accommodate both these people and the wartime refugees from Georgia and South Carolina demonstrates that the laws against slave importation were by no means intended to attack, or even to criticize, the holding of slaves itself.

The portion of the slave code of 1792 dealing with this subject preserved the principles of the act of 1778. But now

---

[1] *Virginia Gazette and Independent Chronicle*, 22 December 1787.

[2] Hening, IX, 471–472.

[3] Jensen, *New Nation*, p. 307.

[4] Hening, X, 307–308.

[5] *Ibid.*, XIII, 62, 121.

fines were set at $200 for the importer and $100 for the buyer, separate fines being chargeable for each slave illegally traded. Again such slaves were to be freed, only this time it was specified that they should be sent away from Virginia. Immigrating slaveholders were obliged to swear the following oath: "I . . . do swear that my removal into the state of Virginia was with no intent of evading the laws for preventing the further importation of slaves, nor have I brought with me any slaves, with an intention of selling them, nor have any of the slaves which I have brought with me, been imported from Africa, or any of the West India Islands, since the first day of November, one thousand seven hundred and seventy-eight. . . ."[6]

An act of 1796 made a further revision in favor of slaveholders. It permitted Virginia residents, or landowners, to bring back into the state any slaves originally born there and removed by them later. However, only original owners were entitled to this privilege; slaves who had been sold since leaving Virginia could not be brought back. Slaves who had been hired out were also refused reentry. The act undertook to discourage kidnappers by declaring that "if any . . . slave or slaves be entitled to freedom under the laws of that state, to which he, she, or they may have been removed, such right shall remain, any thing in this act notwithstanding."[7]

However, Virginia swept away all exceptions in the rigorous act of January, 1806. Slaves simply could not be brought into Virginia legally; anyone bringing a slave into the state must pay a fine of $400, and anyone buying an imported slave must pay the same amount. In keeping with the anti-Negro drift of the law after 1800, contraband slaves were now to be sold for the benefit of the overseers of the poor.[8] This ironclad act was slightly modified a year later, chiefly

---

[6] Shepherd, I, 122.

[7] *Ibid.*, II, 19–20.

[8] *Ibid.*, III, 251.

to avoid prosecuting practices which fell within its strict limits but in no way violated its spirit: citizens leaving the state with intent to return could take and bring back slaves, people owning land crossing state lines could shuffle their slaves back and forth without penalty, and inhabitants of other states who required the help of their slaves to transport goods to market might march them through Virginia. Finally, Virginia citizens received a grace period of six months in which they might bring back to the state any slaves owned by them elsewhere.[9]

The special interests of Virginia in both slavery and the slave trade came out many times, both in the constitutional convention of 1787 and in the Virginia convention for ratification the following year.

Within the Philadelphia convention, George Mason had argued vigorously in favor of the entire nation's adopting the Virginia policy of nonimportation. He warned of the military danger of having a large subject population which might easily be persuaded to join an external enemy. Then he warned the convention that even if only two states, Georgia and South Carolina, were to allow imports, these states could easily become entrepôts for filling up the expanding frontiers of the United States: "The western people are already calling out for slaves for their new lands, and will fill the country with slaves if they can be got through South Carolina and Georgia."[10] Mason's remarks contained so many harsh words against slavery that the logic of his argument seemed to lead toward demanding measures to bring emancipation. Instead, he concluded only that "it is essential in every point of view that the general government should have power to prevent the *increase* of slavery."[11]

---

[9] *Ibid.*, 290.

[10] Quoted from Madison's transcript, in Helen Hill, *George Mason, Constitutionalist* (Cambridge, 1938), p. 203.

[11] *Ibid.*, p. 203. Italics added.

At the Virginia convention for ratifying the Constitution, Mason, now firmly allied with its enemies, repeated his warnings against the twenty-year license for the international slave trade. Then he gave a more urgent warning, which to one confused member seemed rather inconsistent with his first.

There is no clause in the Constitution that will prevent the northern and eastern states from meddling with our whole property of that kind. There is a clause to prohibit the importation of slaves after twenty years; but there is no provision made for securing to the southern states those they now possess. It is far from being a desirable property; but it will involve us in great difficulties and infelicity to be now deprived of them [sic]. There ought to be a clause in the Constitution to secure us that property, which we have acquired under our former laws, and the loss of which would bring ruin on a great many people.[12]

Patrick Henry, most influential of the antifederalists, dwelt with persistent force on the potential threats to slavery contained within the new form of government. At one point he argued that the envisioned centralized authority could prevent Virginians from defending themselves against slave insurrection.[13] This was, on its merits, a foolish argument, but it was Henry's style to play on the most excitable emotions of his listeners.

In a longer speech, Henry pointed out the wide powers which might be used under the authority of the clauses empowering Congress to act for the general defense and for the general welfare. He reminded his fellow Virginians that they had been obliged to free a few slaves for military service during the Revolutionary War, and that some among them had felt they might, in self-defense, be driven to a general emancipation to fill their dwindling ranks. A general govern-

---

[12] Jonathan Elliott, ed., *The Debates in the Several State Conventions on the Adoption of the Federal Constitution* (Philadelphia, 1896), III, 270.

[13] *Ibid.*, p. 423.

ment, Henry warned, whose majority consisted of men with
no sympathy for or interest in slavery, might be expected,
in an emergency, to go much farther in this direction than
had slaveholding Virginians.

Slavery is detested. We feel its fatal effects — we deplore it with
all the pity of humanity. Let all these considerations, at some future
period, press with full force on the minds of Congress. Let that
urbanity, which I trust will distinguish America, and the necessity
of national defense, — let all these things weigh on their minds;
they will search that paper, and see if they have power of manumission. And have they not, sir? Have they not power to provide for the
general defense and welfare? May they not think that these call for
the abolition of slavery? May they not pronounce all slaves free,
and will they not be warranted by that power? . . . As much as I
deplore slavery, I see that prudence forbids its abolition. I deny
that the general government ought to set them free, because a decided majority of the states have not the ties of sympathy and fel-
low-feeling for those whose interest would be affected by their
emancipation. The majority of Congress is to the north, and the
slaves are to the south.[14]

The Federalist Edmund Randolph challenged Henry's position. Given an internal foe so numerous as the slaves might
be, Virginia would be well advised, he said, to bind herself
to a greater power, capable of giving protection well beyond
her own means. He scorned the idea that Virginia delegates
had participated in a convention whose issue could in any
way pose a menace to the future security of slavery: "I believe, whatever we may think here, that there was not a
member of the Virginia delegation who had the smallest
suspicion of the abolition of slavery."[15]

James Madison also claimed that the Constitution, far
from menacing slavery, offered valuable new safeguards for
it. As an example, he cited the clause guaranteeing rights of
extradition of persons "held to service or labor." Under the

---

[14] *Ibid.*, p. 590.
[15] *Ibid.*, p. 599.

Constitution, Virginians could expect to recover their slaves who had escaped to the North. "At present, if any slave elopes to any of those states where slaves are free, he becomes emancipated by their laws; for the laws of the states are uncharitable to one another in this respect."[16]

Then Madison turned to the question of slave imports. He naturally favored an end to them, but he asked his fellow Virginians to consider the point of view of Georgia and South Carolina. Those areas were in a much earlier state of development than Virginia, and contained many citizens who had acquired lands in the hope of improving them with imported slaves. Madison paraphrased the argument he had heard deep-South delegates present to him at the convention: "What would be the consequence of hindering us from [importing slaves]? The slaves of Virginia would rise in value, and we should be obliged to go to your markets." Madison hoped that Virginians should not place themselves in so delicate a position. Friendship and union with the rising states to the south were more important than checking twenty years more of the slave trade.[17]

The Constitution came close to defeat in Virginia, but the various alarms raised over slavery probably had little effect on the close decision. Nevertheless, the treatment of slavery in the debates left a valuable record for anyone inquiring into the tenacity with which Virginians retained slavery. Whether her statesmen tried to show that the Constitution would menace Virginia slavery, or argued that the Constitution would more perfectly sustain and protect it, the various appeals proved that a politician who wanted to carry a point with the ruling class in Virginia had to believe in the protection of slave property. On this everyone agreed. No one said the Constitution was bad because it guaranteed slave property; no one praised it for implied powers to advance the

---

[16] *Ibid.*, p. 453.
[17] *Ibid.*, p. 454.

cause of emancipation. However unfortunate it might be, everyone agreed that slavery must be sustained. And, at the same time, everyone believed that a complete end to the international slave trade would be desirable.

Another landmark often cited as evidence of Virginia antislavery is the Northwest Ordinance, whose restriction derived from Jefferson's famous proposals of 1784.[18] This is another case in which Jefferson had in mind the best interests of white people. The vigorous republics he imagined rising in the west would be blessed, in his view, if they had no Negroes in them whatever. He held, in good Virginia fashion, the belief that the further introduction of foreign slaves would injure America. If he also held — as he certainly did later in life — the view that there should be the largest possible area for the dissipation of Virginia slaves, this principle had to yield to still more urgent considerations. Georgia and South Carolina were admitting foreign slaves, and, as George Mason was to warn in the Philadelphia convention, these sources alone might fill the western country. Furthermore the Spanish empire, with its abundant holdings in slaves, was established along the lower Mississippi, and also threatened to flood the West with slaves. It is significant that Jefferson's prohibition of slavery appears to have been intended for the Southwest as well as the Northwest. It would have constituted an immense barrier against the introduction of foreign slaves. As James Madison explained in 1819, the idea of the Northwest Ordinance had been to limit the number of slaves "by narrowing the space open to them."[19]

While Jefferson proposed the closing of the western territories in general, he does not appear to have opposed the extension of slavery into Kentucky, which remained a part of Virginia until it became an independent state in 1791. Most

---

[18] Jefferson, *Papers*, VI, 604.
[19] Letter to Robert Walsh, 27 November 1819, Madison, *Letters and Other Writings*, III, 155.

of the early settlers of Kentucky were Virginians, and many of the most important ones were personal friends of Jefferson. A minority effort aimed at prohibiting slavery was decisively struck down at the state constitutional convention of 1791. And even in 1784, Jefferson's plan to keep slavery out of the then unorganized western territories did not have the support of many Virginians. Jefferson and his colleagues on a special committee, Jeremiah Townley Chase of Maryland and David Howell of Rhode Island, reported the plan for organizing the West in March of 1784. On April 19, Richard Dobbs Spaight of North Carolina and Jacob Read of South Carolina moved to strike out the article on slavery. On the vote that followed, a motion to retain the article was defeated by a tie in the North Carolina delegation, and negatives from those of Maryland, South Carolina, and, to Jefferson's chagrin, Virginia. Jefferson was outvoted by his colleagues, Samuel Hardy and John Francis Mercer.[20]

In 1785 Congress undertook a revision of Jefferson's plan, though Jefferson himself had left for France and could no longer assist. This time an antislavery provision was introduced by Rufus King of Massachusetts and William Ellery of Rhode Island. It differed from Jefferson's in applying only to the territory north of the Ohio River and also in taking immediate effect, where Jefferson's proposition would have prohibited slavery only after 1800. This time the necessary majority of nine states was attained, but once again the vote of the Virginia delegation was cast against the measure. William Grayson favored exclusion, but Samuel Hardy and Richard Henry Lee did not.[21]

In 1787 Congress finally passed the "Ordinance for the government of the territory of the United States north west of the river Ohio." This time a vote on the antislavery clause

---

[20] *Journal of the Continental Congress*, XXVI, 247. Also, Jefferson's letter to an unidentified correspondent, 25 April 1784, Burnett, VIII, 500.
[21] *Journal of the Continental Congress*, XXVIII, 164.

resulted in its final victory, and this time it had the unanimous support of the Virginia delegation, including Richard Henry Lee.[22] It appeared likely in 1787 that the Northwest Territory would be settled mostly by people who did not want slavery anyway. Nathan Dane wrote to Rufus King that he expected Ohio to be settled "chiefly by eastern people" who had "fully an equal chance of . . . adopting eastern politics."[23] William Grayson wrote to James Monroe that, "The clause respecting slavery was agreed to by the southern members for the purpose of preventing tobacco and indigo from being made on the northwest side of the Ohio, as well as for several other political reasons."[24]

By 1798 some of the representatives of Virginia were subscribing to a new doctrine about slavery in the territories. When a motion was introduced into the House of Representatives to prohibit slavery in the new Mississippi Territory, William Branch Giles spoke against it:

The present motion was brought forward from the avowed motive of furthering the rights of man. [I do] not know whether the tendency of it was calculated to ameliorate the condition of the class of men alluded to; [I believe] not. On the contrary . . . if the slaves of the southern states were permitted to go into this western country, by lessening the number in those states, and spreading them over a large surface of country, there would be a greater probability of ameliorating their condition, which could never be done whilst they were crowded together as they now are in the southern states.[25]

John Nicholas spoke to much the same effect, arguing that the difficulties of slavery would be most easily remedied if slaves were spread as thinly as possible over the largest possible territory. He had a curious rejoinder to the argument

---

[22] *Ibid.*, XXXII, 334, 343.
[23] Letter of 16 July 1787, Burnett, VIII, 622.
[24] Letter of 8 August 1787, *ibid.*, 632.
[25] *Annals of the Fifth Congress*, II, 1308–09.

that keeping slavery out of the new territory must eventually assure its greater happiness. Members of Congress, said Nicholas, "were to legislate for the whole of the Union, and ought to consult the happiness of the whole. It was not for them to attempt to make a particular spot of the country more happy than all the rest."[26]

This was the principle of diffusion, and it remained the fundamental principle of Virginia up to the end of the Jeffersonian period and beyond. Once the federal government had been empowered to end the international slave trade, Virginia's best reasons for closing the West to slavery disappeared. Meanwhile the desire to maintain slave prices and to remove dangerous surpluses of slaves from the state continued and grew stronger. Fully adopting the enlightened principle of diffusion, Thomas Jefferson opposed, in his old age, that part of the Missouri Compromise that closed extensive territories to slavery. Jefferson wrote:

Of one thing I am certain, that as the passage of slaves from one state to another, would not make a slave of a single human being who would not be so without it, so their diffusion over a greater surface would make them individually happier, and proportionally facilitate the accomplishment of their emancipation, by dividing the burthen on a greater number of coadjutors. An abstinence too, from this act of power [prohibiting slavery in the territories] would remove the jealousy excited by the undertaking of Congress to regulate the condition of the different descriptions of men composing a state. This certainly is the exclusive right of every state, which nothing in the constitution has taken from them and given to the general government.[27]

According to the diffusion principle, those slaves were fortunate who were sold from Virginia and carried to, say, Mississippi or Alabama. Also, the best way to reduce slavery was to establish it in as many corners of the United States

---

[26] *Ibid.*, II, 1310.
[27] Jefferson, *Works*, X, 158.

as possible. Experience revealed the absurdity of the first principle: no Virginian ever believed that slaves were as well treated elsewhere. There was some basis, however, for feeling that diffusion would make emancipation easier, for had not Pennsylvania, New York, Connecticut, and other northern states managed to emancipate slaves precisely because the slaveholders themselves were in a small minority and so were their slaves? Virginians did not want the federal government to intervene in abolishing slavery. If local governments were to carry out the proper kind of abolition, it must not be beyond their resources to transport the freed Negroes out of the country. Furthermore, the lower the proportion of Negroes to whites, the less danger there would be of racial warfare.

So much, then, for the principle of slave-free territories, even with the eminent Virginian who has received the credit for its invention. Actually, a number of Virginians tried to circumvent the principle long before the Missouri compromise, and they did so, not in some new territory, but in the Old Northwest. From the end of 1802 until 1810, William Henry Harrison and the so-called "Virginia Aristocrats" in Indiana tried to secure from Congress permission to hold slaves in their territory. These gentlemen demonstrated, as had the settlers of Kentucky, that whatever moral opinions might have been abroad, the advantage of slave labor for clearing a wilderness was simply too attractive to forego.

Many bold Virginians who had followed George Rogers Clark in his conquest of the West understood that they might settle there under Virginia institutions. The French settlers in the area were many of them slaveholders, and had been relieved to hear from Clark that the government of Virginia would protect their property. The passage of the Northwest Ordinance, however, caused a mild panic, so that several settlers removed themselves and their slaves to the Spanish territory on the west bank of the Mississippi. The first territorial governor, apparently after some hesitation, assured the

settlers that the Ordinance did not affect the status of Negroes held as slaves before its passage. On the other hand,
General St. Clair ruled that the children of such slaves, born
after the passage of the Ordinance, must certainly be free.[28]

The first major waves of settlers into the Old Northwest
went, of course, into Ohio. Overwhelmingly these people
owned no slaves and had no desire to own them. The lower
Ohio, on the other hand, was quite attractive to migration-
minded Virginians, offering, as it did, the enormous tracts
of land and potential access to foreign markets so necessary
to plantation agriculture. Nor was there anything objection-
able about the climate. Virginians could easily raise in the
valley of the Ohio the wheat, corn, tobacco, and hemp with
which they were familiar. Between 1790 and 1820 the plantation system, based on slavery, spread rapidly along the
south bank of the Ohio to its confluence with the Mississippi,
and crossed the great river to become established in Missouri.
Free labor and small-homestead settlements, both more numerous and more compact, ran a slower race from Ohio into
Indiana and Illinois.

Therefore it happened that the factor of distribution allowed proslavery forces to control the early politics of Indiana
and Illinois, even though antislavery people were in the great
majority in the Old Northwest. And the special stronghold
of fondness for slavery was in Illinois, but this was part of
the Indiana territory until 1809. It was from the Illinois
country that Congress received in 1796 the first formal petition praying the relaxation of Article 6, a petition which the
Committee on Public Lands of the House of Representatives
refused to countenance on the grounds that it had, after all,
been signed by only four citizens.

The four gentlemen presented arguments of great interest.
They respectfully submitted that the children of their slaves

---

[28] Jacob P. Dunn, "Slavery Petitions and Papers," *Indiana Historical
Society Publications*, II, 447.

were "as much slaves as those born before" the Ordinance, and that they had, in justice, "as fixed and incontrovertible a right to, and interest in, the future issue and increase of such slaves," as to their parents. The slaveholders went on to question the value of Article 6, altogether, "as contrary not only to the interest, but almost to the existence" of their country, which suffered from an acute shortage of labor. Along their remote waters, the petitioners argued,

... laborers can not be procured to assist in cultivating the grounds under one dollar per day, exclusive of washing, lodging and boarding; and ... every kind of tradesmen are paid from a dollar and a half to two dollars per day; neither is there, at these exorbitant prices, a sufficiency of hands to be got for the exigencies of the inhabitants, who, attached to their native soil, have rather chose to encounter these and many other difficulties than, by avoiding them, remove to the Spanish dominions, where slavery is permitted, and consequently, the price of labor much lower.

The petitioners then enticed Congress with their special version of the diffusion principle, holding that they by no means wanted to import any foreign slaves, but rather hoped to draw off "such persons, and such only, as by the laws of [various] states, are slaves therein." Were Congress still unwilling to grant so unobjectionable an extension of slavery, they might at least permit Negroes to be brought in under lifetime indentures, which would "be the means, perhaps, in a great degree, of attaining that object so much wished for by some — 'a gradual abolition of slavery.'"[29]

Rebuffed in 1796, the settlers of the lower Ohio tried again in 1800, this time appealing to the Senate with a petition signed by two hundred and seventy-seven citizens. Here they took the humanitarian approach to the exclusion of all others, asking that they be allowed to import slaves under lifetime indentures, the children of whom, however, should serve only until the males were thirty-one and the females twenty-eight.

---

[29] *Ibid.*, pp. 448–450.

To the adoption of such a modification of slavery, your petitioners can not conceive any well founded objections will be made. It can not but meet with the support of those who are friends to the gradual abolition of slavery, and your petitioners can not entertain the idea that any will be found to oppose a measure which in the course of a few years will, in all human probability, rescue from the vilest state of bondage a number, and without doubt a considerable number, of souls yet unborn.[30]

The senators of the United States placed this petition on the table, which is to say that they dismissed it without taking any formal action. Whether or not there were any sardonic chuckles in the Senate upon the discovery of *amis des noirs* along the shores of Illinois has not been recorded.

Zeal for slavery, or for slavery disguised as indentured servitude, was still on the rise in the Old Northwest. The Governor of the Territory of Indiana, William Henry Harrison, called a convention which met at Vincennes in December, 1802.[31] The fruit of this convention was an appeal to Congress to suspend Article 6 for ten years only. The slaves introduced during this period, and their issue, would continue slaves forever. This petition found its way to the Committee on Public Lands, whose chairman in 1803 was the eccentric John Randolph. This Virginian disappointed the party of Virginia aristocrats in Indiana by writing an unfavorable report, which his committee endorsed:

The rapid population of the State of Ohio sufficiently evinces, in the opinion of your Committee, that the labor of the slave is not necessary to promote the growth and settlement of Colonies in that region; that this labor, demonstrably the dearest of any, can only be employed to advantage in the cultivation of products more val-

---

[30] *Ibid.*, p. 456.

[31] The story of the attempt to introduce slavery is briefly told in McMaster, *History*, III, 523–528, and in Dorothy B. Goebel, *William Henry Harrison* (Indianapolis, 1926), pp. 76–85. The fullest account is Jacob P. Dunn, *Indiana; a Redemption from Slavery* (Boston and New York, 1905).

uable than any known to that quarter of the United States; and the Committee deem it highly dangerous and inexpedient to impair a provision wisely calculated to promote the happiness and prosperity of the Northwestern Country and to give strength and security to that extensive frontier.[32]

Forceful though Randolph's reasoning was, it failed to impress the delegates from Indiana, who secured a vote in the House to have the report recommitted for further consideration. At the next session Caesar Rodney of Delaware submitted a favorable report along with the Indiana petition, and this time the Committee on Public Lands recommended the limited introduction of slavery, with the future issue of slaves to be freed, the males at twenty-five and the females at twenty-one. But the House of Representatives took no action on this report.[33]

Back in Indiana, however, Harrison and his friends proved themselves resourceful. The territory had advanced to the second stage of organization, and had its own legislature. This was controlled by the friends of slavery, who secured an indentured servants act that permitted a de facto slavery to be introduced, and under the protection of this act hundreds of slaves were brought to the north bank of the Ohio.[34] This was a serious matter, for under good republican theory a "sovereign state" had full control of its domestic institutions, and Indiana could, upon the achievement of statehood, easily

---

[32] Quoted in Bruce, *John Randolph*, II, 244–245.

[33] Dunn, "Slavery Petitions and Papers," pp. 473–475.

[34] Francis S. Philbrick, ed., *The Laws of Indiana Territory, 1801–1809* (Springfield, 1930), covers the origins of the "indentured servant" laws in a long and able introduction. The central legislation is "An Act Concerning the Introduction of Negroes and Mulattoes into this Territory," pp. 136–139. Also important are laws on taxation, p. 73; on the sale of alcoholic beverages, pp. 286–287; on the sale of "indentures" under execution, p. 189; on misconduct, pp. 203–204; and on Negro revelry, pp. 657–658. Philbrick's volume is the twenty-first of the *Collections of the Illinois State Historical Society*, edited by Theodore C. Pease.

proceed to legalize slavery forever, the Northwest Ordinance having no further authority in the matter. No one realized this more fully than the antislavery citizens of Clark County, who began a political counterattack which finally triumphed, in the word of the historian of this episode, in "redeeming" Indiana from slavery. But in 1809 the proslavery part of the territory had been detached, to form the new territory of Illinois, where the indentured servant law was maintained until the achievement of statehood in 1818 and where gentlemen were still trying to establish slavery as a domestic institution until they were decisively defeated in an election for a state convention in 1824.[35]

It is interesting that the outstanding leader of the antislavery forces in Illinois was Edward Coles, a migrant Virginia aristocrat who, with considerable inconvenience and annoyance, had led his own slaves into the territory and freed them. And it is especially significant that the prolonged struggle over slavery in Illinois became deeply involved with the national struggle over slavery in the neighboring territory of Missouri. But of especial concern to this study is the fact that, exceptional figures like Coles notwithstanding, the Virginia influence on the Old Northwest was a proslavery influence, and nothing was done by the national government under the Virginians Jefferson and Madison to restrain the proslavery efforts of their migrated countrymen. In the end it proved to be popular sovereignty that prevented the permanent establishment of slavery in Indiana and Illinois. The antislavery majorities in those places certainly drew moral support from the old ordinance, but their triumph resulted because they were, in the end, majorities. Years later the significance of this must have been apparent to the little giant of Illinois and national politics, Stephen A. Douglas.

It must be remembered that the plantation frontier swal-

---

[35] Theodore C. Pease, *The Story of Illinois* (Chicago, 1949), pp. 68–78.

lowed up territory much more rapidly than did the free-labor frontier. A glance at any map of the United States will show that, if the free states in 1860 had much the larger population, the slave states had a much greater quantity of land. What prevented the slaveholding planters from dominating Illinois, and possibly even Indiana, was, of all things, cotton. This marvelous plant, popularly supposed to be the agent of prolonging the life of slavery, probably had the opposite effect, for the majority of slaves in the early republic were held in Virginia and the direction of their early migration was toward Kentucky and the Ohio Valley. But by 1800 cotton was rapidly becoming known as the plantation crop without parallel, and the migration of slavery took a distinct turn toward those latitudes where the growing season would sustain the fibrous plant. The very success of cotton on the lower Mississippi created new opportunities for planters growing grain in the more temperate climates, and slavery was handsomely maintained, for this reason, in Kentucky and Missouri. But planters on the move had little reason to grow grain and hogs in competition with free labor when an obliging government, abetted by eager vigilantes, was continually clearing the Indians from choice cotton lands in the Southwest.

The Virginia dynasty, led by Thomas Jefferson and securely in control of the national government after 1800, surely and expertly exerted its power toward this happy outcome. Flaunting Britain, sacrificing the interests of New England commerce when necessary, and cajoling or threatening France and Spain as the occasion demanded, the Jeffersonian Republicans grasped control of the entire Mississippi Valley, the Floridas, and the vital entrepôt of New Orleans, guaranteeing the security of slavery in the vast Louisiana territory and promoting the greatest and easiest possible access to foreign markets for the rising planters of the deep Southwest.

EPILOGUE

What is left of the idea that slavery in the upper South was headed toward extinction before the rise of King Cotton upset the benign course of history? So far as Virginia was concerned, very little. The spirit of humane progress, doubly embodied in the rational enlightenment and evangelical Christianity of Western civilization, caused all the states from Pennsylvania northward to begin the freeing of their slaves between 1780 and 1800. During this time, when the prophets of emancipation were pressing from one victory to another, Virginia seemed briefly to be going with the tide. But within the decade of the 1780's progress was arrested, and from then until the end of the Jeffersonian era, slavery was defended with increasing vigor, and the activities of abolitionists were increasingly discouraged and restricted.

The triumph of Jeffersonian Republicanism in the election of 1800 was virtually coincident with the shock of Gabriel's rebellion. The latter event seemed to justify anxieties felt over the years, and especially since the successful uprising of the Negroes of Santo Domingo. During the years of Thomas Jefferson's presidency, Virginia discouraged the education of Negroes, required that newly freed Negroes should leave the state, and decided that contraband Negroes should be sold into slavery for the public benefit. When Gabriel proved what many had long suspected, that the Negro could feel the injustice of slavery and yearn for freedom quite as powerfully as the white man, Virginia responded by enacting stronger police measures to control her Negro population. At the same time the Virginia dynasty in national politics, answering to fundamental economic imperatives that transcended any theoretical opposition to slavery, pressed the claims of American planters for wider access to world markets and opened up the rich lands of the lower Mississippi Valley to plantation agriculture.

This demonstrable tightening and extension of slavery occurred at a time when the institution was under criticism and attack from many sources, several of which were within the Old Dominion itself. Statesmen could see that slavery violated the elemental principles of free, republican government. In a more practical way, they could also see that its mere existence drove the most desirable new immigrants toward the free states of the North and many valuable yeomen to the Old Northwest. It was usually agreed that slavery tempted the owning class to luxury, vice, and a tyrannical disposition. Slavery came under further attack from the fervent evangelists, including many Methodists and most Quakers, who held the conviction that holding property in man, even black man, was a grievous sin. Many Quakers succeeded in demonstrating that Negroes could be educated and trained to live as pious, respectable citizens.

Nevertheless, slavery prevailed against these erosive factors. One sound reason for this was that, all observations about the economic wastefulness of slavery notwithstanding, most planters were themselves convinced that they could be wealthy and happy more easily with slaves than without.

Theirs was not a society that identified virtue with manual labor, although it was as convinced as any about the beneficence of agriculture and living on the land. In the absence of either a white peasantry or any prospect of recruiting one, the planters of Virginia relied on their Negro slaves for the amenities of life, and such profits as they could get. Therefore, throughout the Jeffersonian era, the price of slaves remained respectably high compared to all other prices, and Virginia statecraft always held that any depressions that beset the planters resulted from the selfish and monopolistic policies of British traders, rather than from maladjustments within the Virginia economy itself.

A man might have misgivings about building his fortune on slave labor, but if he wanted to remain in Virginia he had little choice. James Madison, hardly a proslavery agrarian in the fashion of John Taylor, demonstrated this to a young correspondent who had sought advice as to whether he ought to sell his slaves and invest his capital in some more innocent pursuit. Madison replied that he fully agreed with the young man "as to the evil, moral, political and economical" of slavery. Nevertheless, he felt that "much improvement" was possible in slave culture, of which "proofs are annually taking place within my own sphere of observation; particularly where slaves are held in small numbers, by good masters and managers." Then Madison argued that, for all its risks, running a plantation with slave labor was still preferable to any of the alternatives facing the young man. Should he buy stocks or bonds, "look at the wrecks everywhere giving warning of the danger." If he should invest in land without slaves, "Will you cultivate it yourself? Then beware of the difficulty of procuring faithful or complying laborers. Will you dispose of it in leases? Ask those who have made the experiment what sort of tenants are to be found where an ownership of the soil is so attainable."[1]

---

[1] Letter to F. Corbin, 26 November 1820, Madison, *Letters and Other Writings*, III, 193–194.

Significantly, Madison did not suggest that the young man might free his slaves and go forth to earn his livelihood by his own efforts. How could he advise anyone to throw away the considerable advantage of a patrimony? Similarly, all over Virginia, planters were bequeathing to their heirs the land and slaves that made up their source and store of wealth, and along with these the often agreeable life based on the plantation economy. When the sons of slaveholders left the state, they therefore went, in the overwhelming majority of cases, to Kentucky, Tennessee, or, later, Alabama, Mississippi, and Louisiana; in brief, they went to other slaveholding commonwealths. A few even tried to carry the plantation system across the Ohio into the Old Northwest.

Efficient or not, slavery proved itself worthwhile for the slaveholders who ruled Virginia, and they were careful that nothing should interfere with it. At the same time they realized that the slaves themselves, if they became too numerous, constituted a deadly threat to their security. Therefore it was sound policy to cut off the flow of slaves into the state, while encouraging the removal of surpluses. Because many white people who were not slaveholders left the state, and because the slaves naturally increased their numbers rapidly, it was desirable to have clear channels for their removal. The only emancipation plans seriously proposed by leading Virginians all had the pleasant attribute of guaranteeing a full slave-labor supply for at least three generations, while helpfully proposing to remove the excessive numbers of freed Negroes which might otherwise engulf the state.

Virginians were disturbed by the possibility of Negroes rising in revenge. They convinced themselves that if Negroes were safely to remain in their state at all, they must be kept under the strict controls of slavery. A more permissive status could easily lead to the dual horrors of civil war and miscegenation. Virginians thus talked themselves out of the only practical solution to their problem. For if they were to be free of the iniquity of slavery, yet retain the labor supply upon which they depended, they must have freed their Negroes and then hired as free laborers those who cared to stay, and experience indicated that most of them would. But only a few radical Quakers and Methodists ever suggested such a course. The great Virginia liberals all agreed that Negroes, if freed, must be removed. By insisting on the impossible, they effectively supported the continued existence of slavery. The Methodist Bishop, Francis Asbury, was not convinced by Virginia rationalizations, as he confided to his journal in 1798:

O! to be dependent on slaveholders is in part to be a slave, and I was free born. I am brought to conclude that slavery will exist in Virginia perhaps for ages; there is not a sufficient sense of religion nor of liberty to destroy it; Methodists, Baptists, Presbyterians, in the highest flights of rapturous piety, still maintain and defend it. I judge in after ages it will be so that poor men and free men will not live among slaveholders, but will go to new lands; they only who are concerned in, and dependent on them will stay in old Virginia.[2]

It was significant that when Virginians rose to speak of slaves in public, they usually referred to them with the euphemism, "species of property." In this way they always reminded their listeners that slaveholders had a basic right of property in their slaves. Often such a reminder would be accompanied by some observation that the tenure of this property was more a burden than an asset, and more painful than pleasurable. But this, in turn, was just as often followed by a confession that either nothing could be done to escape the burden, or that at least an indefinite amount of time would be required for "amelioration." All of which left, for the present, the clear impression that property in slaves deserved quite as much protection from both local and national government as any other legitimate form of property. In this way Virginians managed always to submerge any discussion of the human rights of slaves into considerations of the property rights of

---

[2] Asbury, *Journal and Letters*, II, 151.

slaveholders. So completely had Virginians convinced themselves of their vested rights that one finds even George Washington, perhaps the most fair-minded of them all, arguing that one of his runaway slaves was much less entitled to her freedom than those who stayed loyally at their tasks on his plantation, as if servile labor were an obligation owed by all Negroes to their masters.[3]

When the Quaker abolitionist, Robert Pleasants, asked Madison to introduce a petition against the slave trade into the House of Representatives, Madison declined the commission and submitted to Pleasants the following explanation:

Animadversions such as [the petition] contains . . . are supposed by the holders of that species of property to lessen the value by weakening the tenure of it. Those from whom I derive my public station are known by me to be greatly interested in that species of property, and to view the matter in that light. It would seem that I might be chargeable at least with want of candor, if not of fidelity, were I to make a situation in which their confidence has placed me to become a volunteer in giving a public wound, as they would deem it, to an interest on which they set so great a value.

Madison then advised Pleasants against his plan to send a petition for emancipation to the Virginia legislature. To do so might arouse the foes of emancipation to repeal the act of 1782, or at least to modify it by requiring that all freed Negroes leave the state, "there being arguments of great force for such a regulation, and some would concur in it, who, in general, disapprove of the institution of slavery."[4] Fifteen years later, this restriction became law.

The liberalism of Virginia during this "golden age" proves to have been rather limited. Freedom was, in practice, the birthright of white men only. As for the black men, they were held unfit, either by heredity, or environment, or both,

---

[3] Washington, *Writings*, XXXV, 297.
[4] Letter of 30 October 1791, Madison, *Letters and Other Writings*, I, 542. Brant, *James Madison*, II, 309.

to be trusted with freedom in any measure. Nor was there any firm hope that the Negro might improve, for the classic liberal faith in the improvability, if not the perfectability, of human nature was denied by Virginians when they approached the slavery question. Indeed, it appears that when the Virginian spoke warmly of liberty and its blessings, he was in fact praising his own kind of liberty and its blessings: his personal independence of political or financial suzerains, his own freedom of action, and his own lordship over his acres and his "people."

For the proper understanding of our national development, it is important to know that old Virginia worked out and transmitted, along with the axioms of democratic republicanism, the model theory of American racism. During the Jeffersonian era Virginians rejected the spirit of emancipation and continued the enduring practice of exploiting Negro labor on the one hand while strenuously insisting on the inferiority of the Negro race on the other. Then as later, this interesting position was earnestly, sincerely, and ingeniously explained and justified. But outsiders could never stop wondering whether the racial problem, so deeply stressed, was not an excuse for the exploitation, so manifestly obvious.

Then as later, outsiders were told that they did not "understand" the problem, they were warned that public attacks on slavery could result in nothing but making a bad situation worse, they were asked to help protect property in slaves, and they were instructed that the more territory that was opened to the spread of slavery, the happier everyone would be. The first generation of abolitionists in the United States were mild and pious men, eager to win the love, esteem, and cooperation of slaveholders. In areas where planters were politically dominant, these mild abolitionists made no headway at all toward their goal of complete, however gradual, emancipation. As slavery extended itself, in later years, over the greater portion of settled American territories, it became quickly evident that each new state controlled by planters was, to say the least, as hostile to "meddling" with slavery as old Virginia had been.

In this situation a more vigorous generation of abolitionists excited the public with stories of atrocities, and a passionate indictment of slavery which, if it did not technically damn the southern planter in his character and morals, certainly did so by implication. A somewhat milder breed of antislavery politicians developed finally to unite the North on the principle that the territorial growth of slavery should be, at long last, entirely halted. Both species of men have been widely criticized for their undoubted role in bringing on the showdown of 1860 and the catastrophe of the Civil War. But critics have never demonstrated, nor is it likely that they ever will demonstrate, that anything within plantation society could check its growth or free its slaves. From Old Virginia to the newest cotton lands of Texas and Arkansas, the helplessness of the Negro in any station other than his "normal" one and the virtues of "diffusion" were as much articles of faith as the notion that any public criticism of slavery could produce nothing but mischief. Granting the violence of antislavery in the generation preceding the Civil War, was there any alternative to it other than acquiescence?

No state was more influential than Virginia in transmitting radical doctrines of liberty and equality to Americans of the nineteenth century, and no spokesman for American freedom was ever more eloquent than Virginia's Thomas Jefferson. Is it any wonder that the inspiration of Jefferson's democratic theories made implacable foes of slavery out of men less interested in Negro labor than he, and less influenced by the doctrines of Negro inferiority? The gentlemen of Virginia were somehow able to maintain their radical ideals of human freedom and their institution of Negro slavery without psychic or civil catastrophe, but as ideals and institution grew and ramified, their incompatibility caused the greatest crisis in American history. In some degree the Civil War was the cruel resolution of the conflicting attachments of old Virginia to human liberty and Negro slavery.

DOCUMENTARY SUPPLEMENT

The following documents share several important qualities. They illustrate the thought and feeling of Jeffersonian Virginians (or Kentuckians) either for or against slavery, and they do so in ways that qualify or extend the definitions of such matters in my first edition. They are also relatively neglected, at least up to the present moment of writing. So far as I know, David Rice's excellent antislavery tract of 1792 has not been taken up in the vast reprinting of abolitionist literature that has gone forward in the last ten years. John Taylor's *Arator* has been out of print for 130 years, and his thought on slavery has somehow eluded the kind of systematic analysis which Jefferson's has received in the new literature on American racism. The other items are even more obscure, but it must be remembered that they testify to people who were active and influential in their own time. Many of the papers of Washington, Jefferson, and Madison from which we have reconstructed ideas on slavery and racism were private communications only. Even the *Notes on Virginia* was originally intended for private and foreign circulation only. The documents that follow, however, reflect the public discussion for and against slavery in the Age of Jefferson, a subject which still has not had the full and systematic treatment it deserves.

1. An antislavery statement by a Virginia Quaker, 1782.

In some respects the antislavery sentiments of Robert Williams, communicated to Robert Pleasants and reprinted below, were hackneyed even by 1782. Yet there is something special about the way in which he develops his theme of the depravity of the blacks in their state of bondage. Of course Quakers of the more devout type thought that most of the men and women of the world were caught up with "folly, wickedness, and vanitys." Even so, one can see that a great distance lay between this writer and the objects of his spiritual zeal: he did not at all approve of Negroes as they were. This is not sufficient grounds for impugning his sincere desire to make them free, but it is at least possible that religious abolitionists of Williams's type were likely to limit their own effectiveness. First, they were looking forward to a sort of wholesale religious conversion which was unlikely enough, either among blacks or whites. They were therefore likely to be disillusioned if they freed a black and he pursued "vanitys" all the harder. Second, because they had about the same dismal estimate of the actual character of the Negro that the defenders of slavery held, they left the question of emancipation on the very doubtful ground of whether or not freedom would make him better. Too many white Virginians had formed the opinion that freedom positively made Negroes worse. Unless slaveholders accepted the extraordinary religious beliefs and expectations of the Quakers (or the kindred zealous fringes of the other denominations) they were not likely to accept the antislavery views that so much depended on them. This letter has been copied from the original in the Pleasants Family Papers, Brock Collection, and is printed by kind permission of the Huntington Library.

SOME REMARKS ON SLAVE KEEPING WROTE IN THE
8 MO. 1782
BY ROBERT WILLIAMS

The Devine law that enjoins us to do unto all men as we would they should do unto us, in its moral fitness outweighs any argument that can be advanced for keeping of slaves in bondage. For while we withold their freedom we are in a great measure the cause & the patrons of their Tyrannies, their dissolute lives & conversations. By making a property of their persons, and having the absolute disposal of their labour and time, we fetter the free will, and caus a wrong bias to their understanding: which leads them to lying & thieving, Idleness & deceit; which keeps them in the

Ignorance and forgetfulness of God: in the habit of vain conversation, ungodly lives and profaness. And being obdurate from their state of bondage, and in the constant practice of ill doing it is a thick veil over their minds that prevents the saving light of the gosple from shining effectually into their darkened and benighted souls and not being trained up on the fear of god and good example, they have no pious relish, and think little or nothing of a future state, & the dangerous condition of their Immortal part. Their ignorant kept minds runing cheifly on how to procure means & time to enjoy the folly, wickedness & vanitys of this transatory existence. Again These unhappy people not being brought up in the holy fear of God, and injustice and bad example ever lying before them, their beast like condition & situation leads them also in the way and sinfull practice of whoredom and Adultry. And when a man and woman slaves unites together in the bonds of affection, and come to live together within the bonds of unviolated integrety as man and Wife, yet as Slaves are they ever liable to be deprived of that Happiness by the Cruel despotick unjust tyranny of power: and frequently we have seen a Wife taken away and sold from an Husband, and Husband from a Wife, when in full health, and prime of life in time of peace & publick tranquility: and Children separated from the sight and knowledge of their Parents for ever.

2. Excerpts from a Kentucky antislavery tract, 1792.

The Presbyterian minister David Rice led the antislavery party in Kentucky at the time of the convention which made the Constitution for the new state. Apparently he delivered his message in the form of a speech at the convention itself, and then had it printed. The force of Rice's reasoning and the variety of his arguments prove that he had long been building his case against slavery. Unfortunately his tract is too long to reproduce in its entirely; it is hoped that the following selections represent both the vigor of Rice's mind and the surprising thoroughness with which he reviewed the issue.

Unlike the Quaker Robert Williams, Rice rested his argument as much on the prevailing "natural rights" philosophy of young America, as on the requirements of Christian charity. His discussion of scriptural sanction for slavery proves that the Bible was being used to defend the institution in Jeffersonian times as well as later. It is somewhat surprising, in fact, that proslavery writers continued to use the Bible, for Rice's attack on their position was devastating enough, especially considering the form that Negro slavery in America took. Perhaps the most interesting feature of Rice's pamphlet was the way in which he addressed the bugbear of miscegenation.

There was no problem about freedom of speech on this issue. The antislavery party had a full hearing. The Convention then proceeded to make Kentucky a slave state, proving once again that good ideas do not always triumph where they run against considerable interests.

David Rice was a native of Virginia, and had lived there fifty years before moving to Kentucky. It is therefore fair to represent his views as characteristic of the most advanced antislavery thinking in both states. The standard treatment of the enduring antislavery movement in Kentucky is Asa Earl Martin, *The Anti-Slavery Movement in Kentucky Prior to 1850* (Louisville, Kentucky, 1918; reprinted New York, 1970). I am indebted to Jacqueline Bull of the University of Kentucky Library for a facsimile copy of Rice's pamphlet, which was issued in 1956 as *Keepsake Number* 3 of the University of Kentucky Library Associates.

SLAVERY INCONSISTENT WITH JUSTICE & GOOD POLICY, BY PHILANTHROPOS (LEXINGTON, KENTUCKY, 1792).

. . . Is there any need of arguments to prove, that it is in a high degree unjust and cruel, to reduce one human creature to such an abject wretched state as this, that he may minister to the ease, luxury or avarice of another? Has not that other the same right to have him reduced to this state, that he may minister to his interest or pleasure? On what is this right founded? Whence was it derived? Did it come from heaven, from earth, or from hell? Has the great king of heaven, the absolute sovereign disposer of all men, given this extraordinary right to white men over black men? Where is the charter? In whose hands is it lodged? Let it be produced, and read, that we may know our privilege.

Thus reducing men is an indignity, a degradation to our own nature. Had we not lost a true sense of its worth and dignity, we should blush, to see it converted into brutes. We should blush to see our houses filled, or surrounded with cattle, in our own shapes. We should look upon it to be a fouler, a blacker stain, than that with which the verticle suns have tinged the blood of Africa. When we plead for slavery, we plead for the disgrace and ruin of our own nature. If we are capable of it, we may ever after claim kindred with the brutes, and renounce our own superior dignity.

From our definition it will appear, that a Slave is a creature made after the image of God, and accountable to him for the maintenance of innocence and purity; but by law reduced to a liableness to be debauched by men, without any prospect or hope of redress.

That a Slave is made after the image of God no christian will deny; that a Slave is absolutely subjected to be debauched by men, is so apparent from the nature of slavery, that it needs no proof. This is evidently the unhappy case of female slaves; a number of whom have been remarkable for their chastity and modesty. If their master attempts their chastity, they dare neither resist, nor complain. If another man should make the attempt, though resistance may not be so dangerous, complaints are equally vain. They cannot be heard in their own defence; their testimony cannot be admitted. The injurious person has a right to be heard, may accuse the innocent sufferer of malicious slander, and have her severely chastised.

A virtuous woman, and virtuous Africans no doubt there are, esteems her chastity above every other thing; some have preferred it even to their lives: then forcibly to deprive her of this, is treating her with the greatest injustice. Therefore, since law leaves the chastity of a female Slave entirely in the power of her master, and greatly in the power of others, it permits this injustice; it provides no remedy; it refuses to redress this insufferable grievance; it denies even the small privilege of complaining.

From our definition it will follow, that a Slave is a free moral agent legally deprived of free agency, and obliged to act according to the will of another free agent of the same species: and yet he is accountable to his creator for the use he makes of his own free agency.

When a man, though he can exist independent of another, cannot act independent of him, his agency must depend upon the will of that other; and therefore he is deprived of his own free agency: and yet, as a free agent, he is accountable to his maker for all the deeds done in the body. This comes to pass through a great omission and inconsistency in the legislature. They ought farther to have enacted, in order to have been consistent, that the Slave should not have been accountable for any of his actions; but that his master should have answered for him in all things, here and hereafter.

That a Slave has the capacities of a free moral agent will be allowed by all. That he is, in many instances, deprived by law of the exercise of these powers, evidently appears from his situation. That he is accountable to his maker for his conduct, will be allowed by those, who do not believe that human legislatures are omnipotent, and can free men from this allegiance and subjection to the king of heaven.

The principles of conjugal love and fidelity in the breast of a virtuous pair, of natural affection in parents, and a sense of duty in children, are inscribed there by the finger of God; they are the laws of heaven: but an inslaving law directly opposes them, and virtually forbids obedience. The relation of husband and wife, of parent and child, are formed by divine authority, and founded on the laws of nature. But it is in the power of a cruel master, and often of a needy creditor, to break these tender connexions, and forever to separate these dearest relatives. This is ever done, in fact, at the call of interest or humour. The poor sufferers may expostulate; they may plead; may plead with tears; their hearts may break; but all in vain. The laws of nature are violated, the tender ties are dissolved, a final separation takes place, and the duties of these relations can no longer be performed, nor their comforts enjoyed. Would these Slaves perform the duties of husbands and wives, parents and children? The law disables them, it puts it altogether out of their power.

In these cases, it is evident that the laws of nature, or the laws of man, are wrong; and which, none will be at a loss to judge. The divine law says, Whom God hath joined together, let no man put asunder: the law of man says, to the master of the Slave, Though the divine law has joined them together, you may put them asunder, when you please. The divine law says, Train up your child in the way he should go: the law of man says, You shall not train up your child, but as your master thinks proper. The divine law says, Honour your father and mother, and obey them in all things: but the law of man says, Honour and obey your master in all things, and your parents just as far as he shall direct you.

... The slave is then a member of society, who is, properly speaking, in a state of war with his master, his civil rulers, and every free member of that society. They are his declared enemies, having, in him, made war upon almost every thing dear to a human creature. It is a perpetual war, with an avowed purpose of never making peace. This war as it is unprovoked, is, on the part of the Slave, properly defensive. The injury done him is much greater than what is generally esteemed a just ground of war between different nations; it is much greater than was the cause of war between us and Britain.

... Let us turn our eyes to the West-Indies; and there learn the melancholy effects of this wretched policy. We may there read them written with the blood of thousands. There you may see the sable, let me say, the brave sons of Africa engaged in a noble conflict with their inveterate foes. There you may see thousands fired with a generous resentment of the greatest injuries, and bravely sacrificing their lives on the altar of liberty.

... Young Gentlemen, who ought to be the honour and support of the State, when they have in prospect an independent fortune consisting in land and slaves, which they can easily devolve on a faithful overseer or steward, become the most useless and insignificant members of society. There is no confining them to useful studies, or any business that will fit them for serving the public. They are employed in scenes of pleasure and dissipation. They corrupt each other; they corrupt the morals of all around them: while their slaves, even in time of peace, are far from being equally useful to society with the same number of free men; and, in time of war, are to be considered as an enemy lodged within our walls. I said they were useless insignificant members of society. I should have said more; I should have said, they are intolerable nuisances, pernicious pests of society. I mean not to reproach men of fortune; I mean only to point out the natural tendency of slavery, in order to shew, how inconsistent it is with good policy.

The prosperity of a country depends upon the industry of its inhabitants; idleness will produce poverty: and when slavery becomes common, industry sinks into disgrace. To labour, is to slave; to work, is *to work like a Negroe*: and this is disgraceful; it levels us with the meanest of the species; it sits hard upon the mind; it cannot be patiently born. Youth are hereby tempted to idleness, and drawn into other vices: they see no other way to keep their credit, and acquire some little importance. This renders them, like those they ape, nuisances of society. It frequently tempts them to gaming, theft, robbery, or forgery; for which they often end their days in disgrace on the gallows. Since every state must be supported by industry, it is exceedingly unwise to admit what will inevitably sink it into disgrace: and that this is the tendency of slavery is known from matter of fact.

. . . The destruction of chastity has a natural tendency to introduce a number of vices, that are very pernicious to the interest of a commonwealth; and slavery much conduces to destroy chastity, as it puts so great a number of females entirely in the power of the other sex; against whom they dare not complain, on peril of the lash; and many of whom they dare not resist. This vice, this bane of society, has already become so common, that it is scarcely esteemed a disgrace, in the one sex, and that the one that is generally the most criminal. Let it become as little disgraceful in the other, and there is an end to domestick tranquility, an end to the public prosperity.

. . . You say, a law of emancipation, would be unjust, because it would deprive men of their property: but is there no injustice on the other side? Is no body intitled to justice, but Slaveholders? Let us consider the injustice on both sides; and weigh them in an even ballance. On the one hand, we see a man deprived of all property, of all capacity to possess property, of his own free agency, of the means of instruction, of his wife, of his children, of almost every thing dear to him: on the other, a man deprived of eighty or an hundred pounds. Shall we hesitate a moment to determine, who is the greatest sufferer, and who is treated with the greatest injustice? The matter appears quite glaring, when we consider, that neither this man, nor his parents had sinned, that he was born to these sufferings; but the other suffers altogether for his own sin, and that of his predecessors. Such a law would only take away property, that is its own property, and not ours; property that has the same right to possess us, as its property, as we have to possess it; property that has the same right to convert our children into dogs, and calves, and colts, as we have to convert theirs into these beasts; property that may transfer our children to strangers, by the same right that we transfer theirs.

. . . Making prisoners of war slaves, though practiced by the Romans and other nations, and though still practiced by some barbarous tribes, can by no means be justified; it is unreasonable and cruel. Whatever may be said of the chief authors and promoters of an unjust war, the common soldier, who is under command and obliged to obey, and as is often the case, deprived of the means of information as to the grounds of the war, certainly cannot be thought guilty of a crime so heinous, that for it himself and posterity deserve the dreadful punishment of perpetual servitude. It is a cruelty that the present practice of all civilized nations bears testimony against. Allow then the matter objected to be true, and it will not justify our practice of inslaving the Africans. But the matter contained in the objection is only true in part. The history of the Slave trade is too tragical to be read without a bleeding heart and weeping eyes.

A few of these unhappy Africans, and comparatively few, are criminals, whose servitude is inflicted as a punishment for their crimes. The main body are innocent, unsuspecting creatures, free, living in peace, doing nothing to forfeit the common privileges of men. They are stolen, or violently borne away by armed force, from their country, their parents, and all their tender connections, treated with an indignity and indecency shameful to mention, and a cruelty shocking to all the tender feelings of humanity; and they and their posterity forced into a state of servitude and wretchedness forever. It is true, they are commonly taken prisoners by Africans; but it is the encouragement given by Europeans that tempts the Africans to carry on these unprovoked wars. They furnish them with arms, and purchase the spoil. In this case, who is the most criminal, the civilized European, or the untutored African? The European merchants know, that they themselves are the great encouragers of these wars; as they are the principal gainers by the event. They furnish the sinews, add the strength, and receive the gain. They know that they purchase these slaves of those, who have no just pretence to claim them, as theirs. The African can give the European no better claim than he himself has; the European merchant can give us no better claim than is vested in him; and that is one founded only in violence or fraud.

. . . Another frightened objection to my doctrine is, That should we set our Slaves free, it would lay a foundation for intermarriages and an unnatural mixture of blood, and our posterity at length would all be mulattoes.

This effect, I grant, it would produce. I also grant, that this appears very unnatural to persons labouring under our prejudices of education. I acknowledge my own pride remonstrates against it; but it does not influence my judgment, nor affect my conscience.

To plead this, as a reason for the continuation of slavery, is to plead the fear that we should disgrace ourselves, as a reason why we should do injustice to others: to plead that we may continue in guilt, for fear the features and complexion of our posterity should be spoiled. We should recollect, that it is too late to prevent this great imaginary evil; the matter is already gone beyond recovery; for it may be proved, with mathematical certainty, that, if things go on in the present channel, the future inhabitants of America will inevitably be mulattoes.

How often have men children by their own Slaves, by their fathers' Slaves, or the Slaves of their neighbours! How fast is the number of mulattoes increasing in every part of the land! Visit the little towns and villages to the Eastward; visit the seats of gentlemen, who abound in Slaves; and see how they swarm on every hand! All the children of mulattoes will be mulattoes, and the whites are daily adding to the number; which will continually increase the proportion of mulattoes. Thus this evil is coming upon us in a way much more disgraceful, and unnatural, than intermarriages. Fathers will have their own children for Slaves, and leave them as an inheritance to their children. Men will possess their brothers and sisters as their property, leave them to their heirs, or sell them to strangers. Youth will have their grey headed Uncles and Aunts for Slaves, call them their property, and transfer them to others. Men will humble their own Sisters, or even their Aunts, to gratify their lust. An hard hearted master will not know, whether he has a blood relation, a Brother or a Sister, an Uncle or an Aunt; or, a stranger of Africa, under his scourging hand. This is not the work of imagination; it has been frequently realized.

The worst that can be made of this objection, ugly as it is, is that it would be hastening an evil in an honest way, which we are already bringing on ourselves, in a way that is absolutely dishonest, perfectly shameful, and extremely criminal. This objection then can have no weight with a reasonable man, who can divest himself of his prejudices and his pride, and view the matter as really circumstanced. The evil is inevitable; but as it is a prejudice of education, it would be an evil only in its approach; as it drew near, it would decrease; when fully come, it would cease to exist.

Another objection to my doctrine, and that esteemed by some the most formidable, still lies before me: an objection taken from the sacred scriptures. There will be produced on the occasion, the example of faithful Abraham, recorded Gen. 17: and the law of Moses, recorded in Lev. 25. The injunctions laid upon servants in the gospel, particularly by the Apostle Paul, will also be introduced here. These will all be directed, as formidable artillery, against me, and in defence of absolute slavery.

From the passage in Genesis, it is argued, by the advocates for perpetual slavery, that since Abraham had servants born in his house and bought with money, they must have been servants for life; like our negroes: and hence they conclude, that it is lawful for us to purchase heathen servants, and if they have children born in our houses, to make them servants also. From the law of Moses it is argued, that the Israelites were authorized to leave the children of their servants, as an inheritance to their own children, for ever: and hence it is inferred, that we may leave the children of our Slaves as an inheritance to our children forever. If this was immoral in itself, a just God would never have given it the sanction of his authority; and, if lawful in itself, we may safely follow the example of Abraham, or act according to the law of Moses.

None, I hope, will make this objection, but those who believe these writings to be of divine authority; for if they are not so, it is little to the purpose to introduce them here. If you grant them to be of divine authority, you will also grant, that they are consistent with themselves, and that one passage may help to explain another. Grant me this; and then I reply to the objection.

In the 12th verse of the 17th of Genesis, we find that Abraham was commanded to circumcise all that were born in his house, or bought with money. We find in the sequel of the chapter, that he obeyed this command, without delay; and actually circumcised every male in his family, who came under this description. This law of circumcision continued in force; it was not repealed, but confirmed by the law of Moses.

Now, to the circumcised were committed the oracles of God; and circumcision was a token of that covenant by which, among other things, the land of Canaan, and their various privileges in it, were promised to Abraham, and his seed; to all that were included in that covenant. All were included, to whom circumcision, which was the token of the covenant, was administered, agreeably to God's command. By divine appointment, not only Abraham and his natural seed, but he that was bought with money of any stranger that was not of his seed, was circumcised. Since the seed of the stranger received the token of this covenant we must believe that he was included, and interested, in it; that the benefits promised were to be conferred on him. These persons bought with money were no longer looked upon as uncircumcised and unclean, as aliens and strangers; but were incorporated into the church and nation of the Israelites; and became one people with them, became God's covenant people. Whence it appears; that suitable provision was made by the divine law that they should be properly educated, made free, and enjoy all the common privileges of citizens. . . .

But it is further objected, that the Apostle advises servants to be contented with their state of servitude, and obedient to their masters; and, though he charges their masters to use them well, he no where commands them to set them free.

In order rightly to understand this matter, we should recollect the situation of christians at this time. They were under the Roman yoke, the government of the heathen; who were watching every opportunity of charging them with designs against the government, in order to justify their bloody persecutions. In such circumstances, for the Apostle to have proclaimed liberty to the slaves, would probably have exposed many of them to certain destruction, brought ruin on the christian cause, and that without the prospect of freeing one single man; which would have been the height of madness and cruelty. It was wise, it was humane in him not to drop a single hint on this subject, farther than saying, *If thou mayest be made free, use it rather.*

Though the Apostles acted with this prudent reserve, the unreasonableness of perpetual, unconditional Slavery may easily be inferred from the righteous and benevolent doctrines, and duties taught in the New Testament. It is quite evident, that Slavery is contrary to the spirit and genius of the christian religion. It is contrary to that excellent precept laid down by the divine author of the christian institution viz. *Whatsoever ye would that men should do to you, do ye even so to them.* A precept so finely calculated to teach the duties of justice, to inforce their obligation, and induce the mind to obedience, that nothing can excel it. No man when he views the hardships, the sufferings, the excessive labours, the unreasonable chastisements, the separations between loving husbands and wives, between affectionate parents and children, can say, were I in their place, I should be contented. . . .

This evil is a tree that has been long planted, it has been growing many years, it has taken deep root, its trunk is large, and its branches extended wide; should it be cut down suddenly, it might crush all that grew near it; should it be violently eradicated, it might tear up the ground in which it grows, and produce fatal effects. It is true, the slaves have a just claim to be freed instantly: but by our bad conduct, we have rendered them incapable of enjoying, and properly using this their birthright; and therefore a gradual emancipation only can be adviseable. The limbs of this tree must be lopped off by little and little, the trunk gradually hewn down, and the stump and roots left to rot in the ground.

The legislature, if they judged it expedient, would prevent the importation of any more slaves: they would enact that all born after such a date should be born free; be qualified by proper education to make useful citizens; and be actually freed at a proper age.

It is no small recommendation of this plan, that is so nearly coincides with the Mosaic law, in this case provided; to which, even suppose it a human institution, great respect is due for its antiquity, its justice and humanity.

. . . The Slavery of the negroes began in iniquity; a curse has attended it, and a curse will follow it. National vices will be punished with national calamities. Let us avoid these vices, that we may avoid the punishment which they deserve; and endeavour so to act, as to secure the approbation and smiles of heaven.

Holding men in Slavery is the National vice of Virginia; and while a part of that state, we were partakers of the guilt. As a separate state, we are just now come to the birth; and it depends upon our free choice, whether we shall be born in this sin, or innocent of it. We now have it in our power to adopt it as our national crime; or to bear a national testimony against it. I hope the latter will be our choice; that we shall wash our hands of this guilt; and not leave it in the power of a future legislature, ever more to stain our reputation or our conscience with it.

3. John Breckinridge defends slavery by ridiculing the abolitionists of Kentucky, 1798.

John Breckinridge (1760–1806) was a native of Virginia, where he had lived as friend and neighbor of Jefferson in Albemarle County until 1793, when he decided to try his fortune in Kentucky. In the years 1798 and 1799 he was simultaneously engaged in defending Republicans from the Alien and Sedition Acts, aristocratic planters (such as himself) from the democratic advocates of a new state constitution, and slaveholders (such as himself) from the antislavery movement. These issues were not quite as distinct as they may at first appear. Federalism had a slight aura of antislavery about it, and there was considerable overlap between the constitutional reformers and the abolitionists.

Breckinridge's biographer, Lowell Harrison, suggests that the slavery issue itself was fairly well under control, and that Breckinridge actually used it to discredit other, more possible, reforms. Whether it was the result of feeling secure on this issue, or a generally tranquil disposition, Breckinridge managed to write about slavery and antislavery with an absence of melodramatics that is worthy of close attention. The issue was of course a serious one for him, but he betrayed no signs of guilt or anxiety, and his tactic of lampooning the abolitionists was surely effective.

John Breckinridge defended the holding of slaves because they were property and because their use was expedient. Along with the less successful advocates of slavery in early Indiana and Illinois, he saw Negro slaves as the best practical answer to the shortage of labor on the frontier. In his satire on the abolitionists, he argued that they were simply trying to avail themselves of this advantage by political revolution, being unable to do so by more wholesome means. Breckinridge may seem callous when compared to Jefferson and Madison, who responded to the moral wrong of slavery in thought and feeling, but his indifference at least spared him from that moral inversion whereby the holding of slaves was made into a sort of good. He did not point with horror to the possibility of Negroes' destroying the white race either by interbreeding or by war. In his moderate way he was one of the most effective promoters of the expansion of slavery the nation was ever to see, presiding in his coordinate roles as purveyor of western lands, lawyer, and politician. The following satire is transcribed from the Breckinridge Family Papers (LC) XVI, 2716–17. The printed version appeared in the Lexington *Kentucky Gazette* for May 2, 1798. The handwritten draft differs in minor respects from the published one, chiefly because the printer preferred not to mention names. For a fuller discussion, see Lowell H. Harrison, *John Breckinridge, Jeffersonian Republican* (Louisville, 1969), especially ch. 5.

ATTEND!

The members of "The Society for the Abolition of Slavery" who live in Fayette, are requested to assemble on Saturday the 28th instant at the office of —— ——, Esq., Attorney at Law, and after taking a lecture on the subject of a general emancipation, proceed to McNair's tavern, when and where matters of the highest importance will be submitted to them, and which will require their discussion previous to the general election on the Tuesday following.

As the said society was instituted for the purpose of promoting the *general good*, holding in utter contempt all sinister views; and as they have no doubt their numbers would daily increase were the terms and conditions of their association made known; in order therefore that every *good man* may have an opportunity of becoming a member, their Secretary is directed to make the same public, which are as follow:

1. No man who owneth a slave shall be admitted as a member except he be a teacher of the Gospel, in which case he may, because he cannot attend his flock and labor too; and it seemeth meet, that he should have a few slaves to labor for him, for it is very unseemly to take hire for teaching the Gospel, and tithes are an accursed thing.

2nd. No person shall be a member who owns more than 100 acres of land, unless his quantity has been increased to a larger, by *selling* his slaves and laying out the money in said land.

3rd. Any man who never owned a slave, or a slaves worth, and who by his course of life, will in all probability ever remain so, will be readily admitted as a member and no questions asked of him.

4th. People of Color cannot at present be admitted, except such as have actually commenced suits to recover their freedom. For these the Society, agreeable to an old maxim of equity, considers "that as actually happened, which ought to happen."

5th. There shall be but one lawyer in the society at any one time, who upon his admission and for one year afterwards must not own a slave. If he should not be able however to purchase a slave the second year, the society are to buy one for him; and they will then be able to hear what can be said on both sides of the question.

6th. The oath heretofore taken on the admission of members; viz: "I do solemnly swear, that I could not in justice own a single slave were I ever so poor; and if one dozen were given to me as a present, I would immediately emancipate them," is expunged from the regulations of the Society, it being considered as putting a man's conscience to too severe a trial; and moreover as foreign to the main object, which is not what the Society would do if they had slaves, but what *other people ought to do*, who actually have them.

7th. All persons opposed to an immediate call of a convention, would more easily find their way to Heaven, than into this Society.

8th. Of course, all persons who are for tearing down the old Constitution to the foundation and building up a new one, shall be entitled to a seat, although they may own a slave or so, because, as emancipation will be the certain consequence of a convention if that convention is judiciously selected, the presumption is that all who are for a convention, although they will lose their slaves, yet they expect also that in the general shuffle they will gain on some other score more than they would lose on that, and the maxim is, *stabitur presumptione, donce probatur in contrarium.* [Let the assumption stand, until the opposite be proved.]

9th. This is a secret article.

10. As the labors, toils, and watching of the Society in the cause of humanity will be great, and as the labor is always deserving of some hire, the Society propose as a small recompense that so soon as an emancipation does take place, they will each of them (and it will be justified by Scripture, for did not Jacob serve Laban fourteen years?) take indentures on some two or three dozen of —— (perhaps it might be as well to omit this article also).

T. Spinhoop, Secretary
April 21, 1798

4. John Taylor's qualified defense of slave-holding.

John Breckinridge went west to Kentucky and defended slavery with pragmatism and humor. John Taylor stayed in eastern Virginia, rebuilt the soil of his plantations, and defended slavery with stoic idealism. "Negro slavery is a misfortune to agriculture, incapable of removal, and only within the reach of palliation," he wrote at one point. Taylor represented a curious point of transition between the high-minded deprecation of slavery of his old law teacher, George Wythe, and the high-minded defense of slavery of his own disciple, George Fitzhugh. Like most of the statesmen of his generation (he was born in 1753 and died in 1824) Taylor believed that the introduction of slaves had been a tragic mistake, but that any effort to free the Negroes must be followed by their rapid and complete removal to distant lands. Like Jefferson, Taylor supposed that a terrific insurrection would follow if the Negroes were freed and allowed to stay in Virginia, and that the doings of abolitionists threatened the country with slave insurrections. He therefore favored the colonization of all free blacks, and urged the advocates of antislavery to keep quiet.

While holding that slavery was bad in itself, Taylor set down, in his *Arator* papers, a detailed program for making a good thing of it. "Slaves are docile, useful and happy, if they are well managed," he wrote in Arator No. 29. Indeed, so far as material things were concerned, slaves nurtured according to Taylor's directions would have been among the best fed, clothed, and housed laborers on earth. He believed that one would get the most work out of slaves who were fed a varied and nutritious diet, and lived in snug, fireproof quarters. He also believed that withholding part of their supplies was a much more effective system of punishment than whips or irons. The slave, as Taylor would have him, lived like the average citizen of Plato's Republic, kept happily and usefully at work by his moral and intellectual superiors.

It was in his positive view of this master-slave relationship that Taylor broke with the views of his contemporaries Jefferson and St. George Tucker, and fully anticipated the thinking of Thomas R. Dew, Edmund Ruffin, and George Fitzhugh. All of these Virginia apologists for slavery may be presumed to have read the *Arator* papers, which circulated in newspapers for years before they were published as a book in 1813, and quickly went through five editions. Ruffin himself revived them in 1841. When one considers that Jefferson was extremely reluctant to have his *Notes on Virginia* published in America, for fear of offending slave-holders, and that Taylor, who partly refuted him, wrote precisely for a Virginia audience, which bought out several editions of his work, the evidence does seem very strong that Taylor, rather than Jefferson, came closest to stating the planters' ideas on slavery.

The two quotations above, and the paper reproduced below, are from *Arator: Being a Series of Agricultural Essays Practical and Political . . . By a Citizen of Virginia* (Georgetown, 1813) 57, 119, and 61–67.

ARATOR NUMBER 14.
SLAVERY, CONTINUED.

Societies are instituted to control and diminish the imperfections of human nature, because without them it generates ignorance, savageness and depravity of manners. Those best constituted, cannot however cure it of a disposition to command, and to live by the labor of others; it is eternally forming sub-societies for acquiring power and wealth, and to these perfidious, ambitious, avaricious or unconstitutional sub-societies, the liberty and property of the rest of the body politic has universally fallen a prey. They are of a civil or military complexion, or of both, as the circumstances of the case may require fraud or force. Anciently, the general ignorance of mankind, caused the frauds of superstition to suffice for working the ends of traitorous sub-societies. As these became exploded, the more intricate pecuniary frauds were resorted to. Now, on account of the increasing knowledge and more prying temper of mankind, military force is united with pecuniary frauds. And hitherto the most perfect society for the public good, has never been able to defend itself against sub-societies in some form for advancing the wealth or power of a faction or a particular interest. Combine with this universal experience, that is is impossible to conceive a form of society better calculated to excite and foster factions or sub-societies, than one constituted of distinct colors, incurable prejudices, and inimicable interests, and the inferences are unavoidable. If the badges of foolish names can drive men into frenzy without cause, will not those which powerfully assail both reason and the senses, create deadly factions?

The attempt will undoubtedly terminate according to the nature of man, as it has once already terminated; but its catastrophe ought rather to be courted than avoided if the author of the Notes on Virginia is right in the following quotations. "The whole commerce between master and slave," says he, "is a perpetual exercise of the most unremitting despotism on one part, and degrading submissions on the other. The parent storms, the child looks on, catches the lineaments of wrath, puts on the same airs in the circle of smaller slaves, gives a loose to his worst of passions, and thus nursed, educated and daily exercised in tyranny, cannot but be stamped by it with odious peculiarities. The man must be a prodigy who can retain his manners and morals undepraved by such circumstances. . . . The Almighty has no attribute which can take side with us in such a contest." Such is the picture exhibited in the Notes on Virginia of the "manners" of the people, without a single palliating circumstance; and Winterbotham in his history of America has quoted and varnished it anew.

No man has been less accustomed than the author of the Notes on Virginia to paint his opinions, for the same reason that an Indian paints his body; and yet from reading the whole chapter on the manners of that state, a stranger would hardly form a more correct idea of them, than a stranger to Indians would of their color, on seeing one painted coal black. Circumstances affect the mind, as weather does beer, and frequently produces a sort of moral fermentation, which throws up bubbles of prismatic splendor, whilst they are played upon by the rays of some temporary effervescence, but destined to burst when the fermentation ceases. The Notes on Virginia were written in the heat of war for liberty; the human mind was made still hotter by the French revolution; and let those who were insensible of the mental fermentations and moral bubbles generated by these causes, censure Mr. Jefferson. I should be unjust to do it.

If Mr. Jefferson's assertions are correct, it is better to run the risk of national extinction, by liberating and fighting the blacks, than to live abhorred of God, and consequently hated of man. If they are erroneous, they ought not to be admitted as arguments for the emancipating policy. The considerations, which this chapter of impassioned censure of slaveholders inspires, are too extensive for a hasty essay, but a few of them may be noticed. I shall pass over the enlistment of the Deity in the question with an humble hope that his justice and mercy do not require the whites and blacks to be placed in such a relative situation, as that one color must extinguish the other; and as inclining to think the enrolment of his name on the side of the slaves somewhat like a charge of inattention to his own attributes, in apparently siding with masters throughout all ages and among most nations hitherto, the liberating St. Domingo masters excepted, and not a little tinged with impiety. Slavery was carried farther among the Greeks and the Romans than among ourselves, and yet, these two nations produced more great and good patriots and citizens than, probably, all the rest of the world. In the United States it is also probable that the public and private character of individuals is as good, as in the countries where loco-motive liberty and slavery to a faction exist; nor do the slave states seem less productive of characters in whom the nation is willing to confide than the others. Even the author of the quotation himself may be fairly adduced as an instance which refutes every syllable of his chapter on Virginia manners, unless indeed this refutation, and an abundance of others like it, can be evaded by forming the best citizens into a class of prodigies or monsters, to evade the force of eminent virtues towards the refutation of erroneous assertions.

These facts are referred to the consideration of the physiologist. To me it seems that slaves are too far below, and too much in the power of the master to inspire furious passions; that such are nearly as rare and disgraceful towards slaves as towards horses; that slaves are more frequently the objects of benevolence than of rage; that children from their nature are inclined to soothe, and hardly ever suffered to tyrannize over them; that they open instead of shut the sluices of benevolence in tender minds; and that fewer good public or private characters have been raised in countries enslaved by some faction or particular interest, than in those where personal slavery existed.

I conjecture the cause of this to be that vicious and mean qualities became despicable in the eyes of freemen from their association with the character of slaves. Character, like condition is contrasted, and as one contrast causes us to love liberty better, so the other causes us to love virtue better. Qualities, odious in themselves, become more contemptible, when united with the most degraded class of men, than when seen with our equals; and pride steps in to aid the struggles of virtue. Instead therefore of fearing that children should imbibe the qualities of slaves, it is probable that the circumstance of seeing bad qualities in slaves will contribute to their virtue.

For the same reason the submission and flattery of slaves will be despised, and cause us rather to hate servility than to imbibe a dictatorial arrogance; and only inspire the same passion with the submission and flattery of a spaniel. It is the submission and flattery of equals, which fills men with the impudent and wicked wish to dictate, and an impatience of free opinion and fair discussion. This reprehensible temper is a sound objection against any species of human policy, which generates it, and applies most forcibly against that conferring on an individual a power, so to dispense money and honors, as to procure submission and flattery from the highest ranks and conditions in society, a thousand times more genial to pride than the submission and flattery of a poor slave; and ten thousand times more pernicious to nations.

Virtue and vice are naturally and unavoidably coexistent in the moral world, as beauty and deformity are in the animal; one is the only mirror in which the other can be seen; and therefore in the present state of man, one cannot be destroyed without the other. It may be thus that personal slavery has constantly reflected the strongest rays of civil liberty and patriotism. Perhaps it is suffered by the deity to perform an office without which these rays are gradually obscured and finally obliterated by charters and partial laws. Perhaps the sight of slavery and its vices may inspire the mind with an affection for liberty and virtue, just as the climates and deserts of Arabia would make it think Italy a paradise.

Let it not be supposed that I approve of slavery because I do not aggravate its evils, or prefer a policy which must terminate in a war of extermination. The chapter on the manners of slave-holders before quoted concludes with an intimation that the consent of the masters to a general emancipation, or their own extirpation, were the alternatives between which they had to choose. Such a hint from a profound mind is awful. It admits an ability in the blacks, though shackled by slavery, to extirpate the whites, and proposes to increase this ability by knocking off their shackles. Such a hint adds force to the recommendation in the previous essay for separating the enslaved and free blacks, as some security against the prognosticated extirpation. And after such a hint, "with what execration should the statesman be loaded" who thus forewarned, should produce the destruction of the most civilized portion of society, and repeople half the world with savages. If

England and America would erect and foster a settlement of free Negroes in some fertile part of Africa, it would soon subsist by its own energies. Slavery might then be gradually reexported, and philanthropy gratified by a slow reanimation of the virtue, religion and liberty of the Negroes, instead of being again afflicted with the effects of her own rash attempts suddenly to change human nature.

5. A dialogue between a Virginia justice of the peace and a constable on the subject of teaching slaves to read.

The dialogue is excerpted from a collection of tracts and sermons, edited, compiled, and partly written by the Rev. William Meade, later Bishop of the Protestant Episcopal Church in Virginia, *Sermons Addressed to Masters and Servants and Published in the Year 1743 by the Rev. Thomas Bacon, Minister of the Protestant Episcopal Church in Maryland, Now Republished with Other Tracts and Dialogues* (Winchester, Virginia, 1813) pp. 151–56. It would be wrong to suppose that there was a fixed and unrelieved trend toward stiffening slavery in Virginia after Gabriel's rebellion. Although no single religious group threw its weight wholly against slavery besides the Quakers, there remained antislavery minorities in the South, and especially in the border, or upper South. The Reverend William Meade (1789-1862) perhaps reflected the overall trend toward conservatism, for in his youth he actually freed some slaves, and encouraged others to do so. He was the most energetic and effective agent the ill-fated American Colonization Society ever had, serving the organization in its early years, from 1817 to 1820. Later he ceased to advocate emancipation, and at the end of his life he acquiesced in secession and became presiding bishop of the Confederate Episcopal Church. (For further information, see P. J. Staudenraus, *The African Colonization Movement, 1816–1865* (New York, 1961), pp. 70–74, and Rt. Rev. John Johns, *Memoir of the Life of the Rt. Rev. William Meade, D.D.* (Baltimore, 1867), pp. 76–77.)

The following tract represents more than the moderate efforts of a Virginia priest to carry the gospel to slaves. It reflects something of the social deference that was expected in polite Virginia society; the constable was bound to be instructed by the justice of peace in a matter where the law was by no means clear. Indeed, if anything, the justice was in favor of setting aside a law which he felt was foolish or worse. The southern churches have often been blamed for not taking a strong position against slavery or, since the Civil War, against segregation. But in the case of William Meade, even when he ceased to advocate emancipation, he continued in what he considered his major and essential task, the preaching of the Word to black as well as white, and some may agree with Charles Williams, that where all are Christians slavery is nonsense. Or to put it another way, if slavery did not corrupt Christianity, Christianity was bound to undermine slavery by reforming it out of existence.

Meade's argument is cast in the form of a dialogue between a pious gentleman, recently "induced to serve as a justice of the peace that he might be useful in the neighborhood," and "the constable in the village, who was rather an ignorant man."

A Dialogue

Constable. Sir, I think it proper to acquaint you of what I have observed going on in the village that it may be stopped in time—some of the neighbours are a good deal alarmed about it, and said I ought to state it to you, and besides some of your own people, certainly without your knowledge, are concerned in it. A man of Mr. Wilkins, is actually keeping a school for black people, and teaching them to read. As soon as it was reported to me, I went to the place and found what they were at, and as I said before, two or three of your servants were among them. Now sir, you know best how to proceed in such a case in order that it may be broken up.

Justice. Well, if this is wrong, let us see how it can be prevented; you know we must go according to the law.

Constable. Why sir, you know our laws prevent the unlawful assembling together of slaves, and you can issue your warrant to disperse them.

Justice. But we must first see if this is an unlawful assembly; what do they do?

Constable. Why sir, they are learning to read—surely there is a law against that.

Justice. I am not so clear that that is an unlawful purpose provided that is their real object. Do they disturb the neighbourhood?

Constable. No other ways sir, that I hear of but by learning to read. But will not that disturb the neighbourhood?

Justice. I can't see that it will, unless they read unseasonably loud.

Constable. As for that they are very still about it. And that convinces me that they will be plotting some mischief and laying their plans to steal; I dare say we shall have work enough if they are suffered to go on.

Justice. Nay, if that was their business they would be more cautious about it and not meet where children and others were whom they would not know they could trust. Besides I cannot think learning to read informs people in roguery; as well as I can recollect most rogues we have had to deal with, could not read at all. You remember poor Dick Drone, who was hung for breaking open Mr. Speedwell's house; he complained that he had never been taught to read and that therefore when he was not at his work, he had nothing else to do but to loiter in idleness about the streets or lounge in the dram shops, and that was the reason why he began to drink, and at last to steal.

Now I think if these people were taught to read they might be less tempted to idleness and bad habits, and would stay at nights and other times at home with their books instead of getting into bad company.

Constable. But sir, slaves should be kept to their work and ought not to have any leisure times. I have often thought this of Sundays and holydays when I have been so often called on, and you too sir, to keep them in order.

Justice. Then you thought wrong I think. You would not surely deny them all holydays and keep them at work on the Sabbath. This would be using them worse than the beasts.

Constable. Well, they should be kept at home at such times.

Justice. And even then they might get into mischief unless you locked them up, and at nights too, unless they were secured in the same way, you would have to employ people to watch them. I think your plan would be rather troublesome if not impracticable, to say nothing of the injustice of it.

Constable. But people will not like their negroes to read, they have no time for such things, and if they neglect their work for their books, their masters would have cause to complain.

Justice. They need not neglect their work, they have leisure enough, as you allow, at nights and Sundays, and holydays, besides other little odd times; and is it not better they should have good books to employ their minds at such times when they are resting their bodies, than that they should be giving, by their misconduct, you and me the trouble you have just complained of?

Constable. Aye, but they will get bad books.

Justice. That may be prevented by their masters who may take them away and give them good ones; they will read such books as are given them, not being generally able to buy books; and good people are more apt to give away good books than bad people are to give away bad ones. Besides, if your objection is a good one, nobody ought to learn to read, for fear they may get bad books: you ought to take your children from school.

Constable. But they say it makes them impudent, and to my certain knowledge, there's Ashford's Jack, that's the impudentest fellow in the whole country, and does not mind master or overseer a pin, and he can read as glib as a lawyer.

Justice. But are you sure he would not have been just as impudent, without learning to read? As I said of your other objection, so of this, if reading makes people impudent, take your children from school. But I can't conceive how learning to read can make people impudent.—There are some of us in the village who can read, and I believe we are quite as civil and well-behaved, as the few vagabonds among us, who don't know a letter. And why should it be otherwise with them? Of the few among them who have been taught to read, some may be bad; but reading did not make them so, and I believe more are good. People learn to be bad without books; books are not necessary to teach them to steal, and lie, and swear, and drink. These lessons are acquired without books, by heart as one may say.

Constable. Well sir, as you seem to be in favour of it, I hope it is right; but the people talked so against it, that I thought I would speak to you about it.

Justice. To tell you a secret about it, I knew of it before you did, and have been instrumental in getting Mr. Wilkins to let his man (who bears an excellent character, and though he can read, neither neglects his master's work, nor is he at all impudent,) come in from his work an hour earlier than usual, of an evening, that such of us who choose to have our people brought up differently from our cattle, may have the means of having them taught; and I doubt not but in a little time, I can induce all the neighbors (as I already have some of them,) to come into the plan.

Constable. You will find it a hard task with some of them, I heard two or three talk mightily against it.

Justice. They will understand it better, and they will see the good effects of it; and if they become religious they cannot help approving of it. Do you believe that our slaves will be judged by the same bible that we shall?

Constable. Why, if the bible says so, I suppose—though I never thought about that.

Justice. "Great and small, black and white, master and slave, shall stand together before the judgment seat of CHRIST." If on that day, I should be condemned, if I am found guilty of having withheld from my slaves the means of preserving their bodies, what will become of me if I have denied them the means of preserving their souls? If my slave who is to be judged by the bible, knows nothing about the bible, and I am the cause of this ignorance, what will be my sentence?

Constable. Well, sir, as I said before, I did not speak of this to you of myself, and I never thought of it so before, and now I must say it seems so right, that upon consideration, I don't see how any body, much less a Christian person, can help agreeing to what you say.

Justice. What will that master have to say for himself whose slaves have never known that bible?—These are the words of eternal life, and to these words he has given his slaves no access.

STATISTICAL TABLES

Considering the relative ease of moving in the early United States, the rapid growth of Virginia in the period 1790–1820 may be taken as at least suggestive that the area was not in rapid decline. Even most of the Tidewater counties continued to grow in population; it was only in the counties of the "northern neck" and the two counties of the eastern shore where stagnation definitely set in, and these accounted for very little of the total land mass of Virginia. It should be noted, however, that the old agricultural heartland of Virginia, the valleys of the James and York, had quite different growth records. This was surely determined by geography. The southwestward position of the Blue Ridge simply made the area drained by the James larger, so there was more room for the extensive type of agriculture practiced by Virginians.

There are excellent discussions of the economic system of colonial and Revolutionary Virginia in three books: Robert E. and B. Katherine Brown, *Virginia 1705–1786: Democracy or Aristocracy?* (East Lansing, Michigan, 1964), especially chapter 3, "The Impact of Slavery on White Society"; Jackson Turner Main, *The Social Structure of Revolutionary America* (Princeton, 1965), especially chapter 2, "The Economic Class Structure of the South"; and Gerald W. Mullin, *Flight and Rebellion: Slave Resistance in Eighteenth-Century Virginia* (New York, 1972).

For purposes of comparison, the following tables, which are derived from United States census figures, also show the growth of slavery in the rest of the United States for the period 1790–1820. Of striking interest here is the record of Maryland, which had roughly 40 percent as many slaves as Virginia by 1820, but actually had three thousand more free blacks. Maryland and Virginia had the largest free black populations in the union, and their increase—especially that of Maryland, suggest that the defenses of slavery against the erosion of time were not as great as we of the "neo-abolitionist" persuasion once thought.

The tables are the work of David Bennetts, whose efforts were supported by a grant from the Research Board of the University of Illinois.

TABLE 1. REGIONAL DISTRIBUTION OF SLAVES IN VIRGINIA, 1790–1820

	1790	1800	1810	1820
Tidewater				
Total Population	271,274	260,208	256,577	298,740
Slave Population	131,176	133,946	132,198	143,230
Percentage Slave	48+	51+	51+	48+
Percentage of Va.'s Slaves	44+	38+	33+	33+
Piedmont				
Total Population	346,918	418,517	441,247	470,541
Slave Population	146,273	185,947	214,126	236,504
Percentage Slave	42+	44+	48+	50+
Percentage of Va.'s Slaves	49+	53+	54+	55+
Valley				
Total Population	84,451	91,307	115,801	131,561
Slave Population	10,320	13,418	19,529	24,567
Percentage Slave	12+	14+	16+	18+
Percentage of Va.'s Slaves	3+	3+	4+	5+
Trans-Allegheny				
Total Population	59,211	110,168	160,997	159,591
Slave Population	4,858	12,485	26,665	17,767
Percentage Slave	8+	11+	16+	11+
Percentage of Va.'s Slaves	1+	3+	6+	4+

Tidewater Counties: Accomac, Charles City, Elizabeth City, Henrico, James City, Isle of Wight, Norfolk, Nansemond, Northampton, Warwick, York, Northumberland, Gloucester, Lancaster, Surry, Westmoreland, New Kent, Middlesex, King and Queen, Princess Anne, Essex, Richmond, King William, Prince George, Hanover, King George, Caroline, Southampton, Sussex, Greensville, Mathews.

Piedmont Counties: Stafford, Spotsylvania, Goochland, Prince William, Brunswick, Orange, Amelia, Fairfax, Louisa, Albemarle, Lunenburg, Culpeper, Cumberland, Chesterfield, Dinwiddie, Halifax, Prince Edward, Bedford, Loudoun, Fauquier, Amherst, Buckingham, Charlotte, Mecklenburg, Pittsylvania, Henry, Fluvanna, Powhatan, Campbell, Franklin, Nottoway, Patrick, Grayson, Madison, Nelson, Floyd, Rappahannock, Greene, Carroll.

Valley Counties: Frederick, Augusta, Botetourt, Montgomery, Washington, Rockbridge, Rockingham, Shenandoah, Wythe.

Trans-Allegheny: Hampshire, Berkeley, Monongalia, Ohio, Greenbriar, Fayette, Jefferson, Lincoln, Harrison, Nelson, Hardy, Mercer, Bourbon, Russell, Randolph, Pendleton, Woodford, Kanawha, Bath, Lee, Brooke, Wood, Monroe, Tazewell, Jefferson, Mason, Giles, Cabell, Scott, Tyler, Lewis, Preston, Nicholas, Morgan.

TABLE 2. GEOGRAPHICAL DISTRIBUTION OF SLAVES IN VIRGINIA ALONG
MAJOR RIVER SYSTEMS, 1790–1820

Region	1790	1800	1810	1820
Counties of the Rappahannock/Potomac River System:				
Total Population	142,608	157,383	158,314	158,721
Slaves	60,472	70,294	71,453	71,568
Percentage Slave	42	44	45	44
Percentage of Va.'s Slaves	20	20	18	16
Counties of the York River System:				
Total Population	104,358	104,929	112,510	116,375
Slaves	57,259	58,512	63,544	65,740
Percentage Slave	54	55	56	56
Percentage of Va.'s Slaves	19	16	16	15
Counties of the James River System:				
Total Population	218,130	244,229	271,113	298,808
Slaves	103,378	117,135	137,531	147,277
Percentage Slave	47	47	50	49
Percentage of Va.'s Slaves	35	33	35	34
Counties of Accomac and Northampton:				
Total Population	20,848	22,456	23,217	23,671
Slaves	7,506	7,607	7,892	7,803
Percentage Slave	36	33	33	32
Percentage of Va.'s Slaves	2	2	2	1
Counties East of the Blue Ridge and South of the James River System:				
Total Population	117,999	151,633	165,556	171,706
Slaves	47,781	67,247	91,606	86,987
Percentage Slave	40	44	55	51
Percentage of Va.'s Slaves	16	19	23	20

In 1790 the Counties of the three river systems had 78 percent of Virginia's slaves. In 1800, 1810, and 1820 the percentages were 72, 71, and 66. These figures include the Eastern Shore counties of Accomac and Northampton.

TABLE 3. AGGREGATE POPULATIONS BY STATES AND TERRITORIES, 1790–1820

States and Territories	Free White Males 16 and over	Free White Males under 16	Free White Females	All Other Free	Slaves Male	Slaves Female	Slaves Total	Percentage Population Slave	Free Colored	Total
1790										
Maryland	55,915	51,339	101,395	8,043			103,036	32 +		319,728
Virginia	110,936	116,135	215,046	12,866			292,627	39 +		747,610
North Carolina	69,988	77,506	140,710	4,975			100,571	25 +		393,751
Georgia	13,103	14,044	25,739	398			29,264	35 +		82,548
Kentucky	15,154	17,057	28,922	114			12,430	16 +		73,677
Territory of U.S. South of Ohio R., July, 1791.										
Washington Dist.										
Washington	1,009	1,792	2,524	12			535			5,872
Sullivan	806	1,242	1,995	107			297			4,447
Greene (partial)	1,293	2,374	3,580	40			454			7,741
Hawkins	1,204	1,970	2,921	68			807			6,970
S. of French Broad (partial)	681	1,082	1,627	66			163			3,619
Mero District										
Davidson (partial)	639	855	1,288	18			659			3,459
Sumner	404	582	854	8			348			2,196
Tennessee	235	380	576	42			154			1,387
Territory Totals	6,271	10,277	15,365	361			3,417			35,691

continued

Table 3, *continued*

States and Territories	Free White Males 16 and over	Free White Males under 16	Free White Females	All Other Free	Slaves Male	Slaves Female	Slaves Total	Percentage Population Slave	Free Colored	Total
1800										
Maryland, including Washington County	59,194	54,494	108,310	19,987			107,707	30+		349,692
Virginia										
East District	86,119	83,835	166,335	18,194			322,199			676,682
Dist. of Colum.	861	1,209	2,124	383			1,172			5,949
West District	43,072	49,103	85,816	1,930			23,597			203,518
Total	130,052	134,147	254,275	20,507			346,968	38+		886,149
North Carolina	81,457	90,191	166,116	7,043			133,296	27+		478,103
South Carolina	47,349	50,567	95,339	3,185			146,151	42+		345,591
Georgia	25,658	28,310	48,293	1,919			59,699	36+		162,686
Kentucky	42,642	51,319	85,915	741			40,343	18+		220,959
Tennessee	20,759	26,421	44,529	309			13,584	12+		105,602
Mississippi Territory							3,489	39+		8,850

Table 3, continued

States and Territories	Free White Males 16 and over	Free White Males under 16	Free White Females	All Other Free	Slaves Male	Slaves Female	Slaves Total	Percentage Population Slave	Free Colored	Total
1810										
Maryland	63,108	57,102	114,907	33,927			111,502	29+		380,546
Virginia	139,342	140,696	271,496	30,570			392,518	40+		974,622
North Carolina	90,275	98,357	187,778	10,266			168,824	30+		555,500
South Carolina	52,725	56,862	104,609	4,554			196,365	47+		415,115
Georgia	35,892	39,953	69,569	1,801			105,218	41+		252,433
Kentucky	76,867	91,938	155,432	1,713			80,561	19+		406,511
Tennessee										
East Tennessee	20,803	26,010	44,668	510			9,376	9+		101,367
West Tennessee	29,296	35,654	59,444	807			35,159	21+		160,360
Total							44,535	17+		261,727
Territory of Orleans				7,585			34,660			76,556
" " Mississippi				240			17,088			40,352
" " Louisiana				607			3,011			20,845
" " Indiana				393			237			24,520
" " Illinois				613			168			12,282
District of Columbia				2,549			5,395			24,023

continued

Table 3, continued

States and Territories	Free White Males 16 and over	Free White Males under 16	Free White Females	All Other Free	Slaves			Percentage Population Slave	Free Colored	Total
					Male	Female	Total			
1820										
Maryland	75,541	60,463	128,479		56,373	51,025	107,398	26 +	39,730	407,350
Virginia	168,154	149,725	298,343		218,274	206,879	425,153	39 +	36,889	1,065,366
North Carolina	110,992	108,400	209,556		106,551	98,466	205,017	32 +	14,612	638,829
South Carolina	64,249	59,526	113,765		127,115	124,668	251,783	51 +	6,714	490,309
Georgia	52,432	50,187	91,162		75,916	73,740	149,656	43 +	1,763	340,989
Kentucky	115,025	119,054	210,948		63,914	62,818	126,732	22 +	2,759	564,317
Tennessee	84,629	96,243	166,327		39,747	40,360	80,107	18 +	2,727	422,813
District of Columbia					3,007	3,370	6,377	19 +	4,048	33,039
Alabama	24,205	23,384	39,612		21,780	20,099	41,879	32 +	571	127,901
Mississippi	13,018	11,320	18,890		16,850	15,964	32,814	43 +	458	75,448
Louisiana	26,910	16,527	32,051		36,566	32,498	69,064	45 +	10,476	153,407
Missouri	17,369	14,933	24,987		5,341	4,881	10,222	15 +	347	66,586
Illinois	15,933	14,781	24,387		548	369	917	1.6 +	457	55,211
Territory of Arkansas	3,895	3,405	5,581		820	797	1,617	11 +	59	14,273

SOURCES:
1790 figures: *Return of the Whole Number of Persons Within the Several Districts of the United States according to 'An Act Passed for the Enumeration of the Inhabitants of the United States,' Passed March the First, 1790.* Printed by Childs and Swaine, Philadelphia: 1791, pp. 47, 48–50, 51, 52–53, 55, 56.
1800 figures: *Return of the Whole Number of Persons Within the Several Districts of the United States, according to 'An Act providing for the second Census or Enumeration of the Inhabitants of the United States,' Passed February 28, 1800.* Printed by Order of the House of Representatives, Washington: 1801, p. 1.
1810 figures: *Book I of the Third Census. ... Made According to Law, in the Year 1810.* Washington: 1811, p. 1.
1820 figures: *Book I of the Fourth Census for 1820.* Printed by Gales-Seaton, Washington: 1821, p. 1.

ESSAY ON SOURCES

The period of Virginia history covered by this investigation may be traced through more than enough sources to divert a lifetime. My inquiry has been a modest one, and I found that four major repositories of documents largely satisfied my curiosity. One reason for this is the excellence of the holdings of the Library of Congress, the University of Virginia, the Virginia State Library, and the Virginia Historical Society. Another is the abundance of published sources, and a third is the extensive biographical writing on Virginians of this era. Only the accidents of situation caused me to choose this group of repositories while neglecting such fine collections as those of the Huntington Library, the Institute for Early American Culture at Williamsburg, and the Southern Historical Collection at Chapel Hill.

The records convinced me that there is little to challenge in the present treatment of the social history of Virginia, at least as it is represented in serious works such as David Mays's *Edmund Pendleton*. Quite a different situation exists in economic history. The extent of mercantile activity in Jeffersonian Virginia has not received its proper attention. A way of demonstrating this is to consult Bray Hammond's widely respected treatise on banking in the early United States. Thorough as it is, it tells nothing about the banks of Alexandria and Richmond. Similarly, general economic histories neglect the extensive development of water transportation in Jeffersonian Virginia, which may well have had more miles of canals and improved river channels than any other state in 1800. In brief, it seems quite likely that the most rewarding work remaining to be done with these Virginia sources is to use them for the writing of serious and thorough economic history.

Here is a small suspicion: the records suggest a surprisingly high incidence of success in planting and trading, but this may be misleading. It is possible that the careful preserving of records was most often a habit of the most prudent and industrious Virginians. Still, the evidence of personal papers, when combined with that of the estate inventories preserved at the Virginia State Library, surely demonstrates prosperity by any historical standards.

Personal Papers

Among the most interesting sources to me were the Pocket Plantation Papers and the Journal of Leneaus Bolling. These disclosed men who were wealthy, but not aristocratic in manners or attitudes. Their records disclose the remarkable extent of trade in the upper Piedmont, and further suggest that neither sharecropping nor the crop-lien system were innovations of the Reconstruction era. Frontier merchants rented land, and then conveyed supplies to their tenants on credit, which was repaid by tobacco, grain, or some other staple. All the elements of the later situation existed, except for a quantity of landless free Negroes.

John Tayloe, not to be confused with his contemporary, John Taylor, has left some of the finest plantation records for the period. Minute books kept by his subordinates account for the labor of his slaves every working day of the year. The Commonplace Book of John Page is much less systematic and thorough than Tayloe's minute books, but also more fun to read because of poetic musings and occasional essays in metaphysics. The papers of Thomas Massie display the business of milling grain, mercantile affairs, and the westward-moving game of making investments in land. The Carr-Cary Papers are valuable both for general social history and for data on the domestic concerns of Thomas Jefferson. James Minor's papers present interesting glimpses of medical training and practice. The most impressive collection of mercantile records are in the Ellis-Allan Papers.

The papers of the first John Breckinridge (1760-1807) are equally splendid for political, social, and economic history. Breckinridge was a lawyer, a politician, a land speculator, and one of the most important figures in early Kentucky. He was as responsible as any man for the translation of Virginia institutions to the West.

None of these collections seem to be widely known, which is the chief reason for mentioning them here. There is no such neglect of the published personal papers of the nationally famous Virginians of the period, so it is quite sufficient merely to list them in the formal bibliography following this essay.

Collections of Public Papers

The Virginia State Library holds microfilm or photostat copies of all the county court will books and minute books that have survived into the modern era. The minute books are of little use for the social history of the Jeffersonian period, for they omit substantive discussion of the causes being tried. The will books and, sometimes maintained separately, the estate inventories, constitute the best single source available. One finds in the inventories detailed information about the age and abilities of slaves, and often thorough accounts of the livestock, farm equipment, home furnishings, musical instruments, books, jewelry, clothing, and weapons owned by Virginians. The wills are often quite personal documents, for the pragmatic lawyers of the period had not reduced them to the standard and sterile legal dialect that was so distasteful to Thomas Jefferson.

Frequency of citations more than sufficiently demonstrates the importance of Hening's and Shepherd's collections of *The Statutes at Large in Virginia,* and Helen T. Catterall's *Judicial Cases Concerning Slavery.* The limitations of these collections should be kept in mind. The laws passed are never identical to the laws observed, and therefore are no sure guide to the behavior of Virginians. On the other hand, the laws are clear and direct evidence of the intention of the effective majority in the legislature, and, when laws are repeatedly enacted upon the same subject, a true guide to the most pressing problems of the commonwealth which admitted of legislative remedy in the minds of the Virginians themselves. Mrs. Catterall's collection contains no criminal cases involving Negroes, because Virginia law provided that all such cases should be settled in the county courts, without appeal. As has already been mentioned, the county court records contain no particulars. But suits between citizens of Virginia over Negro property could go to the higher courts, and it is these that Mrs. Catterall offers. They are quite instructive for illustrating the ardor of many Virginians for protecting or acquiring property in slaves, and for presenting the opinions on slavery of Virginia's leading jurists, George Wythe and St. George Tucker.

The published journals of the Virginia legislature are a disappointment, for they maintain no records of debates. They are, in fact, the sparsest sort of minutes. It is a pity that the excellent series, *Messages and Papers of the Governors*, does not extend beyond the close of the American Revolution. As it is, it constitutes, along with the Fitzpatrick edition of Washington's papers, the best printed repository for sketching the annoying dislocation of slave property during the Revolutionary War. The commanding position of Virginia in the politics of the early nation accounts for the value of such standard published sources as Burnett's *Letters of the Members of the Continental Congress*, the *Journals of the Continental Congress*, and Gales and Seaton's *Annals of Congress*. For revealing the political attitudes of Virginians on the slavery question, the best published source is volume three of Jonathan Elliott's *Debates ... on the Adoption of the Federal Constitution*. In Congress Virginians almost never initiated the discussion of slavery, and when others introduced it they spoke so as to diminish and dismiss the topic as quickly as possible. Quite different was their behavior at their state ratifying convention. There the anti-Federalists argued most ingeniously about the possible effects of the new constitution on the vulnerable institution of slavery. The Federalists were necessarily obliged to answer, and the results are conclusive.

Published documents are especially abundant for the early years of the Indiana and Illinois territories, during which emigrants from Virginia undertook to introduce slavery and President Jefferson's administration neither offered encouragement nor undertook to see that the old antislavery clause of the Northwest Ordinance was preserved. Clarence Edward Carter's *Territorial Papers*, Volume VIII, covers the period of slavery's ascendency. Also valuable are

Logan Esarey's *Messages and Papers of William Henry Harrison* and Francis L. Philbrick's *The Laws of Indiana Territory, 1801-1809*. The most thorough historian of slavery in early Indiana, Jacob P. Dunn, has edited a large collection of "Slavery Petitions and Papers," for *Indiana Historical Society Publications,* Volume II.

The newspapers of Jeffersonian Virginia are for most purposes disappointing. Their news columns are almost all simply lifted from other papers, and their political essays represent party inspiration rather than an enlightened and independent journalism. Most useful for the social historian are their advertisements. Those describing runaway Negroes afford one of the best sources available to us on the personal characteristics of slaves. Much of the newspaper material on slavery has been collected by Carter G. Woodson and published in the earlier volumes of the *Journal of Negro History.*

Travel accounts are especially valuable for Jeffersonian Virginia. Peerless among many is the *Voyage dans les États-Unis d'Amerique* by the Duc de la Rochefoucauld-Liancourt. Two of his eight volumes were devoted to Virginia, and they abound with carefully gathered information on the economy, technology, legal usages, and politics of the state. Informed and detached, the Duke created the most balanced and least biased account of Virginia in the 1790's to have seen the printed page. Less sympathetic in tone and more impressionistic in manner, Dr. Johann Schoepf wrote at the end of the Revolutionary War, which may have accounted for much of the despondency reflected in his pages. His narrative has been translated by A. J. Morrison and published as *Travels in the Confederation.*

Two more French accounts deserve mention. Of these Moreau de St. Mery's is both racier and more accessible, having been translated and published in recent years by Kenneth and Anna M. Roberts. Brissot de Warville, however, was a more serious student of Virginia, with a valuable interest in the tobacco industry and in slavery. There is an eighteenth-century edition in English of his narrative, entitled *New Travels in the United States of America, Performed in 1788.*

Isaac Weld, Jr., and Robert Hunter are the most informative of the English travelers. Unfortunately, Weld is not available in a modern edition. Both travelers represented English commercial interests which gave them access to the homes of the wealthier traders of Virginia. Harry Toulmin's account, recently published as *The Western Country in 1793*, is the most ambitious effort by an Englishman to describe society in all of its aspects. This is promotional literature, written originally by Toulmin to convince a number of his countrymen that they ought to migrate to Kentucky. Therefore he dwells fondly on the high level of wages, the cheapness and fertility of land, the abundance of food, and the general prosperity. He neglects the depressing aspects of the institution of slavery, the widespread sickness in parts of Virginia, and the great difficulties involved in transportation. Still less serious is the section on travel in Virginia in Benjamin Latrobe's *Journal*, which was obviously written to entertain rather than to edify. But Latrobe should be read if only for his description of Virginia debauchery observed when he attended some horse races. Charles William Janson's *The Stranger in America*, republished in 1935, is very good indeed, but its author spent most of his time in Norfolk and saw little of either the Virginia back country or of the rustic aristocracy which ruled it. His is an excellent account of Norfolk and its neighborhood. Full references to these and less consequential travel accounts are contained in Thomas D. Clark, *Travels in the Old South: A Bibliography*, Volume II.

Secondary Accounts

Biography dominates the published literature on Jeffersonian Virginia. There are whole libraries on Washington and Jefferson, at the head of which now stand Douglas Southall Freeman's seven volumes on our first president and Dumas Malone's three volumes on our third, with more promised. Irving Brant has published six sympathetic volumes on the career of James Madison. These are excellent books, but they were undertaken in the first place more because of the prominence of their subjects in national affairs than because of an interest in Virginia herself. As these volumes have appeared the fund of knowledge about the home state of the patriots has not been greatly enlarged.

More useful for the study of Virginia are two thorough biographies of politicians who remained more closely identified with their region: William Cabell Bruce's *John Randolph,* and David J. Mays's *Edmund Pendleton,* each of which fills two generous volumes. The older work by Bruce is episodic and amateurish, but the work of a thorough and dedicated author. His habit of publishing long excerpts from original sources represents poor style, but enhances the value of the book for the researcher. The only shortcoming of Mays's book is that its subject died in 1803, and was at the peak of his career in the late colonial and revolutionary years. Pendleton's life, therefore, can only illuminate the background and the early part of the period of this study.

General Histories

The assessment of Virginia society presented here has been shaped by, and is in harmony with, that presented in three excellent volumes of the *History of the South* series, edited by W. H. Stephenson and E. M. Coulter. These are John R. Alden's *South in the American Revolution,* Thomas Perkins Abernethy's *South in the New Nation,* and Charles S. Sydnor's *Development of Southern Sectionalism.* Strictly speaking, the volumes by Alden and Sydnor fall on either side of the period of this study, but their surveys of southern society apply to the Jeffersonian era. So much is this the case that Professor Abernethy, whose book was the last of the three to appear, presents only a minimal social analysis, and refers his readers to the other volumes.

Professor Abernethy has little to say about Virginia, and less to say about slavery itself, and yet his book, indeed all of his books, forcefully demonstrates the vitality and expansiveness of the southern plantation society, including its fundamental labor institution. For Abernethy's great subject has been the expansion of southern society from the eastern seaboard across the Appalachians and into the lower Mississippi Valley, and to a considerable degree this has been expansion from Virginia. His books have been, by implication, a running refutation of the more romantic theories of Frederick Jackson Turner and his followers. The western movement of the South, as described by Professor Abernethy, produced succeeding waves of new planter aristocracies.

Merrill Jensen's book, *The New Nation,* demonstrates that the

United States was by no means in a state of economic and political disintegration in the 1780's, but was, on the contrary, enjoying a decade of overall growth and prosperity. As this was as true of the southern states as the northern, Jensen has incidentally made a strong if indirect demonstration of the vigor of plantation agriculture. The most thorough case for the effectiveness of slavery as a labor system is in Lewis C. Gray, *History of Agriculture in the Southern United States to 1860*, Volume II. Most ambition analyses of the efficiency of slavery concentrate on the cotton area during the generation before the Civil War. Gray's is the only intensive study that includes colonial and early national data.

Stanley Elkins has written a survey of the major literature on American slavery up to 1958, *Slavery; a Problem in American Institutional and Intellectual Life*. The book serves as an introduction to the field, and offers an independent and modern view of slavery as a social system. A more detailed and historical account of slavery written from a contemporary point of view is Kenneth M. Stampp, *The Peculiar Institution*. Ulrich B. Phillips, *Life and Labor in the Old South*, has become a part of American intellectual history, but remains as rich a volume as any for information about slavery. Founded in the racial attitudes of his generation, Phillips' work assumes the suitability of Negroes for serfdom, and finds in the considerable adjustment of Negroes to slavery a triumph of civilization, not a lapse. But the book is neither apology nor euphemism.

Several works by Jackson T. Main already published, and another near completion, offer the best printed accounts of the property held by Virginians during the 1780's. The most thorough of these now available is *The Antifederalists*. Professor Main has demonstrated both the reduction of the great landed estates of the colonial period and the upward mobility of poorer white Virginians.

The main purpose of this essay has been to indicate collections and books of great value, and not to complain about failures. Three books that are now unsatisfactory must be mentioned, however, because they have so much to do with the study of slavery and Jeffersonian Virginia: James C. Ballagh, *A History of Slavery in Virginia*, John H. Russell, *The Free Negro in Virginia, 1619–1865*, and Mary S. Locke, *Anti-Slavery in America . . . 1619–1808*. All of

232

these were published before World War I, all of them were based on research which would now be considered entirely inadequate, and two of them are little more than a review of legislation. The best things one can find in print about the abolitionists of Jeffersonian Virginia are in denominational histories and in biographies of eminent churchmen. There is happily a good volume on the remarkable Quaker, Warner Mifflin, by Hilda Justice. It includes Mifflin's own long explanation of his conduct toward slaves. Unfortunately there is practically nothing in print about Robert Pleasants, who, indeed, is not even mentioned in the *DAB*. The early abolitionists of the South were part of a pious and humanitarian movement that was still more forceful in the middle and northern states and in England. Some account of this may be found in several of the biographies listed below. Early abolitionists in the North are described in Leon Litwack, *North of Slavery*.

Richard Beale Davis has just published his award-winning *Intellectual Life in Jefferson's Virginia, 1790–1830* (Chapel Hill, 1964). It has appeared too recently to inform these pages, but ought certainly to inform the readers of them.

BIBLIOGRAPHY

Manuscript, Microfilm, and Photostat Sources

Albemarle County Order Book, 1791–93, VSL.

Albemarle County Will Book no. 4, 1798–1809, VSL.

Barbour Family Papers, UVL.

Barbour, Philip Pendleton, Papers, VHS.

Berkeley Papers and Berkeley-Noland MSS, UVL.

Bolling, Leneaus, Journal, UVL. An earlier journal is owned by the Huntington Library.

Book List for Virginia, 1812–22, UVL.

Bryan Family MSS, UVL.

Campbell County Will Book no. 1, 1782–1800, VSL.

Campbell–Preston Papers, LC.

Caroline County Minute Book, 1787–91, VSL.

Carr-Cary Papers, UVL.

Chesterfield County Will Book no. 5, VSL.

De Butts Family Letters (microfilm of typed copies), UVL.

Ellis-Allan Papers, LC.

Eppes Deposit, UVL.

Erskine, David Montague, Travel Diary: a copybook of letters written to his father, UVL.

Fairfax, Ferdinando, Diary (1792), UVL.

Halifax County Will Book no. 6 (1798-1804), VSL.

Henry, William Wirt, Papers, VHS.

Lee, Richard Bland, Papers, LC.

Lunenburg County, lower district: Register of Free Negroes, UVL.

McKean, William, Letterbook, 1809–18. McKean was a Scot who operated Roslin Plantation in Chesterfield County for its absentee owner, James Dunlop of Glasgow.

Massie Family Papers, VHS.

Middlesex County Wills, 1675–1798, Part 2, VSL.

Millan, William, Collector in Truro Parish: Sheriff's Book for 1797, LC.

Minor, James, Papers, UVL.

Minute Book of the Vestry of St. George's Parish, Spotsylvania County, UVL.

Nelson-Kinlock Papers, UVL.

Nicholas, Wilson Cary, Papers, LC.

Nicholas, Wilson Cary, Papers, UVL.

Northampton County Will Book no. 32, 1802–07, VSL.

Page, John, Commonplace Book, kept in a copy of *Benjamin Bannaker's Pennsylvania, Delaware, Maryland and Virginia Almanac for 1795*, VHS.

Pleasants, Robert, Letter Book (transcriptions), Quaker Records, Volume IV, the Valentine Museum, Richmond.

Pocket Plantation Papers, UVL.

Prince William County Will Book I, with inventories and accounts, Reel 19, VSL.

Randolph, Edmund, Letter to James Madison of 19 May, 1789, VHS.

Randolph, John, Papers, UVL.

Rives, William Cabell, Papers, LC.

Tayloe Family Papers, VHS.

Virginia Legislative Petitions: Inhabitants of Cumberland County to the House of Delegates, 2 December, 1778, UVL (photostat), VSL (original).

Woodson, Carter G., Collection of Negro Papers, LC.

Wormeley Papers, UVL.

Newspapers

The Virginia Argus, Richmond, published by Samuel Pleasants, Jr., 1795–1814, and by successors for two more years.

The Virginia Gazette and General Advertiser, Richmond, published by Augustine Davis, 1790–1809.

The Virginia Gazette and Independent Chronicle, Richmond, published by John Dixon and John H. Holt, 1783–89.

For historical details about these papers, and present location of copies, see Clarence S. Brigham, *History and Bibliography of American Newspapers, 1690–1820* (Worcester, 1947), II, 1142–48.

Published Sources

Anburey, Thomas, *Travels Through the Interior Parts of America* (Boston, 1923).

Annals of Congress: Gales and Seaton's Debates and Proceedings in the Congress of the United States.

Asbury, Francis, *Journal and Letters,* edited by J. Manning Potts, Elmer T. Clark, and Jacob S. Payton, 3 vols. (London and Nashville, 1958).

Benton, Thomas Hart, *Abridgement of the Debates of Congress,* 16 vols. (New York, 1857–61).

Bernard, John, *Retrospections of America, 1797–1811,* edited from the manuscript by Mrs. Bayle Bernard, with an introduction, notes, and index by Laurence Hutton and Brander Matthews (New York, 1887).

Brissot de Warville, J. P., *New Travels in the United States of America Performed in 1788,* translated from the French by anon. (Dublin, 1792).

Burnett, E. C., ed., *Letters of Members of the Continental Congress,* 7 vols. (Washington, D.C., 1921–34).

Carter, Clarence Edwin, ed., *Territorial Papers of the United States,* vol. VIII: Indiana, 1800–10 (Washington, D.C., 1939).

Catterall, Helen T., ed., *Judicial Cases Concerning Slavery and the Negro,* vol. I: Cases from the Courts of England, Virginia, West Virginia, and Kentucky (Washington, D.C., 1926).

Davis, John, *Travels of Four Years and a Half in the United States of America* (1798–1802), edited by A. J. Morrison (New York, 1909).

Dunn, Jacob P., ed., "Slavery Petitions and Papers," *Indiana Historical Society Publications*, vol. II (Indianapolis, 1895), pp. 447–529.

Elliott, Jonathan, ed., *The Debates in the Several State Conventions on the Adoption of the Federal Constitution*, 5 vols. (Philadelphia, 1896).

Harrison, William Henry, *Messages and Letters*, edited by Logan Esarey, *Indiana Historical Collections*, vols. VIII and IX (Indianapolis, 1922).

Hening, William Waller, *The New Virginia Justice* (Richmond, 1799).

———, *The Statutes at Large in Virginia*, vols. IX-XIII (Richmond, 1821–23; Philadelphia, 1823).

Journal of the Continental Congress, edited by Gaillard Hunt and others (Washington, D.C., 1904–37).

Hunter, Robert, Jr., *Quebec to Carolina in 1785–1786*, edited by Louis B. Wright and Marion Tinling (San Marino, 1943).

Janson, Charles William, *The Stranger in America*, edited by Carl S. Driver (New York, 1935).

Jefferson, Thomas, *Notes on the State of Virginia* (London, 1787).

———, *Papers*, edited by Julian Boyd, to July 4, 1790, 16 vols. (Princeton, 1950–).

———, *Works*, edited by Paul Leicester Ford, 10 vols. (New York, 1892–99).

La Rochefoucauld-Liancourt et d'Estissac, François-Alexandre-Frédéric, Duc de,*Voyage dans les États-Unis d'Amerique*, vols. IV-V (Paris, 1799).

Latrobe, Benjamin Henry, *Journal*, edited by J. H. B. Latrobe (New York, 1905).

Lear, Tobias, *Observations on the River Potomack* (New York, 1793).

Lee, Richard Henry, *Letters*, edited by J. C. Ballagh, 2 vols. (New York, 1914).

McIlwain, H. R., ed., *Official Letters of the Governors of the State of Virginia*, vol. III: Letters of Thomas Nelson and Benjamin Harrison (Richmond, 1929).

Madison, James, *Letters and Other Writings of James. Madison,* published by order of Congress, 4 vols. (Philadelphia, 1865).

Mayo, Bernard, ed., *Thomas Jefferson and His Unknown Brother Randolph* (Charlottesville, 1942).

Monroe, James, *Writings,* edited by Stanislaus Hamilton, 7 vols. (New York, 1898–1903).

Moreau de Saint-Méry, Médéric-Louis-Elie, *Moreau de St. Mérys American Journey* (1793–98), translated and edited by Kenneth Roberts and Anna M. Roberts (New York, 1947).

Morrison, A. J., *Travels in Virginia in Revolutionary Times* (Lynchburg, 1922).

Orr, Lucinda Lee, *Journal of a Young Lady of Virginia, 1782,* edited by Emily V. Mason (Baltimore, 1871).

Philbrick, Francis S., ed., *The Laws of Indiana Territory, 1801–1809; Collections of the Illinois State Historical Society,* Theodore C. Pease, general editor, vol. XXI (Springfield, 1930).

Price, Richard, *Observations on the Importance of the American Revolution* (Dublin, 1785).

Schoepf, Johann David, *Travels in the Confederation* (1783–84), translated and edited by Alfred J. Morrison, vol. II (Philadelphia, 1911).

Shepherd, Samuel, *The Statutes at Large in Virginia, 1792–1806,* 3 vols. (Richmond, 1835).

[William Loughton Smith and Oliver Wolcott], *The Pretensions of Thomas Jefferson to the Presidency Examined and the Charges Against John Adams Refuted* (Philadelphia, 1796).

Thorpe, Francis N., ed., *The Federal and State Constitutions, Colonial Charters, and Other Organic Laws,* 7 vols. (Washington, D.C., 1909).

Toulmin, Harry, *The Western Country in 1793,* edited by Marion Tinling and Godfrey Davies (San Marino, 1948).

Tucker, St. George, *Blackstone's Commentaries* (Philadelphia, 1803).

——, *A Dissertation on Slavery, with a Proposal for the Gradual Abolition of It, in the State of Virginia* (Philadelphia, 1796).

——, "Letters Concerning Slavery to Dr. Jeremy Belknap," *Collections of the Massachusetts Historical Society,* 5th series, vol. III (Boston, 1877).

Twining, Thomas, *Travels in India a Hundred Years Ago,* edited by the Rev. W. H. G. Twining (London, 1893). The title is misleading. Thomas Twining wrote about travels in the early United States as well as in India.

Washington, George, *Diaries*, edited by John C. Fitzpatrick, 4 vols. (Boston, 1925).

——, *Writings*, edited by John C. Fitzpatrick, 39 vols. (Washington, D.C., 1931–44).

Weld, Isaac, Jr., *Travels Through the States of North America, and the Provinces of Upper and Lower Canada, During the Years 1795, 1796, and 1797*, 3rd ed., vol. I (London, 1800).

Wirt, William, *The Letters of the British Spy*, 10th ed. (New York, 1832).

[Woodson, Carter G., ed.], "Eighteenth Century Slaves as Advertised by Their Masters," *JNH* I (April, 1916), 163–216.

——, "Travelers' Impressions of Slavery in America from 1750 to 1800," *JNH* I (October, 1916), 399–443.

Secondary Accounts

Abernethy, Thomas P., *From Frontier to Plantation in Tennessee* (Memphis, 1955).

——, *The South in the New Nation* (Baton Rouge, 1961).

——, *Three Virginia Frontiers* (Baton Rouge, 1940).

Adams, Henry, *History of the United States of America*, 9 vols. (New York, 1931).

Alden, John R., *The South in the Revolution, 1763–1789* (Baton Rouge, 1957).

Ambler, Charles Henry, *Sectionalism in Virginia from 1776 to 1861* (Chicago, 1910).

Anderson, Dice Robins, *William Branch Giles: A Study in the Politics of Virginia and the Nation from 1790 to 1830* (Menasha, Wisconsin, 1914).

Aptheker, Herbert, *American Negro Slave Revolts* (New York, 1943).

——, *The Negro in the American Revolution* (New York, 1940).

Ballagh, James C., *A History of Slavery in Virginia* (Baltimore, 1902).

Bangs, Nathan, *The Life of the Reverend Freeborn Garrettson*, 2nd ed. (New York, 1830).

Barnhart, John D., *Valley of Democracy: The Frontier Versus the Plantation in the Ohio Valley, 1775–1818* (Bloomington, 1953).

Beard, Charles A., *Economic Origins of Jeffersonian Democracy* (New York, 1915).

Bell, Whitfield J., "Thomas Anburey's 'Travels Through America': A Note on Eighteenth-Century Plagiarism," *Papers of the Bibliographical Society of America*, XXXVII, no. 1 (1943), 23–26.

Boyd, Julian P., *The Murder of George Wythe* (privately printed, Philadelphia, 1949).

Brant, Irving, *James Madison*, 6 vols. (Indianapolis, 1941–61).

Bridenbaugh, Carl, *Myths and Realities: Societies of the Colonial South* (Baton Rouge, 1952).

Brookes, George S., *Friend Anthony Benezet* (Philadelphia and London, 1937).

Bruce, Kathleen, *Virginia Iron Manufacture in the Slave Era* (New York, 1931).

Bruce, William Cabell, *John Randolph of Roanoke: 1773–1833*, 2 vols. (New York, 1922).

Clark, Thomas D., *Travels in the Old South: A Bibliography*, vol. II, 1750–1825 (Norman, 1956).

Cox, Theodore S., "George Wythe," *Dictionary of American Biography*, XX, 586–589.

Craven, Avery O., *Soil Exhaustion as a Factor in the Agricultural History of Virginia and Maryland, 1606–1860* (Urbana, 1925).

Craven, Wesley Frank, *The Southern Colonies in the Seventeenth Century, 1607–1689* (Baton Rouge, 1949).

Cunliffe, Marcus, *George Washington, Man and Monument* (Boston, 1958).

Drake, Thomas Edward, *Quakers and Slavery in America* (New Haven, 1950).

Drew, Samuel, *The Life of the Reverend Thomas Coke, LL.D.* (New York, 1818).

Dunn, Jacob P., *Indiana; a Redemption from Slavery*, rev. ed. (Boston and New York, 1905).

Elkins, Stanley, *Slavery; a Problem in American Institutional and Intellectual Life* (Chicago, 1959).

Freeman, Douglas Southall, *George Washington*, 7 vols., of which the last was written by Mr. Freeman's collaborators, John Alexander Carroll and Mary Wells Ashworth (New York, 1948–57).

Galbreath, Charles B., "Thomas Jefferson's Views on Slavery," *Ohio Archaeological and Historical Quarterly*, XXXIV (1925), 184–202.

Gewehr, Wesley M., *The Great Awakening in Virginia, 1740–1790* (Durham, 1930).

Goebel, Dorothy B., *William Henry Harrison* (Indianapolis, 1926).

Gray, Lewis C., *History of Agriculture in the Southern United States to 1860*, vol. II (Washington, D.C., 1933).

Griggs, Earl Leslie, *Thomas Clarkson, the Friend of Slaves* (London, 1936).

Harrison, Lowell H., "John Breckinridge: Western Statesman," *Journal of Southern History*, XVIII (1952), 137–151.

Hill, Helen, *George Mason, Constitutionalist* (Cambridge, 1938).

Jenkins, William S., *Pro-Slavery Thought in the Old South* (Chapel Hill, 1935).

Jensen, Merrill, *The New Nation; a History of the United States During the Confederation, 1781–1789* (New York, 1950).

Justice, Hilda, *The Life and Ancestry of Warner Mifflin* (Philadelphia, 1905).

Kelsey, Rayner W., "Warner Mifflin," *Dictionary of American Biography*, XII, 608–609.

Kennedy, John Pendleton, *Memoirs of the Life of William Wirt*, new and rev. ed. (Philadelphia, 1854).

Link, Eugene Perry, *Democratic-Republican Societies, 1790–1800* (New York, 1942).

Litwack, Leon F., *North of Slavery; the Negro in the Free States, 1790–1860* (Chicago, 1961).

Locke, Mary S., *Anti-Slavery in America, from the Introduction of African Slaves to the Prohibition of the Slave Trade, 1619–1808* (Boston, 1901).

Long, Charles M., *Virginia County Names* (New York, 1908).

McDonald, Forrest, *We the People: The Economic Origins of the Constitution* (Chicago, 1958).

McMaster, John Bach, *History of the People of the United States*, vols. I-IV (New York, 1883–95).

Main, Jackson T., *The Antifederalists* (Chapel Hill, 1961).

———, "Distribution of Property in Post-Revolutionary Virginia," *Mississippi Valley Historical Review*, XLI (1954), 241–258.

———, "The One Hundred," *William and Mary Quarterly*, 3rd series, XI (1954), 354–384.

———, "Sections and Politics in Virginia, 1781–1787," *William and Mary Quarterly*, 3rd series, XII (1955), 96–112.

Malone, Dumas, *Jefferson and His Time*, 3 vols. (Boston, 1948–62).

Mays, David J., *Edmund Pendleton, 1721–1803*, 2 vols. (Cambridge, 1952).

Mudge, Eugene T., *The Social Philosophy of John Taylor of Caroline* (New York, 1939).

Phillips, Ulrich B., *Life and Labor in the Old South* (Boston, 1929).

Pease, Theodore C., *The Story of Illinois* (Chicago, 1949).

Pole, J. R., "Representation and Authority in Virginia from the Revolution to Reform," *Journal of Southern History*, XXIV (1958), 16–50.

Robinson, Morgan P., "Virginia Counties," *Bulletin of the Virginia State Library*, IX (1916).

Russell, John H., *The Free Negro in Virginia, 1619–1865* (Baltimore, 1913).

Shulim, Joseph I., *The Old Dominion and Napoleon Bonaparte* (New York, 1952).

Simms, Henry H., *Life of John Taylor* (Richmond, 1932).

Smith, James Morton, *Freedom's Fetters: The Alien and Sedition Laws and American Civil Liberties* (Cornell, 1956). Useful here is chapter 15, "Sedition in the Old Dominion: James T. Callender and *The Prospect Before Us*."

Stampp, Kenneth M., *The Peculiar Institution* (New York, 1956).

Sydnor, Charles S., *The Development of Southern Sectionalism* (Durham, 1948).

Tansill, Charles C., *The United States and Santo Domingo, 1798–1873* (Baltimore, 1938).

Tyler, Alice Felt, *Freedom's Ferment* (Minneapolis, 1944).

Webster, Homer J., *William Henry Harrison's Administration of Indiana Territory, Indiana Historical Society Publications*, IV: 3 (Indianapolis, 1907).

Wirt, William, *The Life of Patrick Henry*, 6th ed. (New York, 1833).

Woodson, Carter G., *The Education of the Negro Prior to 1861* (New York, 1915).

Wright, Louis B., *First Gentlemen of Virginia* (San Marino, 1940).

Supplementary Bibliography

Bancroft, Frederic, *Slave Trading in the Old South* (New York, 1959).

Brown, Robert E. and B. Katherine, *Virginia, 1705–1786: Democracy or Aristocracy?* (East Lansing, 1964).

Cohen, William, "Thomas Jefferson and the Problem of Slavery," *Journal of American History* LVI (1969).

Craven, Wesley Frank, *White, Red and Black: The Seventeenth Century Virginian* (Charlottesville, 1971).

Davis, David Brion, *The Problem of Slavery in Western Culture* (Ithaca, 1966).

———, *Was Thomas Jefferson an Authentic Enemy of Slavery?* (Oxford, 1970).

Davis, Richard Beale, *Intellectual Life in Jefferson's Virginia, 1790–1830* (Chapel Hill, 1964).

Degler, Carl N., *Neither Black nor White: Slavery and Race Relations in Brazil and the United States* (New York, 1971).

Foner, Laura, and Genovese, Eugene, *Slavery in the New World: A Reader in Comparative History* (Englewood Cliffs, 1969).

Jackson, Luther Porter, *Free Negro Labor and Property Holding in Virginia, 1830–1860* (New York, 1969).

———, "Religious Development of the Negro in Virginia from 1760 to 1860," *JNH* XVI (1931).

Johnston, James Hugo, *Race Relations in Virginia and Miscegenation in the South, 1776–1860* (Amherst, 1970).

Jordan, Winthrop D., *White over Black: American Attitudes toward the Negro, 1550–1812* (Chapel Hill, 1968).

Klein, Herbert S., *Slavery in the Americas: A Comparative Study of Cuba and Virginia* (Chicago, 1967).

Main, Jackson Turner, *The Social Structure of Revolutionary America* (Princeton, 1965).

Mullin, Gerald W., *Flight and Rebellion: Slave Resistance in Eighteenth-Century Virginia* (New York, 1972).

Robinson, Donald L., *Slavery in the Structure of American Politics, 1765–1820* (New York, 1971).

Staudenraus, P. J., *The African Colonization Movement, 1816–1865* (New York, 1961).

Tate, Thad W., Jr., *The Negro in Eighteenth-Century Williamsburg* (Charlottesville, 1965).

Weinstein, Allen, and Gatell, Frank Otto, eds., *American Negro Slavery: A Modern Reader* (New York, 1968).

Zilversmit, Arthur, *The First Emancipation: The Abolition of Slavery in the North* (Chicago, 1967).

INDEX

Aberdeen, University of: mathematics teacher in Richmond trained at, 43

Abolitionists: their position compared to that of Virginia statesmen, 36, 131; legal restrictions on, 159–161. *See also* Methodists; Quakers

Accomac County: activities of Daniel and Warner Mifflin in, 155–156

Adams, Henry: quoted on Virginia politics, 56

Adams, John: appointment questioned by southerners because of antislavery views, 86

Africa: transporting of American Negroes to, 87; General Assembly recommends sale of rebel slaves in, 110; route of slaves from, 139; mentioned in oath required of immigrant slaveholders, 166

Aggy, slave of John Hedges, Sr., 68

Agricultural practices in Virginia, 16–18

Alabama: and western expansion, 174, 185

Albemarle County: site of Charlottesville, Jefferson's Monticello, and the University of Virginia, 10–11; court fixes tavern rates, 39; academy in,

42; flour mill in, 51; disposition of slaves in, 143–144

Alexandria: as commercial town, 12; oyster house operated by free Negro in, 74; as refuge for runaways, 96

American Colonization Society: related to Gabriel's Rebellion, 110

American Revolution: advance of antislavery feeling during, 2, 89, 115, 153–155

Ames, Fisher, representative from Massachusetts: quoted on slavery debate in the House of Representatives, 121

Amherst County: Leneaus Bolling leases land in, 28

Anburey, Thomas: describes traveling conditions in Virginia, 37–38

Anderson, Richard: slaves of run away, 96

Anglican Church: disestablished, 10, 36; communicants protest presence of slaves at unregulated prayer meetings, 104

Angora: testamentary provisions for, 143

Antislavery: advance during Revolution, 89, 115, 153–155. *See also* Abolitionists; Jefferson, Thomas; Methodists; Quakers; Tucker, St. George; Wythe, George

policy toward Negroes during American Revolution, 82–87; and runaways, 84–88; John Adams appointed ambassador to, 86; kings held responsible for existence of slavery in Virginia, 116; maintains slave trade, 116–117; emancipation societies of, 119–120; and Jefferson's foreign policy, 181; blamed for the economic troubles of Virginia, 184

Brown, James, merchant of Richmond, 51

Brunswick Circuit of Virginia: preaching of Reverend Freeborn Garrettson on, 149

Buckingham County: residence of Leneaus Bolling, 28

Bullit, Sophia C. M.: arranges for slaves to earn freedom, 144

Caesar, slave freed by General Assembly, 89

Caleb, emancipated Negro, 143

Callaway, Dr. Henry G.: asked to purchase slave, 66

Callaway, James, iron manufacturer in Pittsylvania County, 23

Callaway, John: invites son to buy a slave, 66

Calvert, Obed: testamentary provisions for a slave of, 144

Cambridge, Moll, and Esther, slaves sold by Wilson Cary Nicholas, 68

Campbell County: will of John M. Reynolds of, 79

Carleton, General Guy: shelters runaways, 85–87

Caroline County: academy in, 43

Carr, Dabney, trustee of academy, 42

Carr, John, trustee of academy, 42

Carr, Peter, trustee of academy,

42; studies languages, 44; misgivings over sale of slaves, 67; endows newlyweds with slaves, 78

Cary, Wilson Miles: sells timber lands, 51

Castro, Fidel: attitudes toward compared with attitudes toward Santo Domingo rebels, 112–113

Charles City County: slave uprising in, 107

Charlottesville: location of university at, 10; emancipation in, 143

Chase, Jeremiah Townley, of Maryland: on special committee for western lands of Continental Congress, 172

Chesapeake Bay: influence of on Virginia settlements, 9; project for connecting with Ohio Valley, 55

Chiles, Micajah: provisions for freeing slaves of, 143

Civil War: historical interpretations of, 5; free-state sympathies during, 35; as reflection of tension in Virginia between progressive liberalism and racism, 189

Claiborne, Thomas: supports stronger fugitive slave law, 100

Clark, George Rogers: conquers Northwest Territory, 175

Clark County, Indiana Territory: citizens of petition Congress against introduction of slavery, 180

Clarkson, John, director of colony at Sierra Leone, 87–88

Clarkson, Thomas, British abolitionist, 87

Clay, Henry: and economic nationalism, 33

Cocke, Bowler, of Turkey Island: